POLITICAL
PRISONERS
IN AMERICA

POLITICAL
PRISONERS
IN AMERICA

Charles Goodell

RANDOM HOUSE · NEW YORK

Library of Congress Cataloging in Publication Data
Goodell, Charles E 1926–
   Political prisoners in America.
   Includes bibliographical references.
   1 Government, Resistance to. 2. Political crimes
and offenses—United States. 3. Criminal justice,
Administration of—United States. 4. Liberty of
speech—United States. I. Title.
KF9390.G66   364.1'31   72–11424
ISBN 0-394-47882-7

ACKNOWLEDGMENTS

Passages from Dr. Martin Luther King's "Letter from Birmingham City Jail," Copyright © 1963 Martin Luther King, Jr. Used by permission of Harper & Row, Publishers.

"Compared to What," by Eugene McDaniels, Copyright © 1966 Lonport Music Corp., c/o Sidney A. Seidenberg, 1414 Avenue of the Americas, New York, N. Y. 10019. A portion of the lyrics to "Compared to What" as sung by Roberta Flack is used for the epigraph to Chapter 9 with her permission.

Passages from "Civil Rights and Disobedience to Law," by Harrison Tweed, Bernard G. Segal, and Herbert L. Packer, Copyright © 1964 by *Presbyterian Life*. Used by permission.

A passage from "Civil Rights—Yes: Civil Disobedience—No," by Louis Waldman, is reprinted from the *New York State Bar Journal*, August, 1965, with the permission of the author and the publisher.

ACKNOWLEDGMENTS

I wish to pay special tribute to Michael Smith, without whom this book would not have taken its form or substance. He faithfully and arduously transmuted into type the ideas evolved from our long discussions, as well as contributing many of his own. A New York attorney, Harvard Law School graduate, and Rhodes Scholar, he literally gave a year of his life to this book. His sensitive intelligence and genuine discomfort about injustice make his life's commitment of very special importance.

I would also like to thank Judith Douw, who volunteered her valuable time to the typing of early drafts. My secretary, Evelyn McCargar, suffered loyally through the final typing and did a superb job. Three former members of my staff in the Senate also deserve mention for their assistance: Steven Martindale originally suggested the book and encouraged me every step of the way; Brian Conboy tapped his experience and knowledge to guide the course of the book; and Andrew von Hirsch made many perceptive and helpful contributions. Their unswerving loyalty has been a sustaining force to me.

To my friend, Richard Nixon—
May he do more than listen

Contents

POLITICAL
PRISONERS
IN AMERICA

Introduction

Those who won our independence believed that the final end of the State was to make men free to develop their faculties . . . they believed that freedom to think as you will and to speak as you think are means indispensable to the discovery and spread of political truth . . . that the greatest menace to freedom is an inert people . . . that fear breeds repression; that repression breeds hate; that hate menaces stable government; that the path of safety lies in the power of reason as applied through public discussion; they eschewed silence coerced by law—the argument of force in its worst form.

—Justice Louis Brandeis, concurring in *Whitney* v. *California* (1927)

Why do I write a book on American political prisoners? Why not the usual attempt by a former United States senator to portray the luminous characters and monumental events with which the author has had contact? That for another time. I'm too restless for memoirs, too troubled about my country's future for personalizing the past.

I recall the lilting rhetoric of 1961. The decade was going

3

to soar to new frontiers of hope and realization. For our victims at home as well as overseas, the decade seared more than it soared. Our racial sins finally caught up to us and "Burn, baby, burn" became a literal reality, matched only by the blind brutality of a foreign policy expressed in the wrenching words: "We had to destroy that village in order to save it." Race and war, the two great political issues which gripped America throughout the decade, enmeshed thousands in the criminal process.

In 1970, when I began to refer publicly to Philip and Daniel Berrigan as "political prisoners," an old friend of mine, the man who first organized a movement to draft me for Congress in 1959, abruptly withdrew his support. My friend was a very learned lawyer and he saw it as a simple case: the Berrigans destroyed federal property; that's a crime, and their motive makes no difference under the law. His view reflects the difficulties we all have in thinking about conscientious citizens who are moved by political frustrations to disobey the law.

It seemed to me that his was too narrow a view. Philip Berrigan had sent a long personal letter to me when I was in the Senate. He was in Lewisburg Penitentiary at the time for having poured blood and napalm over draft board records. I intervened on his behalf with prison officials, a friendship sprang up between us, and I spent many hours in conversation with both Phil and his imprisoned brother, Dan Berrigan. I knew them to be conscientious and moral citizens, fully dedicated to the service of their fellow men, in peace. They committed acts which the law defines as criminal, but they were certainly not ordinary lawbreakers. Were they criminal at all? My heart said no, but in my head I kept asking a lawyer's question: "What happens to the rule of law if men, however well-motivated, break the rules at will in order to express a view they consider to be of overriding importance?"

Philip Berrigan pointed out to me that he was trying to penetrate the consciousness of an America impervious to the destruction of human life in Vietnam. He compared his symbolic destruction of federal property to the act of a man who breaks down the door of another's house in order to save children from a fire. That would not result in a prison sentence for breaking and entering. Yet the analogy obviously served the priest's conscience better than a lawyer's need for an objective standard by which to place protest into neat categories: permissible or criminal.

As I puzzled about the propriety or impropriety of civil disobedience, I was becoming increasingly dismayed at the tendency of America's officialdom to view *any* challenge to authority as a crime. The case of the Presidio 27 focused my concern. These men were court-martialed for mutiny—the most serious charge in the Military Code of Justice—and they were sentenced to up to sixteen years at hard labor for participating in a ten minute, nonviolent sit-down demonstration at the Presidio stockade.

Senator Alan Cranston and I looked into the facts. These soldiers imprisoned at the Presidio, mostly for going AWOL and for other minor offenses, had been trying to protest truly unspeakable conditions there. The clogged sewage system, for instance, was backed up into the shower stalls and everywhere there was filth and the smell of human waste. Their appeals for better facilities had been repeatedly rebuffed, and their peaceful demonstration seemed to us clearly justified and inoffensive. We worked to get the sentences reduced. Men who are forced to endure confinement amidst rats, roaches, and floating feces protest with an admirable restraint when they sit and sing "America the Beautiful" and "We Shall Overcome."

My dismay intensified when I heard about Roger Priest. He was a tall and personable seaman. Except for his sailor's proclivity for four-letter words, he seemed to deserve his surname. He had ruffled feathers in Washington with "Om," an amusing but insulting antiwar and anti-Establishment newsletter which he wrote, printed and distributed off-base and off-duty. The Army went after him simply for what he had written. When I first got involved in his case, he faced court-martial and a possible thirty-nine-year sentence on sixteen charges including sedition and promoting disloyalty and disrespect in the armed services. I was beginning to suspect that the urge to repress dissent is boundless, that the First Amendment is all too easily waived and the integrity of our system too often sullied except where circumstance happens to focus public attention on the abuses.

Nevertheless, I was unprepared for the shocking prophecy Dan Ellsberg shared with me as I was leaving the Senate in December 1970. "They're going to get me into jail one way or another," he said, "because I've got to tell the truth about this war." Why jail? All he had done was to try to open some congressional eyes to startling historical facts. He knew more about the war than almost anyone: he had served as an advisor in the Defense Department during the war's escalation, and he had helped prepare parts of *The Pentagon Papers*. It was not until he went to Vietnam that the war, for the first time, came off the drawing boards for him and became an immense human tragedy.

As it turned out, the administration decided that telling the truth about history is a federal crime. Within a year, Leonard Boudin, Charles Nesson, and I were defending Ellsberg in a political trial involving a possible prison sentence of 115 years. When Ellsberg revealed to the public how our political leaders had systematically bypassed the political process for thirty years to escalate an unnecessary, unwinnable and immoral war, the Justice Department found a way to *get* him by twisting old laws into new shapes. The result, the Ellsberg trial, is a sophisticated message to the

American people—anyone who deals this administration a serious political embarrassment will be the target of a concerted effort to punish him.

Being so close to men whose political activity enmeshed them in the criminal process shattered the illusions I had held since civics class in grade school. I began to wonder whether the paraphernalia of our criminal process had always so overlapped with politics. Other incidents sharpened my curiosity. When I was in the Senate, speaking out against administration policies, I learned that my official telephone was tapped and that Military Intelligence agents were following me around the country, building a dossier on my public remarks.

The uncomfortable blurring of the line between dissent and crime forced me to ask myself whether there were political prisoners in America. The very phrase "political prisoner" was difficult for me, just as it is difficult for most Americans—lawyers and laymen alike. The words have the ring of slogan and of propaganda. "Free all political prisoners!" is not the sort of demand we are accustomed to finding in the editorial columns of our newspapers; we find it instead scrawled in revolutionary calligraphy on every kind of public surface. And the images it evokes are distinctly foreign: a consumptive Russian author, perhaps, courageously enduring the privations of numberless Siberian winters for refusing to write the word "God" in the lower case. Or a Greek democrat suffering, without benefit of trial, a harsh exile or imprisonment, or even torture, because his views on the dignity of man worry the junta generals.

It all seems so alien to America. We have always welcomed and given money to international committees trying to help political prisoners in foreign lands. When I was working with others to alleviate the plight of the families of Greek political prisoners, the question again came home:

how do *we* deal with our citizens who challenge the status quo?

The same international committees which we rely upon to monitor foreign abuses are today accusing the United States. Amnesty International, an organization concerned with "prisoners of conscience" everywhere in the world, maintains a fast-growing list of Americans whom they consider, after careful investigation of the facts, are in prison solely for what they believe.

Some countries openly label the expression of certain ideas and criticisms "political crime" and maintain a "political police" to track down violators. Those convicted proceed to "political prisons" or concentration camps. Such rituals are frankly designed to produce "political prisoners." Our own political and criminal processes are not so obviously repressive, but we cannot protect our fundamentally free and nonrepressive system merely by avoiding the labels—words do not have that kind of power over reality.

We are a people who firmly believe that a just and free society need not deal with political questions by resorting to the inflexible and drastic sanctions of the criminal law. Equally strong is our belief that all social conflicts can be resolved "politically," at the ballot box, and that neither repressive coercion by the government nor principled defiance of the law by the governed is proper.

Believing, as I do, that political change is necessary to our nation's stability, I found it difficult to acknowledge that politically pivotal citizens are arbitrarily removed from our political process and jailed, and that important questions of public policy are made into questions of guilt or innocence. How can there be political prisoners in America, where freedom of speech, the presumption of innocence, and a guarantee of fair trial stand in the way of any attempt to put a man behind bars for what he believes and says?

The reality of our political life is not so easily brought into line with the ideal. I have come to acknowledge that we *do* have, and that we always have had, political prisoners in America. In the perennial struggle for political power and in the inevitable conflicts that accompany change, dissenters and government alike have manipulated America's criminal process for political ends. It is through this intercourse of the political and criminal systems that "political prisoners" are born.

From the Boston Tea Party to the most recent destruction of draft records, lawbreaking by citizens pressing for political change and reform has punctuated virtually every important period of American political history. Those with political power, frightened and confused by dissent and unorthodoxy, have just as frequently tried to use the criminal process to control American political life and to repress dissent. President Adams used the Alien and Sedition Acts of 1798 to imprison his critics; grand juries and the ancient doctrines of conspiracy law have been bent to political purposes to silence critics of President Nixon's Vietnam policy.

The word "repression" like the phrase "political prisoner," has almost become the exclusive property of the sloganeers; yet it would sadly deplete our language were we to abandon whatever words they appropriate. I don't know what else to call it but repression when a criminal process is bent from its intended purposes and used to crush dissent, to make would-be critics of the status quo overcautious, and to signal that an unconventional lifestyle or a militant anti-Establishment attitude can lead to a jail sentence.

It is hard, very hard, to hear current American leaders accused of repression, but there is no reason to believe that conditions have changed so much, or mankind matured so far, that we are free of the repressive spirit which drove previous administrations. And we would be foolish to think that the barriers set in repression's way by the bare bones of the Constitution are sufficient, without constant vigilance, to keep that force in check.

In a democratic society, the extent to which the criminal process is corrupted for political gain is one measure of the responsiveness of its political institutions, the stewardship of its criminal process and the urgency of the need to alter policies or laws. Some overlap between the political and criminal processes is inevitable at the margin, but if we are to have a political system which is open to change and a criminal system which actually secures our safety, the overlap must be kept to a minimum. There is no sweeping panacea, but understanding the nature of our problem is an important first step.

In thinking about these problems I have found it useful to recognize that civil disobedients and victims of repression *are* political prisoners, even in America. But I do not agree with the wholesale indictment of our system drawn up by the children of the political poverty for which my generation is responsible. The American system has its faults, and we must expect those obsessed, repressed, or ensuffered by those faults to protest. Those overwhelmed by a singular fault, however, cannot be relied upon to give us a balanced overall assessment of the system, or of the possibilities for overcoming the faults within the system.

I do not agree with those who have come to believe that all laws are merely instruments for political repression and that any crime can be justified as a political act of personal liberation or social revolution. They obscure the real problem and their view is self-indulgent, and dangerous as well.

The radicals aren't the only ones contributing to the confusion. Many liberals, concerned by the failure of politics to eliminate the causes of crime and distressed at the body politic's apathy about the crisis of our prisons, have begun to champion all prisoners as political prisoners. This is an attempt to force us to be conscious of some important truths we all would rather ignore, but in the end it is another unhelpful variation on the cheap sociological argument that all crimes are society's fault and that individual responsibility counts not at all. The real cost of the argument is clarity.

I recognize that social, educational, and economic inequities flow directly from failures of our political process, and I agree that they are related to the incidence of crime. Yet I cannot accept an ordinary burglar's attempt to disassociate himself from his conduct by claiming special status as a political prisoner. Those civil disobedients and victims of repression who accede to such claims by their fellow inmates do themselves a disservice and further diffuse the focus of our concern. The tragic prisoner uprising at Attica impressed on all of us that the politicizing of prisoners is fast becoming a critical issue. Important though it is, however, it is a separate issue, and two types of political prisoners are enough for one book. I am concerned, in this book, with civil disobedients and victims of repression and not with politicized prisoners.

My pride in the good things about America remains undiminished, but from more than a decade in the House and in the Senate, I have come to see that our legal and political institutions are dangerously unresponsive and unyielding to the impassioned grievances of our own people. These grievances are not limited to the poor, the ethnic minorities, and the war resisters; blue- and white-collar America also fervently resist impositions of injustice upon them.

When words of appeal fall upon a seemingly inert system, words give way to action. Large numbers of disenchanted Americans have turned to civil disobedience, and some have turned to violence, in pursuit of their political ends, or simply to vent their spleens. The Establishment has reacted in ways bordering on blind panic, abusing the criminal process to lash back.

Ten years ago I would have told anyone that he was crazy if he had described to me what was about to happen in this country. I always thought our freedoms provided too many safety valves for such things to happen here. Yet, somehow the pressures grew beyond the capacity of our system, the country exploded, and so did my own complacency. I watched America, which prides itself on mass production of material benefits for its people, mass produce political prisoners. The very civil liberties which made our system ultimately responsive in the past, and which distinguish it from police states, were seriously threatened.

These developments weighed heavily on me when I was in the Senate. When the frenetic pace of public life slackened, I determined to try to describe what is happening to us and to place it in the perspective of our past. In the process I discovered that I shared with most Americans a kind of amnesia of patriotism. European friends had often remarked to me that Americans have no historical sense, and it is certainly true that we have no fondness for recalling our own mistakes. Our history is a record of almost two hundred years of unprecedented liberty and progress, but it is also a record strewn with failures—failures of vision, failures of leadership, and failures of our cherished institutions.

Few modern systems of government have survived intact for as long as ours, and few systems have demonstrated such flexibility and peacefulness in periods of political change. Americans are justly proud of this record, but we tend to forget the difficult circumstances of our birth as a nation and some of the sordid events marking our passage to the present. I confess that in writing this book I have been astonished at how much there is on the darker side of

American history that I either never knew, or had too quickly forgotten.

Our failure to confront past realities has left us dangerously unprepared for more recent variations on the political prisoner theme. In any event, I now reflect with more charity on my lawyer-friend who took offense at my use of the term. I'm afraid that all of us tend too much to the sunny view that our political and legal institutions, and the men who administer them, have consistently reflected the constitutional ideal. We have short memories. In the words of Emerson, "Time dissipates to shining ether the solid angularity of facts." Perhaps this book can make some contribution to restoring a useful angularity to the facts.

Part I

POLITICAL PRISONERS IN AMERICAN HISTORY

Ultimately all the questions . . . really boil down to one—whether we as a people will try fearfully and futilely to preserve democracy by adopting totalitarian methods, or whether in accordance with our traditions and our Constitution will have the confidence and courage to be free.

—Justice Hugo Black, dissenting in *Barenblatt* v. *United States* (1959)

1

Political Prisoners at the Beginning

I have sworn upon the altar of God, eternal hostility against
every form of tyranny over the mind of man.
—Thomas Jefferson

The great experiment in popular self-government and representative democracy which sprang from the American Revolution was grounded in the novel idea that, because government derived its legitimacy from the consent of the people, the broadest latitude must be given to all political opinion and expression. Novel and unorthodox ideas, challenging cherished beliefs of the moment, might hold some part of the truth. Truth, it was believed, would prevail over error in the public marketplace of ideas, so long as force was not used to tip the scales.

But even in the system of self-government conceived by the American revolutionaries, some men had to be entrusted with administrative power and the discretion to act to preserve the system. The years immediately following the Declaration of Independence were fraught with dangers: the British army was operating on American soil.

Perhaps it would be unreasonable to have demanded of our founding fathers that they rely, at such a time, on the new notion that all varieties of political opinion could be given free reign. But the consequences of their restrictions of that freedom must also be conceded: there were political prisoners at the beginning.

Early in January 1776, the Continental Congress urged the states to pass laws to prevent the public from being "deceived and drawn into erroneous opinion." Throughout the young nation, criminal laws were passed to curtail expression of Tory sentiments. By 1780, for instance, no resident of Thomas Jefferson's Virginia could lawfully wish health, prosperity, or success to the King, or concede that he was the King's subject. Violators could draw five years in prison and a fine of £20,000. It even became a crime to speak in a derogatory way of the new nation's currency. By 1778 all states had adopted systems of loyalty oaths which overlooked the distinction between loyalty and the ritual of swearing to it. If, for whatever reason, an American refused to submit to this compulsory expression of patriotism, punishment could be severe.[1]

Jefferson, the Revolutionary governor of Virginia, ordered military commanders to imprison not only those who refused to take the oath, but also those they suspected had aided, or *might* aid, the enemy. Some political suspects languished in American jails for months without trial or formal charge.

Pacifism, an ethical doctrine and a way of life, has always had significant political overtones in any society which finds itself at war. Many Quakers had been active in nonviolent resistance to the Stamp Act and to other oppressive British measures. But most of them could not condone revolution, which would inevitably be bloody.

During the war, their deep hostility to the use of force was often mistaken for Toryism by their neighbors. In

September 1777, seventeen Quaker leaders were arrested by Revolutionary authorities and accused of "treasonable relations with the enemy." The accused were hurried off to exile in Virginia where they were held for eight months. The Revolutionary government ignored their demand that they be released from illegal confinement or else tried. They never had a chance to prove in court the baselessness of the charges against them.[2]

Statistics are not available to show how many young Quakers went to jail for conscientious noncooperation with the draft. Some suffered violence at the hands of super patriotic mobs and some were forcibly conscripted and made to march toward the battle with guns tied to their backs. Two Quaker draft resisters were kept in jail in Lancaster, Pennsylvania, for over two years. Most states permitted Quakers and the members of other pacifist sects to avoid military service on the condition that they hire substitutes or pay fines. The Quakers felt, however, that these options could not be exercised without endorsing the war, and many were fined repeatedly for failing to hire substitutes.

Many Quakers also refused to swear loyalty oaths until after the war was over, and would not pay special wartime taxes. A few felt that even to handle the paper currency of the Revolutionary government would unacceptedly compromise their opposition to its war. Such refusal eventually became a capital offense and although no Quaker suffered the death penalty, one was actually sentenced to hang. The property and goods of hundreds of Quakers were seized and sold by authorities when they refused to pay the militia fines or war taxes. By the war's end, the Quakers' pacifism had cost them over £100,000. Eventually many ran out of property to offset the fines, and went to jail.

There were political prisoners at the beginning, but our experience of political imprisonment in America extends back to well before the Revolution. Our attitudes toward repression and civil disobedience have their roots in the pre-Revolutionary struggles.

JOHN PETER ZENGER

To you good lads that dare oppose
all lawless power and might,
You are the theme that we have chose,
and to your praise we write:
You dared to show your faces brave
In spite of every abject slave:
          with a fa la la.

Come on brave boys, let us be brave
        for liberty and law,
Boldly despise the haughty knave,
        that would keep us in awe.

These lines appeared in the *New York Weekly Journal* to celebrate the capture of the New York City Common Council by foes of the Royal Governor, William Cosby, in the municipal election of September 1734. The *Journal*'s printer, John Peter Zenger became the first famous American political prisoner when Cosby, the "haughty knave" of the song, had him imprisoned and tried on charges of seditious libel.[3]

Cosby's administration was unpopular with the British King's subjects in New York City; they responded sympathetically to the *Journal*'s regular satire and reportorial criticism. Instead of answering to the charges of corruption, greed, and illegality in his administration, Cosby lashed out at his critics, branding them lawbreakers who sought "to lead weak and unwary men into *tumults* and *sedition*, to the *disturbance* of the *public peace*, and to the endangering of all *order* and *government.*" The blast is not styled for the 1970s, but we hear the message often enough today.

The Royal Governor, however, had the law on his side. In the British monarchy of 1734, there was no such thing as a "loyal opposition." A man could be punished for the crime of "seditious libel" for any published statement, whether true or false, which criticized the conduct of public officials, the laws, or the institutions of government and *tended* to bring them into "disrepute." In trials for seditious libel, juries were not permitted to return verdicts of "guilty" or "not guilty": they were confined to determining whether the accused had, in fact, published the criticism. Only judges, officers of the government which had been criticized, were empowered to decide whether the words had the evil tendency.

Governor Cosby was at first frustrated in his effort to silence the critical *Journal.* Two consecutive grand juries, composed of city freeholders who thought the criticism justified even if illegal, refused to issue indictments. Cosby finally ordered his attorney general to bring the printer to trial without indictment (an extraordinary step) and had Zenger committed to prison. These highhanded maneuvers further alienated the New Yorkers, as did the unprecedented high bail Cosby's judge demanded for Zenger's release pending trial. Zenger and his friends undoubtedly could have raised the sum, but they played for public sympathy by leaving him in the city jail until his trial in 1735 —eight months later.

At the beginning of his trial, Zenger's lawyers challenged the credentials of the judges assigned to the case. The judges, who served at Cosby's "pleasure," responded by summarily disbarring the lawyers. Judicial highhandedness assured Zenger's trial an important place in our history, because the defense sent to Philadelphia for Andrew

Hamilton, probably the best American lawyer of his day. One contemporary observer of the trial remarked that Hamilton conducted the defense according to the "law of the future." It is well for Zenger that Hamilton did so, because the law of seditious libel in 1735 was squarely against him. Hamilton decided to treat the jury as the embodiment of public opinion and conducted his defense to appeal to them rather than to the law.

The trial began after Hamilton uncovered an attempt to pack the jury with the governor's friends and employees. Gesturing to the crowded courtroom, Zenger's lawyer declared that this was obviously a political trial, involving issues well beyond the formal charges. His purpose being political rather than legal, he argued that society's rulers are merely guardians of the public's interest and that vigorous criticism of government is the people's only safeguard against abuses of power.

The prosecution was determined to keep Governor Cosby's record out of the case. When Hamilton conceded that Zenger had printed the statements and announced that his defense would be to prove them true, the attorney general rose, dismissed the witnesses he had summoned to support the accusation against Zenger, and said: "I think the jury must find a verdict for the King; for supposing Zenger's articles were true, the law says that . . . their being true is an aggravation of the crime."

The judges correctly applied the law of the time and ruled that truth was no defense. Hamilton's final attempt to present the political case against Cosby met with no greater success. He argued that if truth aggravated the sedition, the court should welcome Zenger's proof that his published criticisms were true.

Frustrated, Hamilton turned to the jury: "Then gentlemen of the jury, it is to you we must now appeal for witnesses to the truth of the facts we have offered and are denied the liberty to prove." Hamilton asked the twelve to do what the judges refused to do, and what they ruled the jury had no right to do, to consider Cosby's record as a justification for Zenger's crime. "And this I hope is sufficient to prove," he concluded, "that jurymen are to see with their own eyes, to hear with their own ears, and to make use of their own consciences and understandings in judging of the lives, liberties or estates of their fellow subjects."

Hamilton was, in effect, appealing to the jury as a political institution. Reminding the jurors that they embody the popular will, he urged them to nullify the law as it had been stated by the court,and as it had been applied to Zenger's *Journal.* He called upon them to defy the judges and, by returning a verdict of not guilty, to register their protest alongside Zenger's against the governor's oppressive rule and his repressive use of the criminal law.

Hamilton's "political defense" won the day. The jury ignored Zenger's technical guilt, disobeyed the judges' instructions, and quickly returned with the prohibited general verdict of not guilty. The courtroom erupted with cheers, and Zenger was released the next day from his long imprisonment.

The Zenger trial was a dramatic demonstration of the jury's power to nullify a criminal law when it feels its application by authorities in a particular case is unjust. It brought an end in Colonial America to court trials for seditious libel.[4]

THE BOSTON TEA PARTY: FROM DISSENT TO RESISTANCE

This meeting can do nothing more to save the country.

—Samuel Adams, December 16,
1773, at about nine o'clock in the
evening

Samuel Adams raised his voice to adjourn the Boston meeting with these words so that he could be heard by the men, disguised as Mohawk Indians, waiting in the street outside the hall. For days, Adams had chaired mass meetings of Bostonians seeking, in vain, to remove from their harbor three ships laden with taxed tea. War whoops greeted Adam's signal, and the Boston Tea Party—perhaps the most celebrated act of civil disobedience in American history—was underway. The "Party" was not a spontaneous or frivolous rampage by unruly colonists but a calculated political act. It was designed by its organizers to make vividly clear the depth of colonial feeling against highhanded British rule, and to move disaffected Americans in other colonies from ineffectual, independent dissent to coordinated acts of resistance.[5]

Protests against the unresponsiveness of the King and Parliament had begun to escalate as early as the 1760s, when Great Britain, its treasury depleted by wars in which Americans felt they had no interest, launched a program of colonial taxation. "No taxation without representation" became the dissenters' slogan. Polite protests proved unavailing; petitions to Parliament were not read or answered.

Novel methods were devised to increase Royal revenues. By the Stamp Act of 1765, Parliament required that after November 1 government stamps be affixed to all commercial and legal documents, pamphlets, and newspapers. Nine of the thirteen colonies sent delegates to the Stamp Act Congress in New York in October, and, when their petition was ignored and the Act went into effect, it was met with widespread disobedience. Those who had been appointed to the lucrative stamp-collector posts were persuaded, often by the threat of mob violence, to resign their posts. Since this made the stamps virtually unavailable, even the colonial courts violated the law by accepting unstamped pleadings. More important, American merchants refused to pay the mounting debts to their creditors in Great Britain, for which they would have had to use stamped paper.

William Pitt and other friends of the American colonists in Parliament openly rejoiced at these acts of resistance and demanded repeal of the Act. They succeeded in doing so in March 1766, largely because of the distress of British merchants holding millions in pounds of unpaid accounts. But Parliament immediately passed a Declaratory Act to make it perfectly clear that the Americans' disobedient protest established no right of the unrepresented to be free of taxation.

Parliament's accession to London's commercial interests rather than to colonial political principles soon led to the events in Boston Harbor. The East India Company, which had been brought close to bankruptcy by its own costly wars in India, appealed to Parliament for help. Early in 1773, its tea monopoly was extended to America. Outraged Americans repeated the tactics they had used successfully in the Stamp Act Crisis, and in every port but Boston they persuaded the "consignees," the men appointed to receive the tea, to resign.

In December, the *Dartmouth*, the *Eleanor*, and the *Beaver* lay in Boston Harbor, loaded with 342 chests of tea. The leaders of the Boston tax resistance posted an armed guard at the docks to prevent the consignees from claiming the tea. The law provided, however, that if consignees failed for twenty days to claim the tea, it would be brought ashore by officials and sold at public auction. Adams and the other local leaders recognized that even a forced auction would make tea available and fracture the solidarity of resistance. They held mass meetings, some attended by as many as five thousand, to insist that the ships and their controversial cargo be returned to England. But the Royal Governor refused to let the captains take the ships out of Boston Harbor.

The first tea was to be brought ashore under the twenty-day rule on December 17. Until about nine o'clock on the night of December 16, the people of Boston confined their protest to more mass meetings. At Adams's last-minute signal, however, some seventy or eighty men in half-hearted Indian disguise stormed past the wharf guard, formed three well-organized squads, and boarded the ships. Methodically and carefully they hoisted the tea from the holds, broke open each crate, and cast it and its contents into the water. Thousands watched from the shore as the empty crates sailed out on a light breeze. By the first hours of December 17, the task was finished and the protesters had swept up. The only damage, apart from the sodden tea, was a broken padlock. It was replaced by an anonymous caller the next morning.

Critics of today's civil disobedience demonstrators might be tempted to point to the Boston Tea Party as a spectacular and effective protest against an unjust governmental policy, and as the model for restrained, well-planned, non-violent political demonstrations. It should be pointed out, however, that the archetypal American protest involved crimes of trespass and destruction of private property, and that the perpetrators of these crimes did not step forward to accept punishment at the hands of Royal prosecutors.

Yet the Boston action had the effect desired. In New York, a ship was easily turned back. In Philadelphia, the captain of the *Polly,* carrying 697 chests of tea, retreated at the sight of a crowd of eight thousand on the shore. The residents of Annapolis were more direct: they burned a brigantine, tea and all, to the water line.

It was the dramatic disobedience in Boston, however, which most enraged British authorities. Not only had the patriots prevented unloading of the tea, but the success of the Tea Party helped secure signatures, throughout the colony, to a covenant pledging a boycott of British-manufactured articles.

Great Britain failed to recognize that the Boston Tea Party was a demand, just short of open rebellion, for political and legal change. Several members of Parliament called for putting Boston to the torch; in the face of swelling colonial protest and hardening British reaction, Parliament ordered the Port of Boston closed until its citizens reimbursed the East India Company for its tea. The move seemed to spell disaster for the economy of Boston, which was entirely dependent on the sea. British authorities were again frustrated when other towns and colonies from as far as South Carolina rallied to Boston's support and sent food and supplies by land. The effect of Parliament's intemperate reaction was to push the colonies still closer together and to edge them toward a clear break with British rule.

2

Opening Moves

I have therefore long thought that a few prosecutions of the most prominent offenders would have a wholesome effect in restoring the integrity of the presses.
—Thomas Jefferson

Distinctively American styles of civil disobedience and repression were set soon after the War of Independence, during the administrations of Presidents Washington and Adams. An overlap of the political process with the criminal process became apparent: minorities petitioned Congress, refused to obey laws they felt were unjust, and actively resisted enforcement of those laws. Some were prosecuted and jailed; their political imprisonment served to dramatize the justice of their grievances. Smear campaigns were launched by those in political power attempting to cast their critics as criminals. Criminal laws were passed and administered to make the smears come true. Eventually, objectionable laws were abandoned, obnoxious policies were reversed, and political legitimacy restored, temporarily.

THE WHISKY REBELLION, 1794–1795

When the new Federal Government undertook to pay off at full value the Revolutionary War debts incurred by the several states, the farmers of western Pennsylvania were unhappy for a number of reasons.[1] They had already sold their apparently worthless state bonds to eastern speculators for next to nothing. Alexander Hamilton, Secretary of the Treasury and the leading figure in Washington's administration, made things worse for them by proposing that the bonds be paid off through an excise duty on whiskey and other liquors. As it was uneconomical for farmers west of the Allegheny Mountains to transport their grain over poor roads to distant eastern markets, they earned their livelihood by distilling whiskey from their crops and bartering it for the goods they needed.

When Congress passed Hamilton's excise tax statute in 1791, these farmers protested that the burden fell more heavily on them than on any others, wiping out any possible reward for their labor. When it was clear that their petitions to Congress would bring no relief, they began to violate the law. Their purpose was not so much to protest as it was to prevent collection of the tax. They harassed county inspectors and tax collectors; a few were even tarred and feathered. Throughout 1792 and 1793 the tax went largely unpaid. In 1794 Hamilton, who had turned a deliberately deaf ear, attempted to bring a large number of the distillers to trial for the accumulating unpaid taxes.

The farmers again defied the law. They refused to accept summonses from the federal marshals. Despairing of conventional political remedies, they armed themselves, they forced the surrender of army troops who were protecting the marshal, and they burned a house in which he sought protection. Joined by five thousand militiamen from the western part of the state, the farmers marched on Pittsburgh. An armed confrontation was barely averted when they were permitted to march through the town to voice their demands. They called for an end to the tax on whiskey, the expulsion of federal treasury officials, and the removal of the federal courts and judges responsible for enforcing the statute.

President Washington offered amnesty to the now rebellious farmers if they would agree to pay the tax, to obey the laws, and to submit to civil authority. When his offer was not widely accepted, his administration resorted to military coercion to reestablish federal control of the region.

Fifteen thousand militia were called and Washington himself led the troops. But it was easier to establish the supremacy of the federal government than it was to decide what to do with those who had rebelled. Imprisoning all who had flouted the law or who had challenged the government was hardly possible, and the administration stood to gain little from mass trials of simple farmers who had opposed what they honestly felt was an unjust law. Seventeen of the best-known leaders were jailed for six months and then tried for treason. A few were convicted and imprisoned, apparently in order to justify the administration's uncompromising denial of their political demands, for shortly after they were convicted they were granted presidential pardons.

The anti-Federalist opponents of Washington's administration and of Hamilton's policies did not condone the distillers' defiance of the law, but they were sympathetic to their plight. When Thomas Jefferson became president, he saw to it that the whiskey excise was repealed. Whether or not the farmers would have obtained this relief had they merely petitioned Congress year after year, their disobedience was an ample, and perhaps a necessary, demonstration of the depth of their opposition to the excise and to the unevenness of its burden.

THE FIRST SMEAR CAMPAIGN

The Whisky Rebellion was only one sign of growing dissent in the early Republic. Until 1793, differences over domestic policies such as the excise statute were relatively mild, even if they did entail lawbreaking. Then, as has so often been the case in our history, differences over foreign policy provoked deeper animosities.

By 1793 political parties had emerged and the split between the Federalists and the Democratic–Republicans was clear. The Federalists, who had the power of all three branches of government, naturally tended to stress the importance of stability and tranquillity. As the Establishment of their day—lawyers, clergy, merchants, wealthy landowners, and southern planters—they doubted the people's capacity for responsible self-government. Their concept of good government was elitist and antidemocratic, they deliberately confused dissent and disloyalty, and they were willing to use legal and military power to control public opinion. The Democratic–Republican minority, also called Jeffersonians and anti-Federalists, represented a faith in public opinion and popular government. The Federalists feared anarchy, the Jeffersonians feared tyranny.

Their differences came to a head over the French Revolution and France's war with England. On September 21, 1792, France declared herself a Republic. Louis XVI was executed January 21, 1793. On February 1, 1793, France declared war on Great Britain, Spain, and Holland. The Federalists, having erected a financial system based on revenues collected from commerce with England, sympathized with her and viewed the French, particularly after the Terror, as anarchists whose ideas threatened order and authority everywhere.

The Jeffersonians saw in the French Revolution a victory for liberty, and they tended to identify Britain with the suppression of individual freedoms against which the American Revolution had been fought.

Soon after the European war began, "Democratic Societies" were formed throughout the United States to express support for the French and to oppose Federalist foreign and domestic policy. As the whiskey-distilling farmers of western Pennsylvania had not yet won relief from the 1791 excise statute, it is no surprise that the Societies gained particular strength in their region.

President Washington attempted to place the blame for the Whisky Rebellion on the Democratic Societies and the ideas of the French Revolution. By linking the Jeffersonians to the Societies, our first president sought to brand any organized opposition to his administration's policies as a criminal attack on government itself. Using a style of invective still popular today among those in political power, Washington blasted the "self-created societies," and declared his belief that the "peace of society" is endangered when citizens form permanent groups to pass judgment on, and to influence the policies of, their government.

As the Republicans pointed out, President Washington voiced no such criticism of the Cincinnati Society, an aristocratic military group actively supporting Federalist policy. As James Madison put it: "The game was to connect the Democratic Societies with the odium of the [Whisky] insurrection—to connect the Republicans in Cong[res]s with those societies—to put the P[resident] ostensibly at the head of the other party, in opposition to both." Madison labeled this effort by Washington as "perhaps the greatest error of his political life." Jefferson, with dripping sarcasm, called it "wonderful indeed, that the President should have permitted himself to be the organ of such an attack on the freedom of discussion, the freedom of writing, printing and publishing." And so the Democratic–Republican Party, deriving its name from the societies so vehemently denounced by George Washington, took its place in opposition to the Federalists.

The stage was set for a conflict over the fundamental premises of our political system. To the Federalists, criticism of elected officials undermined the very system by which they had been chosen, and public confidence in the current administration could not be undermined without threatening the stability of the state. It is only natural for those with political power to treat any effort to "throw the rascals out" as an effort to "overthrow the government."

THE ALIEN AND SEDITION ACTS: POLITICAL CRIME

Federalist sensitivity to Democratic–Republican criticism intensified as America's precarious neutrality in the French–English conflict began to falter.[2] In 1794, Jay's Treaty avoided war with England but almost brought on war with the French, who began an aggressive campaign against American shipping. When John Adams won the presidency for the Federalists in 1796 and his efforts to negotiate with the French collapsed in 1798, he began to ready the nation for war. Increasingly, Federalists charged that criticism of the administration was opposition to government itself, and that it threatened the nation's security. The president's wife labeled the Jeffersonians "the French Party"; congressional anti-Federalists were named as tools of the French; and rumors flew that the Philadelphia *Aurora*, the principal anti-Federalist newspaper, was manipulated by the French.

Efforts to discredit the Republican anti-Federalists were designed to eliminate the threat they posed to Federalist dominance of government and society. As the Adams administration prepared for war against the external foe, it launched a security program against the Republican internal foe and against the political unorthodoxy they espoused. Adams, in public pronouncements whipping up passions against France, warned that a foreign influence had appeared in the opposition to his administration. Some of his remarks led the Jeffersonians to believe that the president intended to treat all in their party as traitors if the French invaded. Even Alexander Hamilton moved to tone down the president.

Having raised the specter of an international revolutionary conspiracy directed by a foreign power, the Adams administration moved quickly to protect the young nation from it—and incidentally to defend the political status quo. Several leading Republican publicists and spokesmen were aliens who had not completed the requisite period of residency to obtain citizenship. The Federalists moved first to capitalize on the general hostility to aliens which accompanied degeneration of relations with France. In 1798 the Federalist-sponsored Naturalization Act changed the period of residence required for admission to full citizenship from five to fourteen years. The companion Alien Act authorized the president to deport all aliens he regarded as dangerous to the public peace and safety, or whom he suspected of "treasonable or secret" inclinations.

As it turned out, these two measures did not play a major role in the repression that followed. The Federalists' main weapon was the Sedition Act of 1798. It outlawed any "false, scandalous and malicious" statements about the president or Congress, made with the intent to bring them "into contempt or disrepute" or to stir up opposition to any law or presidential act. Opposition to the Sedition Act itself could therefore be criminal, as some anti-Federalists were to discover.

By itself, the Sedition Act gave President Adams less power than Governor Cosby had had under the Star Chamber doctrine of "seditious libel." "Truth," in 1798, was a defense; and juries had some right to judge the legal issue of whether the statement was seditious, as well as the factual question of whether the accused made the statement. Also, the accused's intent was to be weighed, along with the "tendency" of his words, in deciding whether the statement was designed to bring the government into disrepute. This is much of what Andrew Hamilton had argued for in his defense of John Peter Zenger in 1735.

It quickly became apparent, however, that liberalizing the old doctrine could have the effect of reversing the burden of proof. As the law was applied by Federalist judges, those accused of sedition often had to prove the truth of their opinions; otherwise evil intent would be "obvious," as Supreme Court Justice Samuel Chase was to rule. "Truth" is valueless as a defense when men are prosecuted for their opinions. It is a recurrent disappointment to mankind that political truth cannot be proved, and a recurrent feature of repression that dissenters are punished when they fail to do so.

Enforcement of the Sedition Act was a strictly partisan affair. Republicans were indicted by Federalist grand juries, prosecuted by Federalist prosecutors, and convicted by Federalist juries. Federalist judges used the trials to expound on religion, politics, and morality. They denounced defendants as foes of right-minded American values, and overawed juries into returning guilty verdicts. The presumption of innocence was abandoned, and the burden of proof reversed. Looking back it seems as though the Federalists had never heard of John Peter Zenger.

The most vehement demand for enforcement of the law came from Federalist newspapers which called for prosecution of their Republican competitors and branded the Jeffersonian opposition as treason. Secretary of State Pickering read the Republican press avidly, clipped offensive articles, and sent them to President Adams and to Federal prosecutors. Prosecutions were brought under the Act against the editors of the four leading Republican newspapers and against three of the more outspoken Republican officeholders. There were at least twenty-five arrests, fifteen indictments, and ten convictions.[3] Sentences ranged from a fine of $5 and six hours in jail to $400 and eighteen months. A defendant who was fined $400 and could not raise the money was behind bars for two years.

Vermont's Republican Congressman Matthew Lyon was the first victim. In a letter written to a Vermont newspaper before the Sedition Act was made law, but published after its passage, Lyon stated that under the Federalist administration, "every consideration of the public welfare was being swallowed up in a continual grasp for power, in an unbounded thirst for continual pomp, foolish adulation, and selfish avarice." Lyon established his own newsletter, provocatively entitled *The Scourge of Aristocracy and Repository of Important Political Truths*, and he played a part in the publication of a letter by a New England poet which contained criticism of Adams's character in language less than polite.

Congress, in the election year of 1798, was almost evenly divided between the Federalists and the Republicans, and national attention focused on the Lyon trial. The only question presented to his jury was whether the words Lyon had published would tend to bring the president and government into contempt and disrepute. A Federalist jury had no problem finding him guilty and he was sentenced to four months in jail and fined $1,000.

As is so often the case with repressive prosecutions, the conviction and sentence made Lyon something of a hero, even in New England which was a Federalist stronghold. Far from silenced, the administration critic ran a highly successful campaign from jail and was returned to Congress. His journey back to Philadelphia was marked with triumphant parades and speechmaking.

Some of the prosecutions were even more easily turned to Republican advantage. In Philadelphia, Luther Baldwin was convicted of sedition upon an informer's testimony. The accusation was that upon witnessing a sixteen gun salute to the passing president, the inebriated Baldwin said he did not care if they fired through the "president's ass." The Federalists won the case, but lost face.

In New York, Jedidiah Peck—a minister, a member of the New York Assembly, and a former judge—was indicted and arrested on charges of sedition for circulating a petition favoring repeal of the Alien and Sedition Laws. The Peck prosecution was not pushed to trial, however, when even his arrest made a martyr of the upstate leader and seemed likely to increase his popularity at the polls.

As the elections of 1800 approached, the Federalists met with some successes. They succeeded in silencing the major Republican newspapers in New York including the prominent *Argus*, whose editor, the widow Mrs. Greenleaf, was indicted for sedition. While her trial was pending, Alexander Hamilton brought a libel action in state court for an article in the *Argus* which suggested that he might have had British financial backing in an alleged attempt to buy out the most important Republican newspaper of all, the Philadelphia *Aurora*. The lawsuit forced Mrs. Greenleaf to sell the *Argus* just before the election.

As Mrs. Greenleaf was already under Federal indictment, Hamilton chose to bring his state libel action against the *Argus*'s journeyman printer, David Frothingham, who was not a much better target than the widow. Frothingham earned only eight dollars a week and supported a wife and six children. His lawyer argued that a journeyman printer could hardly be held responsible for the editorial statements of the paper, and that, in any case, no good Federalist (as Hamilton surely was) could be libeled by the suggestion that he wished to shut the Republican *Aurora* down. The jury, after a charge which gave them very little choice, convicted Frothingham and recommended leniency. Frothingham was nevertheless sentenced to four months and $100.

The Federalists attempted to silence the Republican *Aurora* by indicting its editor, William Duane, for having suggested that British money influenced Federalist policy. Duane was in the fortunate position of possessing documentary support for the truth of his allegations. When Duane produced a letter, actually written by Adams, in which the president complained of British influence in the administration, the prosecutor hastily agreed to postpone trial and ultimately dropped the charges.

The Federalists' persecution of Duane caused further embarrassment. After Duane published an account of Federalist attempts to change the election laws to favor Adams in the upcoming contest against Jefferson, the Senate indignantly ordered him to appear before an investigating committee. When the senators attempted to restrict his right to counsel, Duane refused to appear and went underground to avoid an intensive manhunt. Though in hiding, he continued to taunt the Federalists with his critical articles in the *Aurora*.

In the summer of 1800, the bitter campaign between Jefferson and Adams was in full swing. Adams had beaten Jefferson by only three electoral votes in 1796, and the worried Federalists launched a major attack on Republican writers of election literature. Federalist Supreme Court Justice Samuel Chase turned his circuit ride that summer into a blatant effort to curb the Jeffersonian writers.

The trial against James Callendar in Richmond, Virginia, is best remembered because the bias displayed by Justice Chase led to his later impeachment. Callendar had fled from Philadelphia, where he worked for the *Aurora*, the day before President Adams signed the Sedition Act.

When Justice Chase reached Richmond in the summer of 1800, he had Callendar brought to trial for an election pamphlet critical of the president. Callendar had had the temerity to send a copy to Adams himself.

Virginia was a tough forum for a Federalist sedition prosecution; it was Jefferson country, and the citizens themselves raised the money for Callendar's defense. Nevertheless, a Federalist jury was empaneled, and Justice Chase, in preliminary discussion, expressed his belief that the writings were false and the writer's malicious intent "sufficiently obvious." By his rulings, Chase effectively required Callendar to prove his innocence over a presumption of guilt. He ruled that Callendar had to prove the truth of every statement which the prosecution charged was seditious—statements such as "the reign of Mr. Adams has been one continued tempest of malignant passions." Justice Chase so frequently interrupted and made such restrictive evidentiary rulings that he drove Callendar's lawyer from the defense table.

The pamphleteer was sentenced to nine months and $200, and remained in prison until the day the Sedition Act expired. The report of his trial, however, became forceful campaign literature, and from prison he continued to attack the Federalists, Justice Chase, and President Adams.

In the end, the Federalist attempt to silence critics with a repressive criminal law facilitated the spread of opposition. They tried to enforce their view that the only lawful way for the people to express dissent and present grievances against administration policy is through the ballot, by changing representatives in election years. They thought it *necessary* to a stable government that public criticism and opposition to government policy be prohibited in order to protect the legitimacy of the system. That is still a not uncommon view among those who wield political power.

But the actions of leading Republicans pose an interesting question about civil disobedience. Passed by a clear majority of Congress, signed by the president, and upheld by three Supreme Court justices riding circuit, the Sedition Act was the law of the land. Many people, nevertheless, openly and systematically violated this law which, as interpreted, forbade criticism of the Sedition Act itself. Madison and Jefferson (who was vice-president at the time and bound by his oath of office to uphold and enforce the law) secretly urged state legislatures to proclaim the Act null and void. The Virginia and Kentucky legislatures passed such resolutions in what, from the vantage of 1972, appears to be a remarkable act of legislative civil disobedience incited by the vice-president of the United States. The Virginia General Assembly resolved that the Sedition Act

> exercises . . . a power not delegated by the Constitution, but, on the contrary, expressly and positively forbidden by one of the amendments thereto—a power which, more than any other, ought to produce universal alarm, because it is levelled against the right of freely examining public characters and measures, and of free communication among the people thereon, which has ever been justly deemed the only effectual guardian of every other right.

The Virginia and Kentucky Resolutions seem to fit the crime of sedition as it was developed by the Federalist trial courts: they were published statements designed to bring into disrepute a law of the United States and the Congress which passed it. Jefferson and Madison believed that state legislatures had the power to rule on the constitutionality of federal laws.* These two founding fathers violated a

---

*The United States Supreme Court, in 1964, finally commented on the constitutionality of the law: "Although the Sedition Act was never tested in this Court," it said, "the attack upon its validity has carried the day in the court of history." *New York Times Co.* v. *Sullivan*, 376 U.S. 254, 276 (1964).

federal law in order to challenge its constitutional validity, just as Martin Luther King and others were to violate state segregation laws in order to challenge their constitutionality in the Supreme Court.

Although the resolutions stopped short of urging obstruction of attempts to enforce the law, the legislators themselves risked prosecution for passing them. Jefferson's draft for the Kentucky legislature came very close to urging resistance; it recommended that the states take whatever measures were necessary to ensure that federal power to enforce the Sedition Act not "be exercised within their respective territories."[4]

In the fall of 1800, Jefferson was swept into office largely on the strength of public reaction to Federalist repression. The "overthrow" of the governing party and administration leaders did not result in an "overthrow" of the government of the United States.

The new president pardoned violators of the Act when he took office, and Congress eventually repaid their fines. In his First Inaugural Address, Jefferson affirmed the right of Americans "to think freely and to speak and to write what they think." Majority rule must be respected, he said, but "to be rightful [it] must be reasonable."

> If there be any among us who would wish to dissolve this Union or to change its republican form, let them stand undisturbed as monuments of the safety with which error of opinion may be tolerated where reason is left free to combat it.

Those were fine and wise words, but they were not always honored in subsequent American history, not even by Jefferson. Like many champions of civil liberty and popular government, he found that when his humane ideology was conjoined with power, it became possible to justify criminal prosecutions against the political expression of his opponents. Jefferson, in many ways the foremost advocate of the American system of freedom of expression, felt that the system was in constant danger of subversion by enemies at home and abroad. He came to identify himself with the American experiment so completely that he perceived attacks on him or on the wisdom of his policies as threats to the security of the democracy.

In 1802 he wrote to his attorney general, "I would wish much to see the experiment tried of getting along without public prosecutions for *libels*. I believe we can do it." In 1803 he wrote, in answer to a French inquiry, "As yet, we have found it better to trust the public judgment, rather than the magistrate, with the discrimination between truth and falsehood." Two weeks later, in a letter to Governor Thomas McKean of Pennsylvania, Jefferson wrote that the Federalists, who had failed when in power to destroy freedom of the press by direct attack, were now "pushing its licentiousness and its lying to such a degree of prostitution as to deprive it of all credit."

> I have therefore long thought that a few prosecutions of the most prominent offenders would have a wholesome effect in restoring the integrity of the presses. Not a general prosecution, for that would look like persecution; but a selected one.

A selection was quickly made. The Sedition Act itself was no longer in effect, but Henry Croswell, Federalist editor of *The Wasp*, was charged with "seditious libel" under the old New York common-law doctrine which Governor Cosby had so abused. Croswell published a piece accusing Jefferson of having paid Callendar to write attacks on Washington and Adams. As one student of Jefferson's "darker side" has observed, "He had an utterly exquisite constitutional conscience when he was not in power."[5]

The prosecution of Croswell is particularly instructive. Perhaps it is no surprise that, with the roles and interests reversed, Alexander Hamilton now came forward to defend Croswell and made an eloquent plea for freedom of speech and press (a view he had not expressed at David Frothingham's trial). He argued, as had Andrew Hamilton before him, that the common law of seditious libel was outmoded; that publication of the "truth, with good motives, for justifiable ends" should not be a crime. Henry Croswell lacked the good fortune of John Peter Zenger and, confronted with a Jeffersonian court and jury, he was easily convicted.[6]

3

Obeying the "Higher Law"

Now . . . the right of property in a slave is distinctly and expressly affirmed in the Constitution. The right to traffic in it, like an ordinary article of merchandise and property, was guaranteed to the citizens of the United States, in every State that might desire it, for twenty years. And the Government in express terms is pledged to protect it in all future time, if the slave escapes from his owner.

—Dred Scott v. *Sanford* (1857)

Slaves were subjected to imprisoning conditions of the most obvious sort. Not only their silence, but virtually every aspect of their lives was coerced under stiff laws passed by fearful and oppressive whites. Under the law they were property, not persons. Black Codes varied from state to state, but they were generally designed to protect the property rights of slave owners, and to protect whites from the real and imagined dangers that threaten the rulers of any totalitarian system. Slaves had no rights in the courts; they could make no contracts; they were forbidden to own most types of personal property; and they could not strike a white, even in self-defense. The rape of a female

44

slave was considered a crime only because it involved trespassing on the property of another white. Slaves were not permitted to congregate unless a white was present.[1]

The Abolitionists are the best-remembered civil disobedients from that time, but the slaves themselves engaged in widespread resistance. There were over two hundred slave revolts before the Civil War, and all against impossible odds. Denmark Vesey led slaves in Charleston, South Carolina, in a conspiracy to revolt in 1822. The planned uprising was aborted by mass arrests, but in the panic that followed, South Carolina tightened its Black Code. In 1831 Nat Turner's uprising in Southampton County, Virginia, took the lives of sixty whites in twenty-four hours. More than one hundred of the slaves were killed when they were finally engaged by state and federal troops. Others, including Turner, were hanged. A few whites were executed for participating in or helping to plan these and other revolts. Rumors of conspiracies abounded and many slaves were executed on suspicion of plotting against their white owners.

Turner's insurrection, and the stirrings of militant abolitionist sentiments in the North at about the same time, brought renewed tightening of the Black Codes; but slaves continued to engage in disobedience short of insurrection. As individuals who were denied any part in the governance of civil society, slaves were not really "civil" disobedients, but the forms of their resistance are chilling examples of a theoretical limit to disobedient protest. By loafing on the job or feigning illness they disobeyed the law. They engaged in elaborate sabotage, ruining farm tools and destroying crops. They burned forests, barns, and homes. They ran away. The most startling form of disobedience was self-mutilation and suicide. Slaves defied their masters' property rights by cutting off their toes, fingers, and hands.

In 1807, two boatloads of newly arrived slaves starved themselves to death in Charleston.

The Abolitionists opposed slavery on two grounds: it was contrary to the teachings of Christianity, and it subverted the American ideals of freedom and equality.[2] Early in the nineteenth century theirs was a minority view; Abolitionists were hounded and attacked by mobs in the North as well as in the South. Their civil disobedience won them the sympathy, and eventually the support, of their northern neighbors; but in the South, fear of abolition quickly stirred those in power to erect a system of repressive criminal laws.

In Louisiana, a conversation "having a tendency to promote discontent among free colored people, or insubordination among slaves" could lead to a sentence ranging from twenty-one years at hard labor to the death penalty. In 1832, Georgia made death the penalty for printing or disseminating any literature tending to incite slave insurrections. North and South Carolina immediately followed suit. In 1836 Virginia forbade any member of an Abolition Society to enter the state, and in 1849 made it a crime to say "Owners have no right of property in slaves."

Although there was some feeling expressed in the South that these restrictions on political speech were worse than the evil they were designed to prevent, and although sentences were generally lenient, many who voiced an antislavery political view were charged and convicted. However, political conformity was more often, and more efficiently, enforced by mob action: whippings, beatings, and tar-and-feathering of suspected Abolitionists were common. Hundreds were lynched.

Harsh treatment and repression were not reserved for northern Abolitionists who ventured South: in April 1804, Judge Jabez Bowen, addressing a grand jury in Savannah, denounced slavery as an obstacle to the happiness and welfare of the people of Georgia. He ordered the grand jury to investigate the subject and draw up a plan for gradual emancipation of slaves. The grand jurors denounced the judge, accused him of disseminating ideas that would foster "domestic insurrection," and had him arrested on charges of attempting to incite a slave insurrection. He was jailed for two weeks, until his family raised an $80,000 bond, and he was impeached at the next session of the legislature.[3] Before the Civil War, hardly a single voice criticizing the institution of slavery could be heard in the South. By repressing moderate discussion of the most important issue facing the nation, the South ensured its subsequent tragedy.

Abolitionists exhausted all remedies short of disobedience. Petitions to Congress demanding the abolition of slavery trickled in until the House of Representatives adopted the following resolution in 1836:

> Whereas, it is extremely important and desirable that the agitation of this subject should be finally arrested, for the purpose of restoring tranquillity to the public mind, . . . all petitions . . . resolutions . . . or papers, relating in any way . . . to the subject of slavery, or the abolition of slavery, shall, without being either printed or referred, be laid upon the table and that no further action whatever shall be had thereon.

The effect of the "gag-rule" was to eliminate discussion of slavery in Congress, but it swelled the Abolitionist ranks with citizens outraged by the withdrawal of the right to petition. Very quickly the number of petitions tabled reached more than half a million.

The primary target for Abolitionist attack was the Fugitive Slave Law. It required all citizens to help capture and return runaway slaves and it prohibited any interference with slaveholders or federal marshals executing the law. The Constitution itself provided, in Article IV, that "No person held to Service or Labour in one State, under the Laws thereof, escaping into another, shall, in Consequence of any Law or Regulation therein, be discharged from such Service or Labour, but shall be delivered up on Claim of the Party to whom such Service or Labour may be due."

The Supreme Court repeatedly upheld the validity of the Fugitive Slave Law and ruled that it could not be limited by the states, but many citizens simply could not be compelled to assist in recapturing runaway slaves or to stand by while it was done in the name of the law. The "Underground Railroad" grew up in direct defiance of federal authority. Slaves who made their way North were provided with food, shelter, and transportation. Abolitionists helped them to avoid their former owners, the federal agents, and (for those who reached Canada) the laws of the United States itself. In the thirty years before the Civil War, sixty thousand blacks broke the laws which forced them to remain in bondage. Abolitionists were imprisoned in the South for helping to organize escapes, and in the North for obstructing their recapture. All were law-violators unwilling to wait for a change in the law through normal political process.

The Compromise of 1850 involved an alteration of the Fugitive Slave Law. One accused of being a fugitive was no longer allowed to testify in his own behalf; he was limited to a summary hearing, not in court before a judge, but before a federal commissioner. The penalty for aiding a fugitive was increased to $1,000 and six months in jail. These stricter laws, however, led to more and more widespread violations. Abolitionists broke fugitives out of jail and carried them bodily out of hearings before the commissioners. Juries became increasingly sympathetic to all forms of disobedience of this law, and indictments far out-numbered convictions.

In 1851 a group of twenty-four were indicted for having broken a fugitive, William Henry, out of jail in Syracuse, New York. The federal judge in Buffalo heaped scorn on them, calling them "disorderly and turbulent men, the common disturbers of society." When they tried to challenge their indictments on the ground that the marshal had permitted "volunteers" on their grand jury, the judge responded that if they could not in conscience obey the Fugitive Slave Law, they could "seek a residence in some other country." The judge missed the point: the Abolitionist law-violators believed that, as *citizens*, they had an affirmative duty to disobey such a law. The view of the federal judiciary was not widely shared by the people of upstate New York. The government was able to secure only one guilty verdict in the first four trials, and it dropped the charges against the rest.[4]

Boston, the site of the Tea Party, was the heart of Abolitionist disobedience. Crowds of otherwise law-abiding citizens acted swiftly there to protect blacks threatened with reenslavement. In February 1851, a mob broke into the Boston courtroom where a fugitive's hearing was in progress and executed a dramatic rescue. President Millard Fillmore declared a state of emergency in Massachusetts, prepared for the possible use of federal troops, and issued a proclamation calling for the prosecution of all "aiders and abettors." In calling for indictments from a grand jury sitting in Boston, Judge Sprague denounced the Abolitionists as "beyond the scope of human reason and fit subjects either of consecration or a mad-house." The grand jury indicted three of those involved in the rescue, but the government was forced to drop the prosecutions after an acquittal and a series of mistrials.[5]

It became quite expensive for federal authorities to enforce the law in Boston against respectable citizens who were increasingly willing to risk imprisonment. In May 1854, the fugitive slave Anthony Burns was taken into custody. The night before Burns was scheduled to go before a commissioner, Abolitionists called a mass meeting at Faneuil Hall to protest the proceedings. After the prominent leaders called for something to be done, a huge crowd marched on the courthouse. A melee broke out when some marchers forced their way in and were repulsed by federal troops, and a stray shot killed a bystander. Burns turned out to be too well-guarded to be set free that night and by the next day hundreds of federal troops appeared to protect the courthouse. At his summary hearing, Burns was found to be a fugitive and arrangements were made to return him to Virginia. The citizens of Boston, unable to block execution of the despised law, raised the money to purchase Burns and set him free.

In June, Justice Samuel Curtis charged a grand jury to indict those who had attempted to obstruct the law by rescuing Burns. He instructed the grand jurors that the leaders who spoke at the meeting before the march, and those who accompanied the crowd to the courthouse, were equally guilty with those who had actually attempted to free Burns. The grand jury refused to indict.[6]

The increasingly defiant Abolitionist lawbreaking had a major impact on Massachusetts politics. The willingness of respected citizens to violate a law, to face criminal charges, and openly to articulate their reasons for resistance, focused political passions on the slavery issue and drew more and more people to the cause of Abolition. In 1854 a new antislavery party was formed, uniting the Abolitionists with traditionally less radical elements under the party name "Republican." By the next year they elected Charles Sumner to the United States Senate, and in 1858 the new party swept the state.

Developments in other northern states followed a similar pattern. Public violations of law led to widespread sympathy with the antislavery philosophy and molded public opinion. The elections of 1858 went to the Republicans throughout the North, and Abolitionist sentiment ran so high that some state legislatures, governors, and even courts were defying the federal government. As Abolitionist fervor spread and talk of civil war increased, some U.S. marshals trying to enforce the Fugitive Slave Law were arrested, tried, and convicted for assault. Some slaveowners, attempting to exercise their right under the law to retake alleged fugitives without legal process, were arrested, tried, and convicted for kidnapping. In these cases law-enforcement officers, judges, and juries were all disobeying the law of the land. Their lawbreaking seems vindicated by history. The laws they violated are today universally held to be inhuman and immoral. Moreover, their politically motivated lawbreaking proved important in bringing about the political change they desired—abolition of slavery.

The years of the Civil War were unique in our history. With half the nation in open war against it and the capital city threatened, the federal government needed to take extraordinary measures for its security. Some of the devices President Lincoln chose, however, strained our criminal system in ways which were used in later crises, particularly his policy of preventive detention. By suspending the writ of *habeas corpus*, the citizen's ancient protection against illegal imprisonment, Lincoln permitted military commanders to bypass the criminal process even in areas where courts were functioning normally and where there was absolutely no danger of rebellion or invasion. The Supreme Court repudiated this exercise of executive power in a decision handed down after the war, too late to prevent the illegal and all too often vengeful jailing of political dissidents, along with spies and other dangerous individuals.[7]

Thousands were imprisoned on suspicion and rumor and were held, without being charged with any crime, for as long as the administration saw fit. By postponing trials, prosecutors avoided acquittals on the favored charge of treason—acquittals which would have made the preventive-detention policy even harder to justify. The number of political imprisonments by executive arrest during this period is hard to determine. Incomplete records in the War Department show over thirteen thousand cases, but the figure has been put as high as thirty-eight thousand. A like proportion of prisoners to population today would land two hundred thousand Americans behind bars for political unreliability.

A powerful political movement for the emancipation of women reaped its legal arguments and political tactics from the Abolitionist success. The Fourteenth Amendment, adopted in 1868 to establish full citizenship for the formerly enslaved, stated flatly that all persons born in the United States were entitled to the privileges and immunities of citizenship. Leading suffragettes argued that women thereby had been granted the right to vote. Before the Supreme Court dashed their hopes on that score in 1894,[8] the suffragettes' techniques for raising legal, political, and moral issues (particularly their use of courtrooms and jails as political forums) made their movement the prototype for twentieth-century protest.

The most striking incident was the trial of Susan B. Anthony. Federal law made it a crime for anyone to vote without the legal right to do so. In the 1872 election, Susan B. Anthony won access to a polling booth in Rochester, New York, with the considerable force of her personality and a copy of the Fourteenth Amendment. When she was arrested by federal authorities, she immediately became a *cause célèbre*, delivering more than a speech per week until her trial in the summer of 1873. Presiding over the courtroom in Canandaigua, New York, for the occasion was Ward Hunt, a newly appointed Justice of the United States Supreme Court. To prevent Ms. Anthony from using the trial as a forum, he refused to let her conduct her own defense, ruled against her lawyer's attempt to put the Fourteenth Amendment before the jury to rebut the accusation against her, and instructed the jury to find her guilty. To stop her from making it a test case, he prevented an immediate appeal by declining to send her to prison, even when she refused to pay the fine he imposed. Ms. Anthony solicited money and support for the suffrage cause through a widely distributed report of her trial. Her disobedience and Justice Hunt's repressive rulings politicized far more women and helped make the women's vote inevitable.

Justice Hunt's judicial highhandedness was nearly replicated in 1970 by Judge Julius Hoffman's treatment of Black Panther leader Bobby Seale. When Justice Hunt finally permitted Susan B. Anthony to speak on her own behalf, before he passed sentence, she delivered one of the strongest politically motivated verbal attacks in American courtroom history:

> Yes, your honor, I have many things to say; for in your ordered verdict of guilty, you have trampled under foot every vital principle of our government. My natural rights, my civil rights, my political rights are all alike ignored. Robbed of the fundamental privilege of citizenship, I am degraded from the status of a citizen to that of a subject; and not only myself individually but all of my sex are, by your honor's verdict, doomed to political subjection under this so-called Republican government.[9]

4

Political Prisoners and
the "War to End All Wars"

SENATOR STERLING: Could it be said that the natural or probable effect of the circulation of the handbills would have
been to obstruct recruiting or enlistment in the Army?

MR. PANKEN: I think, Mr. Chairman, that the circulation of
the Bible could be interpreted to mean that it would obstruct enlistment. "Love thy neighbor," for instance,
would certainly lead some people to believe that that
would inhibit fighting and war.

—December, 1920

The First World War once again gave a national administration the opportunity to punish criticism of its policies as
attacks on the nation itself. Any dissent, particularly from
those associated with unorthodox political and economic
views, was branded a pro-German threat to our survival.
On April 2, 1917, when President Wilson asked Congress for
a declaration of war, antiwar sentiment was running high
in Congress. Senator Robert La Follette and others maintained that the crisis with the Kaiser was of the administra-

tion's own making. On April 4, the Senate rang with damning phrases: "We are going into war upon the command of gold!" "We are about to put the dollar sign upon the American flag!"[1]

It was not an uncommon view of the war early in 1917. As the debate raged in Washington, the leaders of the Socialist Party were gathering in St. Louis. Their resolution, published on April 7, the day after war was declared, read as follows:

> Modern wars as a rule have been caused by the commercial and financial rivalry and intrigues of the capitalist interests in the different countries. Whether they have been frankly waged as wars of aggression or have been hypocritically represented as wars of "defense," they have always been made by the classes and fought by the masses. War brings wealth and power to the ruling classes and suffering, death, and demoralization to the workers.
>
> We, therefore, call upon the workers of all countries to refuse to support their governments in their wars.
>
> Ruthless as the unrestricted submarine war policy of the German Government was and is, it is not an invasion of the rights of American people as such, but only an interference with the opportunity of certain groups of American capitalists to coin cold profits out of the blood and sufferings of our fellow men. . . . [2]

Inadequate though this was as an analysis of our entry into the war, it, and statements like it, reflected the political sentiments and bolstered the pacifist longings of a surprising number of Americans.

But shortly after the declaration of war the mood of the country shifted; Americans who had had serious misgivings about the venture now felt it was everyone's duty to support it. Passage of the Selective Draft Act in May provided a focus and a vehicle for punishing those who lagged behind. *The New York Times* reflected the rising repressive mood with its June 10 editorial: "The Selective Draft Act gives a long and sorely needed means of disciplining a certain insolent foreign element in this nation." On the Fourth of July, a New Yorker distributed copies of the Declaration of Independence to which he appended the thought: "Does your Government live up to these principles?" He got a ninety-day jail sentence for it.[3] A lawyer was sentenced to five years (and served two) for distributing copies of his *Legal Opinion and Advice on the Conscription Law to American Patriots.*

But it was through a section of the Espionage Act, passed June 15, 1917, that the repressive spirit flowed the strongest. The law provided twenty-year sentences and $10,000 fines for anyone making a false statement with the intent to interfere with military operations or to promote the success of our enemies; for anyone attempting to make soldiers insubordinate, disloyal, or mutinous; and for anyone frustrating the government's recruitment or enlistment of men to fight.

Laws designed to shield society from criticism of one of its endeavors have often been used to eliminate criticism altogether. This wartime Espionage Act, most of which was devoted to provisions for punishing spies and saboteurs, seemed reasonable on its face; but it was used to control the entire spectrum of dissent. Almost two thousand prosecutions resulted; nearly all concerned speeches, newspaper articles, leaflets, and books expressing opinions about the merits or conduct of the war. Punishment was harsh: there were twenty-four twenty-year sentences, six fifteen-year sentences, and eleven ten-year sentences.

The Espionage Act of 1917 was not, of course, the first attempt by the federal government to punish men for their words, and like the Sedition Act of 1798, this law specified that truth was a defense. But in 1918, an amendment, commonly called the Sedition Act of 1918, erased that defense as to certain statements. It provided the same penalties for saying anything—true or not—intended to obstruct the sale of U.S. bonds; saying or publishing anything intended to bring the United States form of government, Constitution, flag, or uniform into contempt or disrepute; saying or printing anything intended to incite resistance to the United States or to promote the cause of its enemies; urging curtailment of the production of anything necessary to the war effort; and supporting, defending, or favoring any such acts or the enemy's cause.

In effect, the 1917 and 1918 laws made it a crime to express opposition to the war, the draft, and the status quo. As the laws were applied, whether a remark was *intended* to harm America's fortunes in the war was resolved not by the accused's statement as to what he intended, but by the opinion of judge and jury as to the *tendency* of the words. Judges and juries were highly influenced by the prevailing war hysteria. No overt act harmful to the country had to be proved, and anyone expressing opinions or facts that ran counter to popular ideas was presumed to intend whatever harmful consequences a hostile and disapproving court most feared.

The laws worked just as the infamous Sedition Act of 1798 worked during the Adams administration. Judges eased the government's burden of proof by ruling that if there was any *possibility* that a critical statement or opinion would reach troops or would fall on the ears of draftable youth, it must have been intended to cause mutiny or obstruct recruitment. To engage in genuine discussion about the merits of the war policies, aims, or leaders was to invite prosecution and heavy penalty.

Men were convicted for urging that war revenues be raised by heavier taxation instead of by sale of Liberty Bonds; for saying (even before the question had been settled by the Supreme Court) that the draft was unconstitutional; for saying that a referendum should have preceded a declaration of war; for saying that war is against Christian teachings; even for criticizing the Red Cross and the YMCA.

The Senate subcommittee hearings on amnesty after the war called attention to the case of William Powell who,

> in private conversation in the home of a relative, expressed his opinion that certain published reports about German atrocities were untrue; that those stories were to some extent war propaganda. He expressed his own dissatisfaction with the policy of the United States and his lack of confidence in the President. He expressed the opinion that this was a rich man's war. This is the substance of the acts that were charged against him, for which he was convicted, sentenced to a fine of $5,000 and 20 years in prison.[4]

Victor Berger, the former mayor of Milwaukee and a U.S. Congressman, was also a founder of the Socialist Party and an editor of the *Milwaukee Leader*. From the floor of the House of Representatives, he had opposed Wilson's request for a declaration of war. From the *Leader*'s pages, he issued a stream of editorials, articles, and cartoons denouncing it. The articles led to his indictment, in February 1918, for conspiring with four others to violate the Espionage Act. Shortly before the trial, he was reelected to Congress. He was then convicted and sentenced to twenty years in prison. When the House of Representatives, in a burst of patriotism, refused to seat Berger in the spring of 1919, the governor of Wisconsin ordered a special election. Berger won again, increasing the Socialist vote by almost 50 percent. The House again refused to seat him, and the people of the Fifth Congressional District of Wisconsin went unrepresented for the remainder of the term. Eventually, in

1921, the Supreme Court reversed Berger's conviction because of the judge's prejudicial conduct at the trial, and the charges were dropped.

When persons were tried under the Espionage Act for thoughtful but unorthodox statements about the political or economic origins of the war, they were frequently confronted in court with self-serving quotations from the president and other members of the administration. The administration version, introduced into evidence, was taken by judges and juries alike to prove that the defendants' statements were knowingly false and intended to undermine the war effort. For instance, the son of the Chief Justice of New Hampshire was charged with writing an open letter contradicting the president and secretary of state. He wrote that, because Germany never had actually promised to cease submarine warfare, it was deceptive for the president to cite Germany's violation of the pledge as justification for the war. He received an eighteen-month sentence.

Others were fined and jailed for the most casual remarks and acts. In 1918, George Freerks was prosecuted, under a Minnesota State law, for having discouraged women from knitting by remarking "No soldier ever sees these socks." The highest court of the state ruled that he would have to stand trial.[5]

E.V. Starr was jailed that year in Montana when he refused to be compelled by an angry mob to kiss the U.S. flag. "What is this thing anyway?" he was accused of saying, "Nothing but a piece of cotton with a little paint on it. . . . It might be covered with microbes." He was sentenced to the penitentiary for not less than ten nor more than twenty years at hard labor. He was still in prison in 1920.[6]

Twenty-seven South Dakota farmers, believing they were bearing an unequal share of the military's manpower and financial needs, petitioned various state officers for new draft quotas and revenue measures and for a referendum on the war. They proffered a rather undiplomatic alternative to granting their demands: defeat for the petitioned officials, for their party, and for the nation. Their overzealousness may have been unwise, but the one-year sentences they received for it mocked the First Amendment right to petition for redress of grievances. Attorney General Gregory called the sentences in this case "one of the greatest deterrents against the spread of hostile propaganda, and particularly that class of propaganda which advanced and played upon the theme that this was a capitalists' war." Their convictions were reversed only when the case reached the Supreme Court.[7]

A prosecution particularly indicative of the times was brought against Robert Goldstein and his movie, *The Spirit of '76*. Goldstein finished production of this film about the Revolutionary War just before the outbreak of hostilities with Germany in 1917. The film depicted the patriotic speech of Patrick Henry and the signing of the Declaration of Independence. It also depicted such scenes as the Wyoming massacre perpetrated by British soldiers. After the film was screened in Los Angeles, it was seized by government agents, Goldstein's business was reduced to bankruptcy, and Goldstein was sentenced to ten years in prison. His crime? Attempting to cause insubordination and mutiny in the armed forces by arousing our troops' hatred of our ally, Great Britain. The sentence was belatedly commuted to three years.

Perhaps the most famous political prisoner of this period was the romantic crusader, Eugene Victor Debs. Debs headed the Socialist Party and was its candidate in a number of presidential elections. Before the war, when muckraking journalists and novelists exposed the injustices of unrestrained and unregulated capitalism, the ranks of the

Socialist Party swelled with liberals and progressives. In 1912, Debs polled 6 percent of the national vote, more than a thousand Socialists were elected to public office, and some cities had Socialist administrations.

Right through our entry into the war, the leadership of the Socialist Party held to its official policy of "continuous, active, and public opposition to the war through demonstrations, mass petitions, and all other means within our power." When liberals and progressives became caught up in Wilson's idealism and infatuated with national honor, Debs and the remaining core of the Socialist Party provided one of the only voices of caution and skepticism. The government responded by raiding the Socialist Party's offices and jailing its leaders. The Socialist Party's resolution, quoted earlier, was used in several trials as evidence of their guilty intent.

Debs was jailed for attempting to incite insubordination in the army and for obstructing recruitment. He had not *actually done* anything of the sort. According to the indictment, he "delivered to an assembly of people, a public speech," *intending* those results. The speech in question was not addressed to troops but to a Socialist convention in Canton, Ohio, and it was mild stuff by most standards. He detailed his belief in Socialist economic views, he pointed to the European war as the supreme curse of capitalism, and he approved draft resisters and other war critics. His most inflammatory words were: "You need to know that you are fit for something better than slavery and cannon fodder."

Debs went to prison in April 1919, at the age of sixty-three. There he remained until President Harding released him on Christmas Day, 1921, over three years after the last shot was fired in Europe. From prison, in 1920, he ran once again for the presidency and polled 919,799 votes, which was more than he had received in 1912. But the Supreme

Court, in an opinion written by Justice Holmes, refused to overturn the conviction. Privately, Holmes was of the view that if Debs's conviction did not offend the Constitution, it, and others like it, certainly offended common sense. To one friend he wrote, "I think it quite possible that if I had been on the jury I should have been for acquittal." "The federal judges seem to me," he wrote in another letter, "to have got hysterical about the war. I should think the President when he gets through with his present amusements might do some pardoning."[8]

But the president did very little pardoning, and only a few of the overzealous prosecutions were reversed when and if they were appealed to the Supreme Court. In *Abrams* v. *United States*,[9] the Court affirmed the conviction of five Russians, all in their twenties, for conspiracy. Unlike the bulk of prosecutions which were brought under the original Espionage Act of 1917, Abrams and his friends were indicted under the more sweeping provisions of the 1918 Sedition Act. In August 1918, they distributed leaflets opposing America's participation in the expedition to Vladivostok and Murmansk in Russia. The young Russians argued, not without some basis, that the expedition was designed to influence the course of the Russian Revolution of 1917, and was not part of the war against Germany. Their leaflets stated their hatred of German militarism, but called for a general strike to force a reversal of the government's policy toward Russia.

Arrested by Military Intelligence Police, they were charged with conspiracy to violate the Sedition Act, despite the fact that we were not at war with Russia. There was no evidence presented at their trial that anyone responded to their call for a general strike, or even that the leaflets, thrown onto the street from an upper-story window, ever reached anyone who worked in a munitions industry.

The Act seemed to require the government to prove that they intended to cripple the war effort against Germany, not against Russia. But the accepted view in America at that time was that the Bolshevists were merely German agents, and the judge and jury were quick to identify pro-Bolshevist with pro-German sentiments. The defense attempted to present the testimony of American military personnel who had been in Russia and knew the Bolshevist leaders well, and of other eyewitnesses to the Russian Revolution. The questions were read into the record, but went unanswered. The judge, ruling the testimony irrelevant, observed that "The flowers that bloom in the spring, tra la, have nothing to do with the case."

The judge refused to instruct the jury that opposition to America's *Russian* policy could not support a conviction, and, early in the trial, he announced his belief that no man could be allowed to stir up hostility to the government's Russian policy in an attempt to get it changed. Throughout the trial he cross-examined witnesses and defendants to underscore this view. No intent to hinder the war against Germany was shown, but five men were convicted of a crime requiring such an intent. Sentences ran from three years to twenty years and fines of $4,000 were imposed. All were finally released in November 1921, on the condition that they would return to Russia at their own expense.

America did not lose its taste for repressing dissent when the war ended. In the autumn of 1919, three Syracuse men were arrested for distributing leaflets which described the ill-treatment of political prisoners, called for a meeting to discuss amnesty, and urged people to write letters to the president and members of Congress. They quoted the First Amendment, a Supreme Court opinion, and a speech by President Wilson. Each got an eighteen-month sentence for "disloyal" language tending to obstruct recruitment and to bring the military, the government, and the Constitution into disrepute.[10]

Repressive laws had been passed and repressive law enforcement had been justified as necessary in wartime to ensure military success. They were used by those in power to silence the mix of empty rhetoric, griping, obnoxious political theories, and important political truths which comprises dissent. But the abuse of discretionary power appealed to the nation's underlying intolerance, and reinforced a habit that is always hard to shake. The prosecution of cases under the Espionage Acts after hostilities ended in Europe was a warning of the peacetime repression that was to follow.

5

Repression of the
International Workers of the World

The working class and the employing class have nothing in common. There can be no peace so long as hunger and want are found among millions of working people and the few, who make up the employing class, have all the good things of life. Between these two classes a struggle must go on until the workers of the world organize as a class, take possession of the earth and the machinery of production and abolish the wage system.

—Preamble to the IWW
Constitution

The IWW was a singularly radical and peculiarly American labor union dedicated to abolition of the wage system and capitalism. Its program was to gain control of all industry and large-scale agriculture for the workers who already had, collectively, control over production. The Wobblies, launched in Chicago in 1905, filled a vacuum in American economic and political life at the time. The AFL was organizing labor's elite, but ignoring the 90 percent of the work force that was unskilled. Vast numbers of fungible, unorganized, and unprotected workers suffered physical and spiritual brutalization in exploitive company towns, perilous mines, and backbreaking harvests. At the end of the first decade of the twentieth century, some thirty-five thousand Americans died each year in industrial accidents. The top 2 percent of the population controlled 60 percent of the nation's wealth. At the bottom, some 65 percent of the population scrambled for 5 percent of the pie.

The Wobblies wanted to turn the economic power structure upside down. They hoped to organize the unskilled, industry by industry, into one big union which would be able to wield the weapon of the general strike. They combined the practice of direct action unionism with the preaching of revolutionary utopianism. The IWW invited repressive law enforcement and political imprisonment by framing its program in militant hyperbole. They spoke of "overthrowing" the economic system by "any and all tactics." The wage system, in the Wobbly lexicon, was nothing less than slavery. They spoke of slowdowns and of other job actions as "industrial sabotage." Unlike other American labor movements, the Wobblies never abandoned their militant tone; their rhetoric and tactics were intended to build solidarity among the workers, not to gain the sympathy of middle-class liberals.

Any attack on capitalism was viewed by many at the time, however, as a cover for a criminal attack on democracy itself.

Ironically, nonviolent resistance to repressive law enforcement was both the IWW's most effective tactic and its undoing. Beginning in Spokane, Washington, in 1909, the Wobblies won a series of "free-speech fights." Wobbly organizers were denied the right to speak and organize on the streets of towns where laborers congregated. They were often attacked by local vigilantes and jailed by the police

for disorderly conduct. The Wobblies fought back by inviting more arrests. Scores of "floating reserves" would de-
scend upon the offending municipality to expose themselves to more beatings and jailings. They flooded the jails
to overflowing until the cost and annoyance forced community concession of their right to speak and organize. In
winning the right to speak, however, they won a reputation
for militancy and a popular belief that they caused or incited violence.

When the IWW was at its peak in 1912, with one-hundred
thousand members, it forfeited the tolerance of the empowered by an impressive demonstration of the potential
power of its hard-won rights. In Lawrence, Massachusetts,
the IWW led thirty thousand previously unorganized tex-
tile workers in a successful strike. Authorities arrested nine
hundred strikers and held them without bail, but their
solidarity and their passive resistance to the employers' use
of overt force revealed the potential political power of direct mass action by the powerless.

The drama of America's counterattack played itself out
on the West Coast, where the IWW undertook the difficult task of organizing migratory labor. Wobbly activity
was the most conspicuous in the winter months when migratory workers congregated in the towns to wait out the
slack season. The IWW organizers also would appear in
order to lay a foundation for the following summer's field
strikes.

The longest free-speech fight of all—nine months—began in San Diego at the end of the summer of 1911. Merchants induced the city council to prohibit street speaking
by the Wobblies on the ground that their rhetoric was
scurrilous and abusive. Two hundred Wobblies were formally arrested, and the police, assisted by vigilante committees, attempted to use beatings and threats of force to keep
suspected Wobblies from entering the town. Speakers who

dared to appear were beaten and jailed. Local editorials agitated for their lynching.

But here the Wobblies had the law on their side. The police could cite no examples of Wobbly violence; they could charge none even with resisting arrest. Frustrated by the state's inability to prosecute the Wobblies under California law, a committee of five hundred conservative Republicans, claiming that ten thousand Wobblies and anarchists were organizing to overthrow the government in California, wrote President Taft that an imminent disaster could be averted only by federal prosecutions. The president authorized Justice Department action, but the ensuing investigation failed to reveal evidence of lawbreaking to support an indictment. It was not against federal law to refuse to work, to threaten general strikes, or to organize a group hostile to capitalism.

In 1913, three thousand workers struck a hop ranch at Wheatland, California. A deputy sheriff fired on a mass meeting and several public officials and workers were killed in the ensuing riot. In an attempt to make a scapegoat of the IWW, California indicted the Wobbly organizers of the meeting. Two were convicted of second degree murder and sentenced to life imprisonment. At this point real sabotage made an ugly appearance: Wobbly sympathizers used every available weapon to press for the release of their martyred "political prisoners." The turmoil after Wheatland cost the targeted agricultural interests as much as twenty million dollars in burned crops and ruined equipment. In October 1915, the governors of California, Oregon, Washington, and Utah requested federal intervention on the grounds that the Wobbly menace was an interstate conspiracy. Again, a careful Justice Department investigation did not bear out the charge.

The strength of anti-Wobbly sentiment in the Pacific Northwest was made brutally apparent in November 1916.

A spreading IWW lumber strike led to a free-speech fight in Everett, Washington. As three hundred Wobbly "floating reserves" arrived at the Everett docks by chartered boats, they were ambushed by hundreds of armed vigilantes. Five Wobblies and two vigilantes were killed. The state held seventy-four Wobblies on charges of first degree murder. When the first Wobbly tried won an acquittal, the state reluctantly released the others.

It was not until the First World War, however, that the *federal* government brought its power to bear against the Wobblies. The Wilson administration threw the army, the navy, and, eventually, the courts into the effort. Anxious to avoid peripheral controversies, the IWW had cautioned its membership against taking a futile anticonscription stance. By and large, the membership filed draft registration forms and focused its energy on industrial organization and action. But by refusing to abandon its right to strike, the IWW insured its suppression under the Espionage Acts.

By displaying *prewar* Wobbly propaganda, which contained antimilitary and antigovernment material, the government justified the use of troops to break IWW strikes. Newspapers perpetuated the belief that the Wobbly strikes were pro-German and carried distorted accounts picturing IWW slowdowns and work stoppages as lawless and violent. The government's use of troops led to virtual martial law in many timber and mining areas in the West. The military made arrests, detained Wobblies without charges, infiltrated the IWW with military intelligence agents, worked in conjunction with company-hired *agents provocateurs*, and raided Wobbly offices and meetings.

A hair-raising account of an incident of such official lawlessness is contained in the 1920 opinion of a federal judge:

From August, 1918, to February, 1919, the Butte Union of the Industrial Workers of the World was dissatisfied with working places, conditions, and wages in the mining industry, and to remedy them was discussing ways and means, including strike if necessary. In consequence, its hall and orderly meetings were several times raided and mobbed by employers' agents, and federal agents and soldiers duly officered, acting by federal authority and without warrant or process. The union members, men and women, many of them citizens, limited themselves to oral protests, though in the circumstances the inalienable right and law of self-defense justified resistance to the last dread extremity. There was no disorder save that of the raiders. These, mainly uniformed and armed, overawed, intimidated, and forcibly entered, broke, and destroyed property, searched persons, effects, and papers, arrested persons, seized papers and documents, cursed, insulted, beat, dispersed, and bayoneted union members by order of the commanding officer . . . and in general, in a populous and orderly city, perpetrated a reign of terror, violence, and crime against citizen and alien alike, and whose only offense seems to have been peaceable insistence upon and exercise of a clear legal right.[1]

Not content with these measures, the Justice Department characterized the IWW as a seditious criminal conspiracy, and on September 5, 1917, FBI agents conducted simultaneous raids on Wobbly headquarters and residences throughout the nation. They seized private correspondence and political and economic propaganda, which became the basis of an indictment charging the Wobblies with calling strikes not in order to win better wages, hours, and working conditions (which would be legal), but in order to oppose execution of the Selective Service Law and other wartime statutes, and to obstruct the war effort generally. The government's theory was that because strikes had a tendency to hinder the raising of an army and the success of overseas military operations, the law must presume the IWW intended that result. It is hard to see why the strikes of the politically more acceptable AFL did not have the same tendency and the same legally presumed intent, but the Wilson administration met hundreds of AFL wartime walkouts and strikes with mediation, conciliation, and concessions.

The files of the Department of Justice reveal that prosecutors were counting on the jingoism and antiradical bias of the middle class to lead grand juries to rubber-stamp indictments and to produce guilty verdicts against Wobblies "as a matter of course."[2] They were not wrong. The whole business was reminiscent of the state of affairs prevailing in 1798–1800, when seditious intent was presumed and men were punished for the supposed bad tendency of their words.

The Chicago trial of "Big Bill" Haywood and one hundred sixty-five other leaders became the prototype. After a four-month trial it took a jury less than an hour to convict the IWW's executive board, its general organizers, its editors, and the leaders of its lumber, mining, and agricultural subdivisions. Prosecutions then commenced throughout the country against lesser Wobbly figures. In some cases, the indictments were simply used as a lever to curtail Wobbly activity—the accused were never brought to trial on the merits. In other cases, the U.S. attorneys secured indictments in order to justify arrests, then left the Wobblies languishing in jail for as long as two years, until their superiors in the Department of Justice forced them to move forward with trial.

The prosecutions drained off the IWW leadership, and consumed organizational energies in defending the criminal charges. Juries took as little as one hour to return guilty verdicts after lengthy trials involving complicated issues of law and fact. Judges, in the presence of the jury, treated defendants to lectures on the union's unpatriotic and dangerous views. Sixty-two defendants, tried in Sacramento, acknowledged the hopelessness of trying to contest the charges seriously in such a hostile forum. They remained resolutely silent throughout the proceedings against them.

Repression often backfires. Political defendants often gain the sympathy of large numbers of previously unconcerned citizens by publicizing their legal defense. The Wobblies, however, were prevented from sending literature through the mails, prevented from soliciting funds for legal costs, and unable to get their side of the controversy into the newspapers. Under wartime discretionary authority, the Postmaster General interrupted and delayed legal defense-fund mailings when he did not seize them outright.

An IWW resolution *against* sabotage was refused admission to the mails because it contained the word "sabotage." The post office maintained a secret index of radical ideas and symbols which made unmailable any material in which they appeared. Because the index was secret, the Wobblies could not know, for instance, that its union emblem, a black cat, which appeared on all official stationary and newsletters, made the defense literature unmailable. Even verbatim reports of the Chicago trial, assertions that it was impossible to obtain a fair trial, and requests for contributions were secretly forbidden by the post office. Independent mail carriers were persuaded not to carry IWW literature. Defense committee offices were ransacked by raiding FBI and military intelligence agents looking for more "evidence." Defense committee workers were arrested and their meetings broken up. Meanwhile, the press, fed by propaganda from U.S. prosecutors characterizing the defendants as seditious and disloyal, consistently portrayed the Wobblies in an unfavorable light.

The program of arrests, indictments, trials, and news control worked. In 1917–1919, over a thousand Wobblies were arrested, some five hundred were indicted, and over one hundred leaders were imprisoned under sentences as long as ten and twenty years. Fines totaled $2 million in the Chicago trial alone.[3] For years following the wartime repression, Wobbly energies were largely devoted to the fight—in court, Congress, and the press—to have their "political prisoners" released.

In California, however, the Wobblies continued to be a viable issue. From 1919 to 1924, over five hundred California Wobblies were arrested and held for bail of $15,000 each. Over half of these were actually tried on charges of "criminal syndicalism" for advocating, teaching, aiding, or justifying crime as a necessary or proper means to bring about economic or political change, or belonging to a group which so advocates or advises.

Sporadic sabotage of farm machinery and burning of crops in California's Central Valley was still presumed to be the work of the IWW and it certainly fueled the prosecutions, but very few of those convicted had even been accused of committing any violence. The force of the law was not applied against those who committed the acts complained of, but against those with improper political ideas. Rural strife might have been halted by providing improved working conditions or collective bargaining. Instead, the state abused the prestige of its criminal law in yet another program of repression, and the jailed Wobblies again became political martyrs. Finally, in 1923, California secured an injunction against the IWW, effectively prohibiting its existence. The injunction was won on the basis of affidavits made by the two former IWW members who had testified for the prosecution in virtually every Wobbly trial in the state since 1919. A third affidavit, made by a former deputy sheriff, stated that incendiary fires had been prevalent in his area five years earlier. He failed even to mention the IWW.

This suspect and outdated evidence of an imminent danger was used to remove the already staggering IWW from the American labor scene. The victory for repression did not, however, run very deep. The Wobbly leaders in California stopped summoning workers to the banner of the forbidden union; but they carried their organizational skills as well as a significant number of former members with them into the young Communist Party. Instead of using the power of law to eradicate the conditions that bred extreme radicalism, repressive officials had responded to a popular hysteria, one largely of their own creation, and had driven embittered radicals from one label to another.

Not until long after the wartime and postwar prosecutions decimated the IWW did the Supreme Court vindicate the Wobbly organizers. In 1923, Harold B. Fiske was convicted under a Kansas "criminal syndicalism" law. The case against him was based on words in the IWW constitution declaring that the struggle between workers and employers would continue until the workers seized the means of production and abolished the wage system. Fiske's jury, like so many others, was prepared to assume this could be accomplished only by force, and that anyone organizing for the IWW must be preparing for and advocating an armed revolution. Although the IWW constitution did not mention violence, and although no evidence was introduced connecting Fiske with violent acts or advocacy of crime, the jury read into the IWW constitution all the popular mythology; Fiske was convicted for the wild things other Wobblies had said and for the violent acts of a few who may or may not have been Wobblies at all. In 1927, the Supreme Court reversed his conviction and, for the first time, held that the individual states were bound by the First Amendment's guarantees of freedom of press, speech, and assembly.[4]

6

The Red Scare
and the Palmer Raids

Give me your tired, your poor,
  Your huddled masses, yearning to breathe free,
The wretched refuse of your teeming shore:
  Send these, the homeless, tempest-tossed, to me:
I lift my lamp beside the golden door.
                              —Inscription on the base of the
                              Statue of Liberty

The United States was gripped by a bomb scare in May and June of 1919. Two dozen infernal devices were discovered and defused in a New York post office where they had been mailed to their intended victims with insufficient postage. Bombings were reported in nine cities, including one in front of the home of Attorney General A. Mitchell Palmer. Two men, apparently the putative bombers, were killed by that blast. The press fed the rising fear that this was the work of ideological radicals, and in August the Attorney General set up a General Intelligence Division in the Department of Justice to identify and deal with them. Ap-

75

pointed to head the new unit was J. Edgar Hoover, who at twenty-five already had two years experience under his belt in the Justice Department's Alien Registration section.

The bombers were never detected, but in November, meetings of the Federation of Russian Workers in eleven cities were raided simultaneously by federal agents, and those present were arrested; no one knows how many. Before Christmas, two hundred and forty-nine of them were put aboard an army transport ship, which the press dubbed the "Soviet Ark." With Hoover standing at dockside to watch the sailing, they were deported.

These first "Red Raids" were the swift opening of the most shocking repressive episode in American history. Within a week, the Attorney General reported to Congress that "a more or less complete history of over 60,000 radically inclined individuals has been gathered together and classified, and a foundation laid either under the deportation statutes or legislation to be enacted by the Congress to move against them."[1]

Just as the ideas of the French Revolution terrified the Federalists at the end of the eighteenth century, the highly energized ideas emerging from the Russian Revolution in 1917 terrified the empowered elements of American society at the end of World War I. In the United States, the return of peace was marked by a dramatic rise in unemployment, widespread labor unrest, and resurgent radicalism. In 1919, over four million workers walked out in labor protests. Since the traditional scapegoat, the IWW, was hopelessly enmeshed in legal battles, postwar repression soon focused on the Communist Party and the Communist Labor Party.

Attorney General Palmer pressed Congress for a federal peacetime sedition act on the model of state criminal syndicalism laws, but Congress turned him down. The Justice Department found also that it could not prosecute radicals under the conspiracy law, for the only evidence was their loose talk and militant rhetoric. "The chief evil of the Red movement, both here and abroad," Palmer wrote in 1920, "consists in the fact that it accomplishes a constant spread of evil thinking."

Who were the "Reds" provoking this concern? In September 1919, the Socialist Party splintered. Some local branches formed together as the Communist Labor Party, others as the Communist Party. Palmer thought this turn of events warranted a massive new federal initiative; but as Federal Circuit Court Judge Anderson later pointed out,

> The great mass of the former Socialists who had thus become alleged Communists had no real comprehension of any important or material change either in their associations or in the political or economic purposes sought to be achieved by their negligibly weak organizations. Social, educational purposes, and race sympathy, rather than political agitation, constituted the controlling motives with a large share of them. They joined the local Russian or Polish or Lithuanian Socialist or Communist Club, just as citizens join neighborhood clubs, social or religious, or civic, or fraternal.[2]

Although evil thinkers could not be punished as criminals, the Supreme Court had ruled, in 1893, that deportation was not technically a punishment, that it was merely a procedure for returning undesirable immigrants to their own countries upon an administrative finding that their continued presence in America would be "inconsistent with the public welfare."[3] The safeguards of criminal due process did not, therefore, apply to deportation proceedings.

Unable to punish evil thinking, the Attorney General was determined to deport it. The position of the Secretary of Labor William Wilson, whose responsibility it was to administer the deportation law, was that members of the

Communist Labor Party were not deportable. He found, however, that alien members of the Communist Party could be deported under a provision which singled out those belonging to an "organization that entertains a belief in, teaches or advocates the overthrow by force or violence of the government of the United States." For evidence of the Communist Party's illicit and violent purpose, he was able to marshal only a few passages from the Party's Manifesto and the Manifesto of the Communist International to which the Communist Party was said to adhere. These documents spoke of a "conquest of capitalism" by "mass action, in the form of general political strikes and demonstrations," "direct conflict with the governmental machinery in open combat," "proletarian mass pressure," "revolutionary use of bourgeois parliamentarianism," and "revolutionary propaganda." It is odd that in our country, where the promises of party platforms go largely unheeded by voters and candidates alike, fearful federal bureaucrats gave then and continue to give so much credence to the bombastic phraseology common to all militant working-class movements since 1848.

Even out of context, the passages cited by the Secretary of Labor suggest the Party's aim at the time was the political use of general strikes as much as they suggest an insurrectionist plot. The power of a strike can, after all, be used to force political change as well as to obtain better hours or wages. Urging workers to press for control of industry may frighten those who would thereby lose control, but it is not the sort of call to violent revolution which a free society punishes. Because the passages seemed to advocate pressing for change without resorting to the ordinary political process, they were presumed to intend violent methods, but nonpolitical methods of overturning a government are not necessarily violent—or criminal.[4]

As was the case in the IWW, some members of the Communist Party certainly would have used force to rid the political process of their opponents. Every political party has such extremist members. George Wallace once declared that he would run over any demonstrator who lay in the street in front of his car. Does belonging to Governor Wallace's party entail advocating violent methods of political control?

The Mitchell Palmer Raids were intended to capitalize on a deeply imbedded popular belief that evil thinking is foreign to America, that it is brought to our shores by immigrants, and that immigrants are the cause of social unrest and the purveyors of ideas which challenge the dearest-held values of the beneficiaries of the status quo. This belief predated Mitchell Palmer. Widespread social and economic unrest during the depressions of the 1880s and 1890s coincided with the arrival of waves of European immigrants. The result was an identification of immigrant and radical in popular mythology. It was reassuring to blame foreigners for the continuing subversion of the promise of the American dream. The stereotype endured into the present century despite the basic conservatism of peasant immigrants whose attachment to tradition, status, and authority led them, in large numbers, to repudiate all sorts of radical movements.

The Immigration Act of 1903 provided for the deportation of any immigrant who, within three years after entering the country, was found by immigration officials to "disbelieve" in organized government. The law was aimed at anarchists. In 1917 and 1918 Congress amended the law, removed the three-year cut-off, and added provisions aimed directly at the Wobblies, many of whom had not bothered to obtain citizenship status despite many years' residence. In order to ease problems of proving individual guilt, mere affiliation with any group found to disbelieve in organized government was made a separate ground for deportation.

In applying the sweeping provisions of the law against the Wobblies, inspectors of the Labor Department's Bureau of Immigration became thought police, probing and cross-examining non-citizens for signs of "dangerous" political and economic philosophy. This was made easy by the absence of the due process safeguards required by the Constitution in conventional "criminal" proceedings.

In practice, the power to deport was a discretionary power of the inspectors. Over the years, Bureau procedures developed not to protect individual rights, but to obtain an administratively satisfying high percentage of actual deportations. The proceedings were characterized by long periods of pre-hearing detention, excessively high bail, unreasonable searches and seizures, denial of counsel and jury, and aggressive cross-examination by inspectors seeking to elicit self-incriminating remarks. Arrests were often made without warrants. Immigrants were not notified of their right to an attorney until the inspector had developed enough material to make out a case for deportation. Individual inspectors, eager to facilitate processing and to confirm their own prejudices and biases, conducted fishing expeditions into immigrants' lives and private thoughts.[5] A man or woman who had resided and worked here for years could be deported on the basis of remarks about his personal philosophy, expressed for the first time under an inspector's grueling and hostile examination.

The use of these deportation techniques to control radical dissent was refined in a wartime drive against Wobblies in Seattle, Washington. In January 1918, despite a ruling by the Secretary of Labor that the organic documents of the IWW disclosed no lawless purpose which would bring individual members within the provisions of the law, the Seattle Immigration Bureau began jailing Wobblies and suspected Wobblies pending deportation hearings. The Secretary of Labor was able to limit the drive only by declining to approve additional detention facilities after Wobblies filled every available jail in western Washington to capacity.

Exasperated by their seemingly endless detention, the jailed Wobblies rioted and launched hunger strikes throughout the fall and winter of 1918, while the authorities tried to apply the deportation law to their cases. One hundred twenty *habeas corpus* suits forced the Bureau to concede the insubstantial nature of most of the charges.

In January 1919, Seattle was threatened with a general strike. Local and federal officials were so unsettled that they foresaw an outbreak of revolution. By the hour set for the strike, they had, as a precaution, put the thirty-six Wobblies still being held in jail aboard the "Red Special" rushing East to Ellis Island and, presumably, to final deportation. The "Red Special" was front-page news as it crossed the continent, creating an atmosphere in which it seemed, more than ever, that political unrest and radical ideas could be deported. However, the IWW aliens on that notorious train fared rather well when they reached Ellis Island because the publicity had also brought New York legal talent to their aid. Volunteer attorneys of the fledgling American Civil Liberties Union forced the Labor Department to review most of the cases. Faced with the misleading, inconsistent, and weak records prepared by inspectors in Seattle, the Department simply released a substantial number of the prisoners. *Habeas corpus* proceedings brought further releases. In the end, only seven of those arrested in the Seattle deportation drive sailed from Ellis Island against their will.

After this fiasco, the Bureau of Immigration sought the assistance of the Department of Justice to make records which, in future deportation drives, would support findings against radicals. Immigration found a more than willing partner in J. Edgar Hoover. Justice Department agents had already infiltrated the Communist and the Communist Labor Parties and Hoover saw an opportunity to make use of the information they were gathering on the membership of these groups. He thought that the inquisitorial procedures of the Immigration Bureau, together with information gathered by his undercover agents, would legally support deportations.

By 1920, with half the staff of the Justice Department's Bureau of Investigation devoted to antiradical activity, Hoover reached an agreement with Immigration on the procedure for a massive crackdown on evil thinking. The plan called for simultaneous raids, secret testimony of undercover informers, seizure of personal and organizational correspondence, lists, and membership cards, cross-examination of suspects without interference by legal counsel, and detention in isolation without bail or under prohibitively high bail. To Hoover, denial of bail was essential to success, because he feared that release pending a hearing would provide lawyers an opportunity to prepare the suspects to resist interrogation.

The Secretary of Labor would not likely have supported a plan entailing such a large-scale abrogation of fundamental rights, but some three thousand warrants were made out in his absence by the Labor Department's lawyer—an appointee of Mitchell Palmer—on the basis of affidavits supplied by Hoover's agents. The agents were then instructed to raid residences of the persons to be arrested and meeting halls where they were likely to be found. Although the deportation law said nothing about arresting U.S. citizens, the agents' instructions expressly provided that all persons, including citizens, found in the company of listed suspects were to be arrested. The instructions called for extensive searches of persons, papers, residences, and meeting halls; but no mention was made of search warrants.[6]

On the night of January 2, 1920, in simultaneous raids in

thirty-three cities across the nation, hundreds of federal agents were assisted by local police in arresting roughly ten thousand suspected radicals. Private homes were combed for literature indicating an interest in radical politics. Seized in the winter night from their homes and meeting halls, citizens and aliens were subjected to the indignities of being searched, were hustled through the streets, and were herded into inadequate and overcrowded detention facilities. At the Hartford, Connecticut, jail, persons requesting to visit friends who had been arrested were seized and jailed too. Their concern was taken to be evidence of affiliation with the proscribed groups. Supposedly incriminating statements were elicited throughout the night from the thoroughly terrified immigrants and were preserved for deportation hearings.

The Department of Justice gave spectacular publicity to the raids to make them appear to be directed at persons whose politics gravely threatened the nation, but the excesses won equally widespread publicity, which doomed the Palmer Raids to failure. Secretary of Labor Wilson returned to his desk and restored suspects' right to counsel before the hearings were completed. Assistant Secretary of Labor Louis Post incurred the wrath of Hoover by requiring strict proof that each alien was actually a member of the Communist Party, and by ruling that not every alien who had labeled himself an "anarchist" could be deported for opposing all forms of government. Deportation orders were secured against only a small portion—about eight hundred—of those who had been taken into custody.

Hoover presented elaborate briefs arguing that mere membership in the Communist and the Communist Labor Parties brought immigrants within the deportation provisions. Wilson and Post regularly ruled against him in reviewing the cases. Hoover requested that the suspects be detained while the Bureau of Investigation searched for more evidence. Wilson and Post refused. They also over-ruled Hoover's request that if the immigrants were to be released it be done only on the condition that they be subject to rearrest if they later engaged in radical activities.

Post's devotion to due process led Hoover to charge publicly that the Assistant Secretary was in sympathy with the radicals, and impeachment proceedings were launched in Congress. Hoover searched military intelligence files, and combed the correspondence seized in the 1918 raids on IWW offices for evidence that Post was a tool of the Wobblies.

In the end, repetition of the Palmer Raids was ruled out by public uproar at the Justice Department's illegally repressive excesses. The Raids were denounced by federal judges and U.S. senators, by liberals and conservatives. Federal Circuit Court Judge Anderson heard the evidence and wrote, of what happened the night of January 2, 1920: "It may . . . be observed that a mob is a mob, whether made up of government officials acting under instructions from the Department of Justice, or of criminals, loafers and the vicious classes."[7] Twelve eminent lawyers and law-school professors, including Dean Roscoe Pound of Harvard Law School, and Felix Frankfurter, later a Supreme Court Justice, issued a *Report upon the Illegal Practices of the United States Department of Justice*, censuring the Department for employing "third degree" torture and making illegal arrests, searches, and seizures; for deploying *agents provocateurs*, and for forcing self-incriminatory statements from suspects unprotected by counsel. There was never another attempt, on such a scale, to deport radicalism, although Congress, in 1920, passed further legislation penalizing alien immigrants for mere financial contribution to or possession of the literature of the proscribed groups.

After the debacle of the Palmer Raids, the federal government shied away from using its law-enforcement power for political control. The Justice Department, unable to act directly, began lending the services of its antiradical investigators and undercover informers to the states. And the states were already taking up the burden of enforcing political conformity. By 1921, over thirty states passed sedition statutes and "Red Flag" laws. The "Red Flag" laws regulated or forebade display of emblems that legislators feared as symbols of socialism, anarchism, bolshevism, or opposition to government. Typical of the sedition laws was Rhode Island's: it provided a ten-year sentence for "language intended to incite a disregard of the constitution of Rhode Island or the United States."[8] Many of the laws had provisions punishing mere membership in any organization found to be seditious. In 1919–1920 alone, an estimated fourteen thousand persons (including the California Wobblies) were arrested, and about three hundred were convicted, under state sedition and "Red Flag" laws.[9]

In fact, although there was nothing at the state law enforcement level during this period to match the systematic repressive spirit of the Palmer Raids, there were plenty of isolated cases in which the politically unorthodox were victimized. But as the continuing controversy about the guilt or innocence of Nicola Sacco and Bartolomeo Vanzetti demonstrates, it is not always easy to label the prosecution of radicals for ordinary crimes "repressive." These immigrant radicals were indicted, tried, convicted, and executed for murdering two payroll guards; but the intense political biases that pervaded the proceedings, the national and international political repercussions of the case, and the strong possibility that the result was politically determined make the 1921 Sacco–Vanzetti trial one of the most remarkably "political" trials of the century.

The beginning of the present century, then, produced a bumper crop of political prisoners. One by one, the right to freedom of speech, the right of assembly, the right to petition, the right to protection against unreasonable searches and seizures, the right to a fair trial, the principle that guilt is personal and cannot be established by evidence of mere association with the guilty, the principle that the law can punish acts but not the possible tendency of words, and the principle that the punishment should fit the crime—all were sacrificed in attempts to preserve political orthodoxy and to protect the status quo.

7

Communists as Political Prisoners

Thomas Jefferson's party was attacked and its members
. . . [charged with intending] to "take arms against the laws
as soon as they dare." History should teach us, then, that in
times of high emotional excitement minority parties and
groups which advocate unpopular social or governmental
innovations will always be typed as criminal gangs and attempts will always be made to drive them out.
                              —Justice Hugo Black, dissenting
                                 in *Barenblatt* v. *United States*
                                 (1959)

America passed through the Second World War without
much of the repressive hysteria that so marred the First. A
shameful aberration was, of course, the senseless intern-
ment on the Pacific Coast of 117,000 Americans of Japanese
ancestry. By and large, however, the war was popular and
the American people were tolerant of political dissent. A
sign of the times was a 1943 Supreme Court decision,
handed down at the peak of America's military effort,
which reversed convictions of individuals who had distributed literature condemning the war, opposing the

draft, and debunking the salute to the flag.[1] Another sign was that, of the approximately six thousand conscientious objectors convicted for draft-law violations, fully 75 percent were Jehovah's Witnesses—pacifists whose refusal to cooperate with the draft system had no political overtones.

After the war, however, we passed through a period of hysteria which bore a superficial resemblance to the post-World War I period. Though the Red Scare dissipated relatively soon in the aftermath of the Palmer Raids, McCarthyism, and the methods of repression which we adopted in the 1950s in the attempt to eradicate the American Communist Party, have left an imprint on our political life and our legal institutions which is strongly felt to this day.

Americans have always suffered a sort of schizophrenia between our pride in our guaranteed freedoms and our reluctance to allow them full flower. Since the bulk of citizens go to and from work and play without testing their freedoms very much, they honestly express amazement when someone points to repression of those who are testers. "It's a free country," a statement oft repeated by our people in a spirit of careless disregard, means, in effect, "If you want to do something that crazy, go ahead!" When the law moves in on someone who seriously challenges our accepted values, the reaction tends to be: "Well, he took his chances; I wouldn't do anything like that, so a government that stops it isn't really inhibiting *my* freedoms." But political imprisonments that are blinked at in one period tend to leave behind handy instruments for attacking the quite different groups targeted for repression the next time around.

Most of us who cherish our freedoms retain a residual disdain and revulsion for international communism, which is not entirely unjustified. But have Americans matured enough as a nation to acknowledge, in the 1970s, that twenty years ago we panicked and overreacted to communism in ways that seriously distorted the fabric of our own freedoms, the very ideals that distinguish ours from the communist system? I wonder.

In the post-World War II period, Czechoslovakia, Korea, Hungary, Berlin, and Cuba gave us good reason to distrust and detest communism. Events amply evidenced that a nearly monolithic communist movement, then dominated by the Kremlin, was an evil and repressive force abroad in the world. Our respective reactions to each communist challenge further fueled our fear and our frustration that a new and expansive totalitarian power posed constant problems for an America that wanted international peace and stability. Although we were making our own mistakes and creating American-made injustices in the world, communism was so obvious an evil that it easily became a simplistic justification for much of what we did.

What we did in the world as a reaction to communism is beyond the scope of this book, although our aping of the enemy in that larger arena actuated some of the internal convulsions which produced a large number of modern American political prisoners.

Let us now, in the 1970s, openly face the fact that our uncertainty about the value of our freedoms led us to deal them away in excesses of repression which produced another bumper crop of communist political prisoners in America. Our fear led us to discard too quickly, on the altar of anticommunism, some of the vital protections that secure the political freedoms of Americans—freedoms we too often take for granted.

I was in the Justice Department in 1954 and 1955 at the height of the so-called "McCarthy era." President Eisenhower, Attorney General Brownell, and Deputy Attorney General Rogers, for whom I worked, resisted the excesses of McCarthyism in a gingerly way. Although they were

reluctant to confront directly the rampant McCarthy phenomenon, they were decidedly uncomfortable with it. In
retrospect I now see that this was a crucial transition period during which the blunt and crude repressive devices
of the past were giving way to the sophisticated techniques
of today. J. Edgar Hoover was frustrated that communists
could not be convicted at quick trials on the simple charge
that they belonged to the Party. To him, that was enough!
He was distressed that his informers, who had laboriously
infiltrated the Communist Party, were destroying their future usefulness by coming forward with testimony and
revealing their identities at long public trials. It was in this
period that Hoover began to conceive of saturation surveillance as a calculated method of political control, one far
more attractive to him than direct prosecution of "subversives." By 1962, according to former FBI man Jack Levine,
there was one FBI informer in the Communist Party for
every 5.7 members.[2]

One type of "public trial," however, exacted no price
from the FBI. Congressional committees subpoenaed witnesses whose names were supplied to them by the FBI and
these individuals were publicly pilloried. Those who
balked could, of course, take the Fifth Amendment and
refuse to answer questions on the grounds that to do so
might incriminate them, but the pressure to name names
was intense. Witness after witness told about everyone
they knew who had belonged to one organization or another on the "Communist front" list. The ones who took
the Fifth Amendment, refusing to be party to such a witch
hunt, often lost their jobs and their reputations. Taking the
Fifth Amendment seemed equivalent to admitting guilt
while hiding behind a constitutional technicality. The
House Un-American Activities Committee, the Senate Internal Security Committee and Senator Joe McCarthy's
Government Operations Subcommittee were willing part-

ners for the FBI. The accepted theme from Capitol Hill became: "If we can't convict them, let's make them stand up in public and admit what they believe, or take the Fifth."

I shared the mild discomfiture of many other Republicans at the time, but somehow it seemed that, whatever the injustices, they were deserved by the victims because they were so naive about the vicious communist enemy. By the time I reached Congress in 1959, open prosecutions were dead, but "McCarthyism" was still very much alive. Admittedly, the Cold War was at its peak, but how different that period looks to me with the hindsight of twenty years.

As a nation we had begun to lose our perspective on this issue in 1939. War appeared imminent and it wasn't difficult to identify the villains of the world in the persons of Hitler, Mussolini, and Hirohito. Antialien legislation was so popular in the troubled depression years that Representative Ford of California remarked, in 1939: "The mood of the House is such that if you brought in the Ten Commandments today and asked for their repeal and attached to that request an alien law, you could get it."[3] It was then that Representative Howard W. Smith of Virginia ("Judge" Smith), responding to popular pressure for more vigorous deportation of radical aliens, proposed a law for the deportation of any alien who "advises a change in the form of government of the United States," or "engages in any way in domestic political agitation."

In its original form, Representative Smith's bill asked for virtual repeal of the First Amendment for non-citizen residents. In an amended version, it became the Alien Registration Act of 1940, or the Smith Act. The Smith Act had little to do with aliens or with registration. Antiradical and anticommunist legislators included provisions making it a federal crime even for citizens to advocate, advise, or teach the "duty, necessity, desirability, or propriety" of overthrowing the government by force or violence. They also made it a crime to organize, belong to, or be affiliated with, any group which had such expression as its purpose.

How serious a threat was the Communist Party? Even before it became law, the Smith Act was an anachronism. It was modeled on state criminal syndicalism statutes passed earlier in the century to punish rowdy Wobblies. The exaggerated rhetoric and militant calls to action characteristic of earlier radical groups, and of the Communist Party at earlier periods in its development, had virtually vanished. By 1940 the Communist Party in the United States was no longer seriously agitating for revolutionary violence against the government.[4]

The Communist Party and its Marxist–Leninist ideology never won an enduring popular reception here; its rigid and convoluted analyses seemed divorced from the actual experience of Americans. The economic crash of 1929 temporarily enhanced the Party's drawing power; in a society which seemed hopelessly adrift, a surprising number of the most idealistic students, for instance, found Party activity and meetings a welcome antidote to the irrelevance of "football, frolics, and fraternities." An impressive array of intellectuals, artists, and writers also found temporary solace in the Party's embrace.

It was also in 1929 that Stalin consolidated his control over the American Communist Party. At the very moment when the Party might have capitalized on the growing alienation of Americans from their system, it ceased to respond to their felt needs and its direction and policy became dictated by the needs of Soviet foreign policy. Those who questioned any part of the ideologically complex and rigid positions dictated by Moscow's interests were drummed out. Others drifted away in disgust. In the turbulent years from 1930 to 1934, for instance, the Party claimed to have recruited almost 50,000 new members, but conceded losing about 33,000 in the same period, leaving its total membership at only 23,000.

The Kremlin's Popular Front policy of the late 1930s led the American Communist Party to tone down its militancy and to seek alliance with important segments of the American public. The Party attracted members by virtually throwing out the principles of communism. *Realpolitik* dictated that the class struggle be subordinated to the Kremlin's strategic needs in the face of invading Nazi armies.

In the United States, the Party's constitution was amended to provide for the expulsion of any member who conspired to subvert or overthrow American democratic institutions. In 1936 and again in 1938, the political necessity of violence was specifically repudiated. The Party abandoned its revolutionary rhetoric and overhauled its visible organization in order to appear as a thoroughly respectable American organization. Party leaders spoke out for the programs of the New Deal and repudiated the necessity of a dictatorship of the proletariat. Some of the Party's efforts to adopt the slogans and paraphernalia of "Americanism" were ironic. The American flag replaced the red flag at the head of Party parades; the strains of the "Star Spangled Banner" displaced those of the "International" at Party meetings.

As a result, the Party itself, not including "Front" organizations, could claim 75,000 members by 1938, and 100,000 in 1939. The *sine qua non* of this success was the Party's nonrevolutionary appearance, its opposition to Naziism and German militarism, and its support of the Western democracies; its greatest influence was through Popular Front organizations which purported to serve as vehicles for common action by communists and noncommunists opposed to fascism.

Announcement of the Hitler–Stalin Pact on August 24, 1939, caused the Party immediately to shift gears and devote its energy and resources to keeping America out of a war against Germany. The Party was suddenly opposed to the Western democracies, aligned with fascism, and repudiated the noble sentiments of the Popular Front period. Such cynicism appalled many in its artificially inflated membership ranks and embittered those who now felt they had been betrayed by the Front organizations. The reversal had an immediate effect—the Party conceded a drop in membership of 15 percent from 1939 to 1940.

This decline was halted when, on June 22, 1941, Hitler's armies invaded Russia and the American Communist Party again reversed its position. The Party became among the most strident voices urging American intervention in the war. It called for total mobilization of the U.S. economy and universal military service. It opposed strikes by workers, and even supported Smith Act prosecutions against members of the Socialist Workers Party who were charged with obstructing the war effort. In 1943 *Life* magazine portrayed the Russians as people who "look like Americans, dress like Americans, and think like Americans." In the same article, *Life* assured its readers that Russia's political police, the NKVD, was now simply "a national police similar to the FBI."

Through appeals to patriotism and vigorous support of the war, the membership again rose, reaching 80,000 by the middle of 1944. But membership in the Communist Party had come to mean something very different than it had in the 1920s and early 1930s. All that was required was payment of Party dues; the "disciplined revolutionaries" were not even required to attend Party meetings.

The wartime popularity of the Communist Party lasted only so long as Russian interests could be fused with American patriotism. The major differences between the Allies which were to characterize U.S.–Soviet relations during the Cold War surfaced at the Yalta Conference in

1945. Gradually, the American Communist Party purged those leaders of the Popular Front period who had espoused postwar peaceful coexistence. Predictably, when the Party began to oppose the Marshall Plan and to portray postwar America as a fascist state (propaganda lines dictated by Moscow's Cold War needs), its membership began to dry up and its influence to collapse. By heaping bitter invective on American institutions and policies the Party serviced Soviet Cold War needs, but forfeited any chance it ever had to build a mass revolutionary movement.

Fear of Soviet espionage and spies, a legitimate fear, particularly that America's atomic secrets would be stolen, was blurred for most of us into a growing disgust with the harmless propaganda. The real object of our rage was the Soviet Union itself, so recently an ally-in-arms and now a frustrating foe of virtually every postwar American foreign policy interest. Out of fear and frustration we condoned a diversionary attack on the American Communist Party, the already discredited shadow of our real enemy.

Fear breeds repression. The original purpose of the Smith Act, suspended during the Popular Front period and during our wartime alliance with Russia, had not been forgotten. In February 1948, Attorney General Tom Clark explained to an impatient House Un-American Activities Committee that there was insufficient evidence to prosecute Communist Party members under the Smith Act. But by July, his Justice Department had indicted the leading members, and after a heated six-month trial in New York, all eleven were convicted and given long sentences.

Because there was no evidence that they had committed any criminal acts, they were charged, in the *Dennis* case, with *conspiring* to organize the Communist Party and *conspiring* to advocate the overthrow of our government by force and violence. The evidence upon which they were convicted consisted of the works of Marx and Lenin and of pamphlets, published by the Party, which confirmed their belief in the economic and social doctrines of Marxism–Leninism.[5]

The belief for which they were imprisoned was that the government would eventually be overthrown and power transferred to the proletariat. They desired this as necessary to any fundamental change; they acknowledged that such a shift in the allocation of power in the society would, when it occurred, involve a struggle in which revolutionary and counterrevolutionary violence would be inevitable; and they believed and taught that circumstances would eventually arise which would be propitious for such a struggle. But they had not urged, as some Wobblies had, an immediate resort to force and violence to bring it about. Their views concerned events which were, as Justice Frankfurter wrote, "still in the womb of time."[6]

Although it is hard now to imagine why such opinions were thought to create a danger to American security sufficiently great to warrant criminal punishment, the Supreme Court upheld the convictions early in 1951 and prosecutions began against the Party's lower echelons. That summer, six new groups were arrested. A year later, in September 1952, three more groups were rounded up in a second wave of arrests, and by 1956 another seven groups were under indictment.[7] Over one hundred twenty persons were prosecuted in fifteen actions for conspiracy to advocate Marxist–Leninist doctrine, and eight individuals were prosecuted merely for belonging to the Party. Ninety-six people were convicted, and in no trial did the government fail to convict at least some.

The prosecutions continued unabated until 1957, when the Supreme Court, in the *Yates* case,[8] reversed the convictions of fourteen members of the Party who had been tried on evidence virtually identical to that used in *Dennis*. Justice Harlan expressed the Supreme Court's view that none of the accused were in any way connected with the "half dozen or so scattered incidents" which the government had used to prove that the Party planned to call sometime for forcible action against the government. "None of them has engaged in or been associated with any but what appear to have been wholly lawful activities, or has ever made a single remark or to have been present when someone else made a remark, which would tend to prove the charges."

The Justice Department quickly dropped most of the other prosecutions still outstanding. Where it attempted to move forward, the courts generally dismissed the charges. In one case, a court remarked that "despite ample opportunity for observation by FBI agents with access to the conspirators' innermost councils," there was no direct evidence of even a single example of criminal advocacy of the use of force or violence to overthrow government.[9] Hoover's saturation surveillance had, indeed, placed informers in positions of trust and even leadership in the Communist Party. It is impossible to believe that there was any real plan to issue a revolutionary "call to action," much less to commit espionage or sabotage, and that the FBI did not know of it. One by one, the prosecutions were terminated, and no new ones were launched.

The *Yates* decision forced prosecutors to abide by the fundamental distinction between inciting people to *do* something illegal and advocating that they *believe* in something obnoxious. But from 1948 to 1957 one hundred forty-one Americans were indicted and twenty-nine served prison terms for the political views they or their Party advocated. They were political prisoners.

8

Modern Political Prisoners: Race

The white man has always *loved* it when he could keep us
black men tucked away somewhere, always out of sight,
around the corner! The white man has always *loved* the kind
of black leaders whom he could ask, "Well, how's things
with your people up there?"

—Malcolm X

Politics and prison have never so obviously been entwined
than during the last decade. In our recent struggles to bring
racial justice to our system and to bring an end to the
senseless war in Vietnam, it was not the work of politicians
or judges, but the political imprisonment of thousands of
Americans, both civil disobedients and victims of repression, that made the difference.

The modern period of political imprisonment began on
the afternoon of December 1, 1955. Mrs. Rosa Parks, riding
the Cleveland Avenue bus home after a long day's work in
downtown Montgomery, refused to give up her seat to a
white man. She was arrested, jailed, convicted of violating
Montgomery's segregation ordinance, and fined. Her routine criminal conviction took on political overtones when

it touched off the Montgomery bus boycott, the protest that gave birth to the civil rights movement and to the leadership of men like Dr. Martin Luther King, Jr.

Montgomery's authorities quickly resorted to instruments of the criminal process to repress the protest. Blacks awaiting car-pool rides were arrested on charges of vagrancy and illegal hitchhiking. Dr. King was arrested and charged with speeding. Then, together with over a hundred others, he was indicted under a nineteenth-century antiunion law for conspiracy to obstruct business.

Instead of halting the boycott, this attempt to characterize protesters as criminals gave them a forum from which to pitch their cause to an even wider audience. Faced with inevitable conviction, they seized upon the trial as an opportunity to present the testimony of more than a score of witnesses, uncovering the moral bankruptcy of the city's case against them. Eighty-nine of those brought to trial were convicted and King was sentenced to pay a fine of $500 or to serve 368 days at hard labor.

The Supreme Court decided that Alabama's state and local laws requiring segregation on buses were unconstitutional; on December 20, 1956, a little more than a year after Mrs. Parks's arrest sparked the struggle, a federal court ordered Montgomery to desegregate its public transportation facilities. The protest had begun with a violation of law, its method was found to be illegal, and the court victory formalized a political victory gained by "direct action" outside the conventional political channels. In his search for a way to apply this power, Dr. King speculated about the possibility of young blacks courting arrest in large numbers by "direct action" to integrate school systems on which the Supreme Court's desegregation order had had no impact.

Dr. King's ruminations were interrupted on February 1, 1960, when four freshmen at all-black A & T College in

Greensboro, North Carolina, went downtown to Woolworth's all-white lunch counter and ordered coffee. Radio reports of their challenge to the traditions of Jim Crow brought other students pouring in to join their vigil. Nationwide coverage of the Greensboro sit-in alerted thousands of young blacks to the possibilities of nonviolent civil disobedience as an agent of social change.

Within two weeks, sit-ins spread to fifteen cities in five Southern states. Within the year, over 3,600 sit-in demonstrators spent time in jail. Their tactics did more than unmask racism, they capitalized in a politically effective way on the economic interests of local merchants and on the moral sensitivity of the managers and stockholders of national commercial enterprises such as the Woolworth chain. By the end of 1961, sit-ins led to the desegregation of several hundred lunch counters in scores of communities. The civil disobedience tactic was applied to stand-ins at segregated movie houses, kneel-ins at churches, and wade-ins at beaches and pools.

But these minor victories were won at tremendous cost. Not only did thousands go to jail, but many made the trip over and over again, and they were attacked in and out of jail. In an effort to keep sit-in participants nonviolent, Dr. King's Southern Christian Leadership Conference (SCLC) spawned the Student Nonviolent Coordinating Committee (SNCC). The new organization's statement of purpose proclaimed: "We affirm the philosophical or religious ideal of nonviolence as the foundation of our purpose, the presupposition of our faith, and the manner of our action." SNCC's faith in nonviolence was sapped by the bitter struggle of the next five years, in which conventional protest and nonviolent civil disobedience were met with repressive brutality; but for the remainder of the sit-in experiment and through the Freedom Rides, SNCC, SCLC, and the Congress of Racial Equality (CORE) kept the demonstrations nonviolent.

The commitment to nonviolence as an agent of social change was sorely tried when lighted cigarettes were pressed into sit-in demonstrator's backs and faces in Nashville; when a protester was stabbed in Columbia, South Carolina; when, as frequently happened, demonstrators were pulled off the stools and beaten and their supporters' homes were bombed. But nonviolence proved critical in minimizing the resentment that inevitably flows from successful challenges of the status quo by the formerly powerless.

Suddenly, in October 1960, national and international attention focused on news of an extraordinary political imprisonment coming out of the sit-in experiment. It is generally conceded to have affected the outcome of the 1960 presidential election. Thirty-seven protesters were arrested and jailed on charges of trespassing when they tried to get service at Rich's department store in Atlanta. Among them was Dr. King. Nothing out of the ordinary occurred until King was taken in handcuffs from the county jail to Reidsville State Prison to begin serving a four-month sentence at hard labor.

His incarceration at Reidsville is an important lesson in the criminal system's vulnerability to the hunger of empowered interests for continuing political control. It also shows how, on rare occasions, repression misses its mark, enhances the prestige of the victim, and brings the administration of justice into disrepute.

King's imprisonment was contrived. Several months after he had moved from Montgomery to Atlanta, he had been arrested for driving with his out-of-state license. For that oversight, the judge had fined him $25 and placed him on probation for twelve months. In an extraordinary abuse of judicial discretion, the judge now decided that King's sit-in at Rich's department store violated the earlier probation, and he imposed the four-month sentence.

The White House was deluged by telegrams demanding

federal intervention, but President Eisenhower remained silent and candidate Richard Nixon declined to comment. John Kennedy on the other hand, with an eye on the election just days away, called Dr. King's wife, Coretta, and expressed his concern. Robert Kennedy called the judge, urging him at least to release King on bail. When the judge granted the request, representatives of the press flew to the rural prison to capture Dr. King's words as he stepped through the gates.

In the spring of 1961, civil rights activists again risked abuse and jail. A 1958 Supreme Court decision holding that segregation of interstate travel facilities was illegal had had virtually no impact in the South. James Farmer, the new national director of CORE, organized a Freedom Ride in which biracial groups were to travel by bus to New Orleans, attempting to use bus terminal facilities along the way.

Buses were ambushed, burned, and boarded by thugs who attacked members of the groups. Local police gave them no protection, and carnage at Anniston and Birmingham, Alabama, ended the first Freedom Ride; no driver could be found to take the test on to Montgomery. The young leaders of SNCC energized the next phase; they felt that to abandon the Ride would be to let violence overcome nonviolence.[1]

A group succeeded in boarding a Birmingham bus for Montgomery on May 20. Alabama responded to a personal appeal from President Kennedy and gave the bus a police and helicopter escort. But the escort disappeared when the Freedom Riders disembarked into an angry crowd at the Montgomery terminal. In the fifteen to twenty minutes before police arrived, they were savagely attacked by a mob of over one thousand.

But these Freedom Riders finally reached Jackson, Mississippi, with an escort of three airplanes, two helicopters, and seven patrol cars. Within seconds after disembarking in Jackson, they were arrested and charged with breach of the peace. All twenty-seven were convicted, given two-month suspended sentences, and fined $200. When they refused, on principle, to pay the fines, they were taken to jail where some were beaten. Attempts by local authorities to stifle the protest by blinking at violence backfired, however, and even as the National Guard was escorting the first Ride into Jackson, more riders were announcing plans to join in a summer-long confrontation of conscience.

Rabbis, ministers, seminarians, lawyers, legislators, couples with and without their children, teen-agers with and without their parents, professors, and students followed. Through June, July, and August 1961, over a thousand people made the long trip to Jackson, prepared to submit peaceably to arrest for spending a few seconds at the Jackson terminal lunch counter. By the end of the summer over three hundred had been imprisoned.

The Freedom Riders were not treated as ordinary prisoners. At one point, a four-bunk cell in the Hinds County Jail held twenty-four of them. Mounting arrests finally compelled authorities to transfer them to Parchman State Penitentiary. The riders reported later that when they arrived there they were spat at, cursed, and threatened by men brandishing guns. When they sang freedom songs or, in one case, the "Star Spangled Banner," their mattresses were confiscated and they were left to sleep on filthy cell floors.[2]

Those who rode to prison in the summer of 1961 were a fair cross section of that part of the national conscience which was growing troubled about the failure of our political process to accommodate the aspirations, even to recognize the existence, of a vast black portion of the body politic. They escorted us further into the current period in which conscience is confronted, mores challenged, and pol-

itics shoved into new and fluid shapes. In carrying their
political and moral principles to prison, they also won
some formal victories. Freedom Riders who appealed were
vindicated four years later when the Supreme Court reversed their convictions. In the fall of 1961, the Interstate
Commerce Commission finally issued regulations explic-
itly banning segregation in interstate travel facilities, and
terminals in most areas of the Upper South were quickly
desegregated. In the Deep South, change would exact a
greater price.

On the day the ICC ruling went into effect, members of
SNCC tried to sit in the white waiting room of the bus
terminal at Albany, Georgia. They were threatened with
arrest. SNCC's precipitous call for a "direct action" campaign launched the Albany Movement, the first of a historic series of massive, nonviolent, civilly disobedient "direct action" campaigns across the South. Although a rich
combination of the Wobbly's "free-speech fight" tactics,
the grass-roots community organizing learned in Montgomery, the political philosophy of Thoreau and Gandhi,
and the charisma of Martin Luther King, the Albany
Movement nevertheless failed for lack of focus.

At the end of the first month of protest and marches on
Albany's city hall, with nearly five hundred protesters in
jail, Dr. King seemed justified in telling a packed meeting
at Shiloh Baptist Church, "We will wear them down by our
capacity to suffer." In the following day's march, two hundred fifty-seven more were jailed—Dr. King among them
—and the city turned to outlying barns and pastures to
accommodate the swelling number of prisoners.

But as NAACP leader Ruby Hurley remarked, "Albany
was successful only if the goal was to go to jail."[3] The city
would not capitulate. The protests wore on and on; over
one thousand protesters were again in jail by the end of the
first week of seismic marches on city hall in July and Au-

gust 1962. The Albany Movement dissipated its potential power by attacking simultaneously all aspects of a closed society in which those with power were inured to black suffering. It aimed at desegregating lunch counters, cinemas, libraries, park facilities, bowling alleys, and churches, but by the end of 1962 it had succeeded only in closing down the public facilities completely.

Dr. King's 1963 "direct action" campaign in Birmingham, Alabama, a focused combination of moral pressure on the federal government and economic pressure on local business leaders, amply demonstrated how much was learned from the failure of the Albany Movement. 1963 was the centennial year of the Emancipation Proclamation, but in Birmingham segregation remained rigid and intimidation commonplace. The black community had exhausted conventional remedies of petition and negotiation.

On April 3, during the Easter shopping season, the arrest of thirty blacks attempting to integrate downtown lunch counters inaugurated a carefully orchestrated series of escalating sit-ins, boycotts, and mass marches. At first it appeared that Birmingham's police had also learned from past experience: beginning April 6, and continuing for thirty-four days, protesting marchers headed for city hall were nonviolently herded into Police Commissioner Bull Connor's waiting vans. The city went to court, and on April 10 secured an injunction prohibiting further marches. Two days later, on Good Friday, when Dr. King and fifty volunteers violated the court order, he was simply placed in solitary confinement and cut off completely from his followers.

Once again Dr. King's imprisonment pricked the nation's conscience. President Kennedy arranged for King's isolation to be broken long enough to call his wife. In his cell, the prisoner began writing on slips of paper the thoughts provoked in him by an "Appeal for Law and

Order" which had been published by eight white Birmingham clergymen. They urged King and his followers to confine their search for social justice to the conventional legal and political process.

King's response, "Letter from Birmingham City Jail," is certainly one of the most memorable documents produced by an American political prisoner. "History," he wrote, "is the long and tragic story of the fact that privileged groups seldom give up their privileges voluntarily." By manipulating social and political institutions to block changes in the status quo, privileged groups compel those they have excluded to precipitate a crisis. "Negotiation," King went on, "is the purpose of direct action. Nonviolent direct action seeks to create such a crisis and establish such creative tension that a community that has constantly refused to negotiate is forced to confront the issue." And by insisting that laws be just, by publicly demonstrating a preference for prison over obedience to unjust laws, a civil disobedient "is in reality expressing the very highest respect for law."

The white clergymen had called the Birmingham campaign "untimely." 'Wait,' wrote King, "has almost always meant 'Never.'"

> We have waited for almost three hundred and forty years for our constitutional and God-given rights. . . . When you have seen vicious mobs lynch your mothers and fathers at will and drown your sisters and brothers at whim; when you have seen hate-filled policemen curse, kick, brutalize and even kill your black brothers and sisters with impunity; when you see the vast majority of your twenty million Negro brothers smothering in an air-tight cage of poverty in the midst of an affluent society; when you suddenly find your tongue twisted and your speech stammering as you explain to your six-year-old daughter why she can't go to the public amusement park that has just been advertised on television . . . when you take a cross country drive and find it necessary

to sleep night after night in the uncomfortable corners of your automobile because no motel will accept you; when you are humiliated day in and day out by nagging signs reading "white" and "colored"; when your first name becomes "nigger" and your middle name becomes "boy" (however old you are) and your last name becomes "John", and when your wife and mother are never given the respected title "Mrs."; when you are harried by day and haunted at night by the fact that you are a Negro, living constantly at tip-toe stance never quite knowing what to expect next, and plagued with inner fears and outer resentments; when you are forever fighting a degenerating sense of "nobodiness"; then you will understand why we find it difficult to wait.[4]

On May 2, almost one thousand children were arrested as they marched in wave after wave toward city hall chanting "Freedom!" By this time the depth of Bull Connor's reservoir of nonviolence had been plumbed and, on May 3, snarling police dogs slashed into the marchers' ranks. Police flailed indiscriminately with clubs, and firemen unleashed a torrent of water pressured to strip the bark off trees. Yet on May 7, when over two thousand persons had been imprisoned and Birmingham had exhausted all its detention facilities, several thousand more people were awaiting their turn to march. Still the city refused to negotiate, and demonstrators were that day beaten brutally back into the black district. Leaders lost control of the black teen-agers who loosed a fusillade of rocks, bottles, and bricks at the attacking police. Bull Connor called in 250 state troopers commanded by Colonel Al Lingo, and all parties prepared for what was reasonably expected to be a slaughter the next day.

President Kennedy dispatched Assistant Attorney General Burke Marshall to assist negotiations. Birmingham's business community, confronted with the spectacle of reasonable black demands being repressed with apparently limitless savagery, agreed quickly to SCLC's essential points. The settlement, announced on May 10th, was in part made possible by the efforts of the protest leaders to keep their demands clearly focused and limited throughout: (1) desegregation of downtown public and department store facilities; (2) an end to discrimination in city and industry employment, and an opportunity for blacks to qualify for other than menial jobs; (3) dropping all charges against demonstrators; and (4) formation of a biracial committee to prepare a timetable for desegregating Birmingham's schools.

The Birmingham campaign had political repercussions beyond the concessions won locally. During his presidential campaign, Kennedy had promised that a proposal of major civil rights legislation would be "among the first orders of business" when he took office. The proposal did not come until two and a half years later, when democracy was in the streets. On June 11, 1963, Kennedy announced to the nation that he was requesting Congress immediately to enact the most sweeping civil rights bill since Reconstruction. This was impressive evidence that our representative democracy is often moved to act in controversial areas only when it is compelled to do so. Congress did not move on the Kennedy bill until after 250,000 marchers had converged on Washington on August 23, Martin Luther King had resonated the national conscience with his "I Have a Dream" address at the Lincoln Memorial, and President Kennedy had been shot.

The power of direct nonviolent civil disobedience to cure systematic racial oppression was really very limited. It would not work where the black community lacked significant economic leverage. It could not be effective except where there were at least a few voices in the white power structure responsive to black suffering. It required months of careful planning and organization, tremendous physical sacrifices and spiritual endurance, and a level of discipline and patience almost impossible to maintain in the face of monotonously savage police response. The gains were finite, and each gain was inevitably a settlement for something less than the real goal of full equality.

Direct action campaigns did force concessions from the empowered white community, but civil disobedience left Southern blacks still voteless and without any permanent power base. It became clear that political power for them depended on access to the voting booth. Resistance by entrenched white interests to black voter organization and registration was, if possible, more brutally repressive than their resistance to desegregation had been. The jailings and killings in Mississippi in 1964 and surrounding the Selma march in 1965 were only the most dramatic political preconditions to passage of the Voting Rights Act of 1965. It made possible an end to dictatorial control, by local white officials, of the democratic process; it led to a fundamental political restructuring of the South.

On March 15, 1965, President Johnson, in a nationally televised speech, proposed the Voting Rights legislation to a Congress which had been stirred by the long campaign of civil disobedience and outraged by repeated and blatantly repressive abuses of the criminal process. Acknowledging that out of southern jails had come a fundamental shift in the national consciousness, and summoning the nation to overcome a "crippling legacy of bigotry and injustice," the Chief Executive, a southerner, identified himself with their cause by adopting the protesters' anthem. He punctuated his speech by hurling at a stunned Congress the emotion-laden words, "And we shall overcome."

Among those present when the president signed the Act into law on August 6, was Mrs. Rosa Parks. The political and legal victory, limited though it has proved to be, had cost more lives. Rev. James Reeb of Boston died on the night of March 11, his skull crushed on a Selma street by white vigilantes. Mrs. Viola Liuzzo, a Detroit housewife and the mother of five, was gunned down on the highway while ferrying marchers back to Selma at the conclusion of that march. Like Medgar Evers, Andrew Goodman, James Chaney, Mickey Schwerner, Jimmie Lee Jackson, and others who met their deaths in the effort to bring political change to the South, they were not fortunate enough to be political prisoners.

The Black Panthers, a band of straight-standing angry black men in black berets, powder blue shirts, and black leather jackets, leaped into the American political arena in the fall of 1966. It is still almost impossible to separate fact from fiction in the Black Panther story; both the Panthers and the police have an interest in distorting it. Before the story had fully unfolded, however, it became clear that we learned little from our repression of the Wobblies a half-century earlier. Like the Wobblies, the Panthers filled a vacuum in American political life with hyperbolic rhetoric, grass-roots social services, and novel organizational ploys. Like the Wobblies, repression gave them power through notoriety, and repression wiped them out.

The Panthers flourished in the northern ghettos, where the civil rights campaign had virtually no impact, but their roots went deep into the nonviolent civil disobedience struggle in the South. The Student Nonviolent Coordinating Committee repudiated the pieties of strict nonviolence after the Selma march. SNCC lost interest in appealing to the conscience of moderate whites and in trying to form coalitions with them. The coalitions enabled the black stars of the movement to win superficial legislative gains in Washington, but left local blacks without the indigenous leadership, organization, or élan needed to resist the return of centuries-old social and political patterns when the stars moved on to the next community or the next issue. The young SNCC staff repudiated the "politics of suffering" as a means, and integration as an end. Their goal was to build a power base and to forge a political identity for blacks.

SNCC tested its new tack in Lowndes County, Alabama, which was 80 percent black but where not a single black was registered to vote before 1964 while white voter registration ran at 118 percent of those eligible.[5] SNCC, under the leadership of Stokely Carmichael, founded the Lowndes County Freedom Organization as a black political alternative to the Democratic Party of Governor Wallace, Bull Connor, and Al Lingo. Carmichael set the tone by remarking: "The Negroes won't take it this time. When they go down to vote and they see the white man's got his guns, they're going to go back home and get theirs."[6] For its symbol on the ballot, LCFO chose the black panther: "This Black Panther," explained a spokesman, "is a vicious animal, as you know. Never bothers anything, but when you start pushing him, he moves backwards, backwards and backwards into his corner, and then he comes out to destroy everything that's before him."[7]

The symbol appealed to the sensibilities of Huey Newton, Bobby Seale, and Bobby Hutton, ghetto youths outraged at the everyday brutality and abuses of power by white police in the black areas of Oakland, California. Through them, the Panther symbolism caught the imagination of the nation, sending shockwaves of self-recognition through ghettos where "Black Power," "Black Pride," and other catch phrases were given a hard reality by the nervy young men of Oakland with their guns, their organization, their pride, and their evident lack of fear of whites.

California had no law prohibiting carrying unconcealed weapons, so Newton and the other Panther originals began policing the police. Later, in courtroom testimony, Huey Newton described these early Panther patrols:

We would put three or four people into a car equipped with tape recorder, cameras and weapons and we would patrol the community. . . . If we saw anyone stopped, we would stay a reasonable distance from the person who is stopped by the police. We would have a lawbook with us to read the person his basic rights—his constitutional right to have an attorney present if he is going to answer any questions; and the right to remain silent. We have also followed the police wagons to jails, bailing people out when we thought the person was being done an injustice.[8]

Huey Newton's political thinking was consistent with the military nature of his Panther organization. He characterized the police as an "occupying army . . . recruited from the oppressor race." But "picking up the gun" (a phrase borrowed from Chairman Mao) was a political as well as a military tactic:

Black people can develop Self-Defense Power by arming themselves from house to house, block to block, community to community, throughout the nation. Then we will choose a political representative, and he will state to the power structure the desires of the black masses. If the desires are not met, the power structure will receive a political consequence. We will make it economically non-profitable for the power structure to go on with its oppressive ways. We will then negotiate as equals. There will be a balance between the people who are economically powerful and the people who are potentially economically destructive.[9]

The scenario was fantasy. Newton was not in touch with political realities beyond the block. But grainy newspaper photos of defiant blacks carrying guns struck guilty fear deep into the loins of whites. Like the Wobblies, the Panthers refused to pitch their rhetoric in tones acceptable to middle-gray America. From their own feelings and their experiences on the block they erected a fantasy of revolution, by violence if necessary, with the Panthers as the "Vanguard" party. In order to bolster the theory that theirs was a prerevolutionary time, and to create a sense, consistent with their ideology, that revolutionary violence held the promise of liberation, they condoned violence as a legitimate tool of oppressed people and they openly rejoiced when police were slain.

The rhetorical appeal proved to be as empty a political pitch as any in recent years, and the "fighting words" and military image boomeranged. Panther leaders had trouble controlling recruits attracted by the prospect of violence and ready to plunge ahead with "military" solutions to any problem—including, in some instances, the problem of fund raising. The anticapitalist ideology, the guerrilla psychology, and the fascination with weapons as a source of political and military power led to boasts of revolutionary derring-do and made the Panthers an easy target for repression.

Having achieved some notoriety by "arming for self-defense," the Black Panthers became a full-fledged political party in October 1966, and published a Ten Point Program. Almost one-third of this document is direct quotation from the Declaration of Independence. Its substantive points call for community control (black self-determination); payment of the "overdue debt of forty acres and a mule . . . promised 100 years ago" (reparations); more relevant education; black self-defense to end police brutality; freedom for all black prisoners, since they had not been tried by a jury "of their peers"; draft exemption for blacks so long as they are denied full citizenship; and, finally, "land, bread, housing, education, clothing, justice and peace." As a political program, this list of rather tame demands, couched in a pop melange of Thomas Jefferson, Chairman Mao, Karl Marx, Che

Guevara, and Frantz Fanon, was not likely to capture the imagination of America's militant fringe.

What made the difference for the Panthers was the gun and the guerilla rhetoric. They were immediately portrayed in the press as armed black terrorists. In fairness, it must be said that they courted the sensational publicity. On May 2, 1967, when the California legislature was considering legislation which the Panthers said was "aimed at keeping the Black people disarmed and powerless in the face of police terror, brutality and repression," thirty Panthers appeared, twenty of them armed, in the State Capitol building to "lobby" against the bill. The stunt spurred the passage of tighter gun control laws, but it also shot the Panthers into a position of national prominence which they held for the next three years.

The Oakland police set the style for Panther control. Police brutality decreased with the advent of the Panther patrols only to the extent that the Panthers focused police abuses on themselves. The Oakland police department bulletin board carried a list of twenty "known Panther vehicles," and these were routinely stopped and their occupants subjected to searches and questioning. When a robbery or burglary was reported, Panthers were rounded up as suspects and held for as long as the law allowed before charges had to be brought or the "suspects" released. With the police tailing the Panthers, who were following the police, the mutual hostility was sure to explode.

A year of petty harassment was capped just before dawn on October 28, 1967, when a police cruiser stopped Huey Newton in one of the "known Panther vehicles." There is no satisfactory explanation for what happened next, but Officer Herbert Heames was shot in the arm, Huey Newton was hit with four bullets in his abdomen and one in his thigh, and Officer John Frey was killed by a shot from his own gun. Officer Heames, who admitted shooting Newton, could not recall seeing the Panther with a gun in his hand, and Newton insisted he was carrying only the lawbook. He was charged with murder.

As he awaited trial in the Alameda County Jail, the Panthers threw their energies into a nationwide "Free Huey" campaign. The jurors at Newton's first trial were clearly unable to find facts proving the murder charge. They found him guilty of voluntary manslaughter, a compromise verdict made possible by an error of the judge. Newton served twenty-two months of his fifteen-year sentence before the verdict was reversed by an appellate court because of the error. He was denied bail and kept in prison while California appealed the higher court ruling. A second trial ended, in the summer of 1971, after a jury deliberated for six days and declared itself deadlocked. The third time around, in December 1971, a jury was split six to six after three days of deliberations. The judge dismissed the charges against Newton for good.

At first, the Panthers had succeeded in turning Newton's trials and imprisonment into a political asset. Throughout 1968, the "Free Huey!" campaign appealed to the instincts of ghetto youths familiar with the summary "justice" administered by police on the city streets of America. Panther chapters were formed in a score of cities and the membership surged to perhaps two thousand. But the cost of expanding membership was a loss of control. Among those apparently embracing the Panther political program were incorrigible hoods and police undercover agents—and both types proved to be handy pegs on which to hang the intensifying official repression. The Panthers closed their ranks to new members in January 1969, but it was already too late. Undercover agents may have uncovered a few serious plots, but they also dreamed them up and sometimes they actively tried to recruit individual Panthers to join criminal enterprises so that they could be enmeshed in dragnet conspiracy indictments.

Most of the repression was of low visibility: recruits sent out to hawk *The Black Panther*, for instance, were repeatedly arrested and convicted of assault or some other crime, or were released and rearrested. Panthers were haled into court on trumped up charges made believable by what was becoming, through prosecutorial persistence, an easy identification of "Panther" with "criminal." When police were unable to nab the perpetrator of a crime, they would sometimes report that they had fired at a "fleeing Panther." And a number of the Panthers actually fired upon were not fleeing at all. The mysterious "shoot-outs" (as police characterized them), in which Panther and police deaths mounted alarmingly, climaxed on December 4, 1970, when Illinois Panther Chairman Fred Hampton was shot in the head, from above, as he lay in his bed. Chicago authorities initially described that incident as a twenty-minute "shoot-out": those responsible attempted to suppress the fact that the raiding police fired a barrage of some one hundred bullets into the Panther apartment, and that only one shot was fired back.

With Newton in prison, the Black Panther Party had to negotiate this period of rapid growth as a national party and of mounting police harassment without the counsel of its most politically astute leader. Eldridge Cleaver, the author of *Soul on Ice*, joined the Panthers and became a leading spokesman after he was paroled in 1967 from Soledad Prison, where he had served nine years of a one- to fourteen-year sentence for rape. In March 1968, when riots swept the northern ghettos in the aftermath of Martin Luther King's assassination, the Panthers, led by Bobby Seale, Bobby Hutton, and Eldridge Cleaver, kept Oakland cool.[10] But on April 6, Hutton and Cleaver were arrested following one of those recurrent "shoot outs." Again, it is impossible to know precisely what happened, but Hutton was slain, possibly while he was trying to surrender to the attacking police officers, and Cleaver, a model parolee up to that point, was wounded and charged with three counts of attempted murder and three counts of assault with a deadly weapon.

Authorities did not wait for Cleaver to be tried on the criminal charges and did not even grant him a hearing; they simply revoked his parole and quickly returned him to the enforced silence and isolation of a prison cell for the non-crimes of possessing a gun, associating with people of bad reputation, and "failing to cooperate" with his parole officer. Two months later Cleaver regained his freedom when Superior Court Judge Raymond J. Sherwin found that "the peril to his parole status stemmed . . . from his undue eloquence in pursuing political goals. . . . Not only was there absence of cause for the cancellation of parole, it was the product of a type of pressure unbecoming, to say the least, to the law-enforcement paraphernalia of this State."[11]

Cleaver did not remain free for long. Judge Sherwin's decision was overruled by a higher court on the same day that Huey Newton's first trial ended and he was sentenced to prison. Cleaver's parole was again revoked, and he was ordered to report back to prison. He fled the country instead, claiming that he feared for his life if it was placed again in the hands of California's law-enforcement agencies.

The Panthers never numbered more than a few thousand, but when the Nixon Administration took office, the Panthers were given a whole new series of publicity boosts. Vice-President Agnew, ignoring their politics and their social service programs in the ghettos, lumped them all together as a "completely irresponsible, anarchistic group of criminals"; J. Edgar Hoover called them a "black extremist organization," despite their efforts, unique among black militants, to work with white sympathizers and despite their attempts to carve out a position as the "vanguard" party for the oppressed of all races. Attorney General John Mitchell gave them the ultimate tag: "The Panthers," he said, "are a threat to national security."

The effect of this verbal overkill was to legitimize whatever methods law-enforcement authorities could devise to abort the menace. A Special Panther Unit was set up in the Justice Department under Victor Worheide, who spent the spring and summer of 1969 hopping from city to city to help local police departments bring charges against the Panthers. Panther headquarters in a number of cities were raided and ransacked by local and federal agents. Within a few months, more than a hundred Panthers were already in jail.

With Huey Newton behind bars, Bobby Hutton slain, and Cleaver's exile increasingly distancing him from stateside political realities, the Party's National Chairman, Bobby Seale, was the only original Panther still at liberty. In August 1969, he was arrested in California on charges of conspiracy to kidnap and first-degree murder. The State of Connecticut had indicted him for the "kangaroo trial," torture, and execution of Alex Rackley, a New York Black Panther who had been suspected of being a police informer. Rackley's scalded and beaten body was found in a swamp near New Haven in May and, on May 22, police broke into the New Haven Panther office and arrested seven in connection with the murder. The pretext for the raids on Panther offices across the country between May and August 1969, was a manhunt for George Sams, the Panther who had engineered Rackley's "discipline." When Sams was captured in August, he obligingly implicated Seale in his crime.

Seale's trip to New Haven for the murder trial was

delayed, mid-continent, for him to appear as a defendant in the Chicago Conspiracy Trial which began on September 24. The episode is remembered by many for the Panther leader's attack on Judge Julius Hoffman. Seale's attacks, all verbal, were provoked in nearly every instance by Hoffman's refusal to treat seriously his claim that he was constitutionally entitled either to the trial counsel of his choice or to defend himself. "I have a right to make those demands," he told the judge, "and if you try to suppress my constitutional right to speak out in behalf of my constitutional rights, then I can only see you as a bigot, a racist, and a fascist."[12]

Judge Hoffman routinely delayed trials when an attorney's vacation or some other conflict with the court's calendar was brought to his attention. But when Seale's attorney, Charles Garry, had to enter the hospital for an operation, Judge Hoffman refused to delay the proceedings and insisted on the fiction that William Kunstler was Seale's lawyer. Seale's unyielding assertion of his right, in the absence of counsel, to cross-examine witnesses himself and his persistence in arguing motions on his own behalf at first baffled and then outraged the judge. Hoffman finally ordered Seale gagged and chained to his chair, but he had worked his way into a moral and legal dilemma. On November 5, Judge Hoffman declared a mistrial as to Seale, severed his case from the others, and sentenced him to four years in prison for his contempt.

Under the Sixth Amendment, the constitutional provision which guaranteed Seale a lawyer of his choosing or the right to conduct his own defense, Seale could not be given a sentence for contempt in excess of six months without a trial by jury. Judge Hoffman attempted to circumvent this requirement by characterizing each of Seale's sixteen interruptions as a separate criminal attack on the administration of justice and by dealing out separate three-month sentences for each one. As the Chicago trial proceeded without him, Seale was carried to New Haven.

The Connecticut State's Attorney clearly *believed* that Seale ordered Rackley's execution; the notion fit perfectly with the view, disseminated by public officials from the White House to the precinct stationhouse, that the Panthers were a dangerously disciplined, para-military, terrorist cadre. The Connecticut prosecutor portrayed Rackley's death and Seale's alleged role in it as "typical" of Black Panther Party discipline. George Sams and another New Haven Panther were allowed to plead guilty to second-degree murder, but before Sams was sentenced he was put on the witness stand to testify that he had acted only upon a direct order from Seale.

Sams' testimony was suspect on a number of grounds: he held a grudge against Seale, who had earlier expelled him from the Party for a lapse of discipline; Sams admitted beating other Panthers and taking it upon himself to "discipline" them; and his story stood uncorroborated by the others who had admitted helping him execute Rackley. Sams' medical records, including two psychiatric findings that he was "mentally defective," were not shown to the jury, but his instability and sadism were apparent in his often incoherent, rambling, and ranting testimony. He even broadcast his feelings about Seale in a ten-minute tirade from the witness stand.

This attempt to put the Panther Party and its leadership on trial for murder simply backfired. The State's Attorney failed to convince the jurors that he was conducting a "routine" criminal case; prosecutors do not routinely aim charges so indicriminately, nor do they ordinarily go forward with cases hanging so obviously on their own assumptions and on the testimony of a witness of such evident unreliability. One of the New Haven jurors picked out the political spirit of the prosecution nicely: "There's a war going on here," he said. "When you see [the State's Attorney] wearing a pig on his ties, you know what's going on. [He] is on one side of the war, and he is a leader."[13]

On its very first vote, the jury was agreed on Seale's innocence. He had, however, been brought to trial together with Mrs. Erika Huggins, and she *had* been present during part of Rackley's "interrogation." In the end, one or two of the jurors refused to vote for Seale's acquittal unless the others would agree to convict Huggins on the larger conspiracy counts; on May 25, 1971, they reported to the judge that they were hopelessly deadlocked.

Ordinarily, a hung jury entitles the prosecutor to another chance and the State's Attorney in this case immediately declared: "I'll try them again, absolutely."[14] The following day, however, Judge Mulvey ordered the charges against Seale and Huggins dismissed. As reasons for ruling out a second trial, he pointed to the almost two years each defendant had already served in prison on the charges, the paucity of the state's evidence against them, and the inflammatory publicity which made it "almost impossible to believe that an unbiased jury could be selected."[15]

In the end, police and prosecutors met with only limited success in trying to put their own fantasies on trial. After the killing of Mark Clark and Fred Hampton in Chicago, American juries developed a healthy skepticism about the official view of the Panthers. The New Haven verdict was but one example, and the turning point actually came two weeks earlier, at 4:45 on the afternoon of May 13, 1971. The foreman of a New York jury brought to an end the longest (eight months) and costliest ($2 million) trial in the state's history, by calling out "not guilty" 156 times. In fifteen minutes, thirteen Panthers were acquitted across the board on twelve counts each of conspiracy to bomb department stores, to blow up police stations, and to murder policemen.

Most of these defendants had also been in jail for over

two years. On April 13, 1969, after a series of pre-dawn arrests, District Attorney Frank Hogan had told a shocked New York City of the plot which, he said, was to have been carried out that very day. A judge who set bail at a prohibitive $100,000 for each suspect, emphasized that hundreds of deaths could have resulted had the plot been carried out. The indictment of the New York Panther Thirteen characterized the local Panther chapter as a conspiracy from the moment of its inception in August 1968. Eight hundred joined up in one month of the "Free Huey" campaign and among those present when the chapter was formed were four undercover agents of the New York police department. When the Panther Thirteen were actually brought to trial, seventeen months after the arrests, it became clear that the case against them rested entirely on the stories of the undercover agents, who had risen to positions of leadership in the group they had infiltrated. Their testimony treated each exchange of stilted revolutionary rhetoric as a statement of criminal intent, and took seriously the conspiratorial fantasies with which militants of all stripes regularly feed their egos; they were unable however, to recall any actual *agreement* to go ahead with a plot, nor could they produce any bombs—bombs which certainly would have been in readiness if the plot had been serious. One of the policemen did testify that *he* had led a group of teen-agers on a reconnaissance tour of Manhattan department stores. But there was no hard evidence that anyone else had done more than daydream and brag about dealing a violent blow to the Establishment.

After delivering their "not guilty" verdicts, the Panther Thirteen jurors explained to reporters that the judge had seemed biased, that the informers' testimony could not be believed, and that the informers seemed to have acted as *agents provocateurs*. One juror summed up their view of the case: it was so flimsy that it should never have been brought to trial.

Two of the acquitted Panther Thirteen were not in the courtroom to hear the verdicts; they fled earlier to join Eldridge Cleaver in Algeria. The judge had said that their flight could be considered as evidence of their guilt, but it was evident to the jurors that the two Panthers had substantial reasons to flee, guilty or not. The Establishment press and liberal pundits regularly seize on acquittals such as these for evidence buttressing their faith in the integrity of our system of criminal justice. "The acquittals," intoned the editors of *The New York Times* after the Panther Thirteen case was over, "should put to rest the unfounded comment that it is impossible for a black militant to get a fair trial in the United States." But the jurors themselves felt, as Angela Davis later observed, that when black militants have to wait years in prison before a jury's common sense can pierce the political motivation of a prosecutor, "the only fair trial would be no trial at all."

By the end of 1971, when the Panther's preeminent leader, Huey Newton, was finally freed from the charge of killing Officer Frey, he took active command of an organization which had been decimated by death, repressive prosecutions, internal bickering, and interim leadership which was less than wise. It is impossible to know what course the Black Panthers would have taken had its leadership been free to develop realistic political skills through the day-to-day building of a grass-roots ghetto political organization. There is some evidence that when prosecutions and bullets removed the original leadership, less principled leaders exploited the Panther image, ideology, and membership in a sort of "social banditry" which Newton disdained.[16] Many Panthers broke discipline and committed crimes for which they were justly convicted. But many were the victims of repression, and even while repression was branding the Panthers as anarchistic thugs in the minds of white Americans, their prestige in the black community was steadily rising.

A *Wall Street Journal* survey in January 1970, established that the police raids and the shoddy prosecutions spread sympathy and support for the Panthers among their more conventional black neighbors. In the ghettos, the Panthers were admired for their social service programs of free breakfasts for school children, free medical clinics, legal assistance, and antinarcotic drives. The *Journal* reported that "a clear majority of blacks strongly support both the goals and the methods of the Black Panthers. An even larger percentage believes, moreover, that police officials are determined to crush the party by arresting or killing its key officials."[17]

The black community in America was not ready for revolution during these five years; they were not ready to "pick up the gun" even to protect themselves from police brutality. The Panthers have had, nonetheless, a profound impact on the political consciousness even of those who rejected their guerilla psychology and rhetorical militance. In April 1970, Julian Bond summed up the reaction of many moderate black leaders: "What the Panthers do more than anything else is they set up a standard . . . of aggressiveness, of militance, of just forcefulness, the sort of standard we haven't had in the past. Our idols have been Dr. King who, for all of his beauty as a man, was not an aggressive man."[18] The pride and defiance of the Panthers, standing unyieldingly on their rights, was captured by Eldridge Cleaver for whom it was "love at first sight." One night in February 1967, he was present at a meeting where Bay Area blacks were trying to plan a massive memorial program in honor of Malcolm X on the fourth anniversary of his assassination. Cleaver recalled that paranoia was endemic in the gathering:

> Suddenly the room fell silent. The crackling undercurrent that for weeks had made it impossible to get one's point across when one had the floor was gone; there was only the

sound of the lock clicking as the front door opened, and the soft shuffle of feet moving quietly toward the circle. Shadows danced on the walls. From the tension showing on the faces of the people before me, I thought the cops were invading the meeting, but there was a deep female gleam leaping out of one of the women's eyes that no cop who ever lived could elicit. I recognized that gleam out of the recesses of my soul, even though I had never seen it before in my life: the total admiration of a black woman for a black man. I spun round in my seat and saw the most beautiful sight I had ever seen: four black men wearing black berets, powder blue shirts, black leather jackets, black trousers, shiny black shoes —and each with a gun![19]

In 1972, the Panthers seemed quite clearly on a different track. With Newton out of jail and trying to put an end to the internecine feuding and dead-end posturing of his party, the Panthers are toning down their rhetoric, trying to strengthen their social service programs, and have begun the basic work of all political organizing—voter registration. Mrs. Erika Huggins was elected to membership of a community council in California; Bobby Seale ran for mayor of Oakland;[20] and the Panthers seem to be putting away their guerilla psychology along with their guns.

9

Modern Political Prisoners: War

> Said the President
> (He's got his war
> Folks don't know
> Just what it's for
> No one gives us
> Rhyme or reason
> You have one doubt—
> They call it treason)
> Said
> We're chicken-feathered
> All without one gut.
> Try to make it real
> But compared to what?
> —Roberta Flack

A nation at war is like a tank. It is impossible to change its course without manipulating the internal machinery that powers it. That is why the founding fathers placed the dangerous power to start a war with the deliberative, legislative branch of government, and placed with the president the more limited power to fight what wars Congress may declare. The Vietnam war was undeclared; and, as *The Pen-*

tagon Papers make frighteningly clear, the presidential decisions which committed our national honor and the lives of a generation of our young men to one side of a civil war in Southeast Asia were effectively camouflaged from us for years.

As the human cost of the war rose and its popularity declined, the speed and direction of our course proved virtually uncontrollable by conventional political means. Intimidated by claims of successive presidents that only they had all the facts, and reluctant to challenge the authority of our Commanders-in-Chief in time of war, Congress was unwilling—and perhaps unable—to undo what presidents had done.

A significant minority of the young men who were called upon to fight this war, and compelled by law to do so, could see no good reason for cooperating, and they were given none. Some thought that the war and the draft required to sustain it were illegal under the Constitution. Others thought it an immoral and unjust war. And the horrific spectacle of free-fire zones, search and destroy, "pacification," and all the other brands of indiscriminate killing, provoked a larger percentage than ever before in our history to the conviction that no war could ever claim their support. Their resistance and, as time went on, the resistance of a whole spectrum of our citizenry, led to civil disobedience, repressive laws, and repressive law enforcement. There was much more than this to the antiwar movement, but with the political imprisonments and political trials came an immense and, I hope, an enduring shift in American political attitudes.

The civil disobedients whose "direct action" focused our political process on the legal and moral infirmities of segregation had an easy target by comparison: they could violate segregation ordinances. But a war, even an immoral or unconstitutional war, is not a law, and it cannot be broken.

A warring government demands two things from its citizens: cold cash and warm bodies. The Vietnam War provoked at least twenty thousand Americans, who were over draft age and whose bodies were therefore not warm enough for war, to deny their cold cash. They refused to pay all or a proportionate part of their taxes to support the war, a federal crime for which some of them went to prison.

The numbers are impressive, but obviously insignificant in terms of the military budget. War tax resistance is a very private, very cerebral form of disobedience, a matter between a citizen's conscience, his bank, and the Internal Revenue Service.

Warm bodies are another matter altogether. Even before the Universal Military Service and Training Act was passed in 1948, strenuous objections were raised to giving the Executive Branch of government the power to draft young men in the absence of a Congressional declaration of war. Senator Vandenberg sounded a prophetic warning in 1940: "[P]eace time military conscription is repugnant to the spirit of democracy and the soul of Republican institutions, and it leads in dark directions."[1] It has been wonderful to watch today's liberals take up this line of argument, advanced by their conservative nemesis of thirty years ago. The cycle was actually complete years ago, when Vandenberg was himself reconciled to those "dark directions" and became an aggressive internationalist.

In July 1965, President Johnson announced the first large-scale shipment of troops to Vietnam. On July 29, four hundred New Yorkers were trying, rather ineffectually, to make their protest against the escalations visible by mass picketing. Their target, the Whitehall Induction Center, is one of those buildings hidden in the mass of narrow winding streets of Lower Manhattan. Chris Kearns, a young Catholic pacifist, tried to shed some light on the "dark directions" by sending a draft card up in flames. *Life* ran a picture, and it was immediately clear that burning a little piece of cardboard could be a more effective protest than a picket line or an oration. A week later, the Chairman of the House Armed Services Committee, Representative Mendel Rivers, introduced legislation making destruction of a draft card a felony punishable by five years in prison.

The draft laws already prohibited young men from disposing of their draft cards, but Representative Rivers made no secret of his repressive purpose in calling for new penalties. He wanted a law to punish "a vocal minority in this country [who] thumb their noses at their own government."[2] Thumbing one's nose at government has not been a crime in this country since Luther Baldwin was convicted of Sedition in 1799 for expressing his wish that President Adams get his sixteen-gun salute up his ass. President Johnson signed this new measure into law on August 30, 1965. Outlawing the burning of draft cards had an unexpected result. Every draft-age man in America was now carrying around in his wallet the ingredients for instant civil disobedience of the most dramatic sort, to be used whenever the spirit moved him.

Congress had adopted the Gulf of Tonkin Resolution in 1964 on the president's assurance that the power it gave him was needed to repel an armed attack on American forces and that "the United States intends no rashness and seeks no wider war."[3] By October 1965, not much more than a year later, the president's commitment to a wider war had increased draft call-ups tenfold. Having lent its war-making power to the president, Congress made no move to get it back, and resistance to the draft itself was viewed by many as a restraint of last resort against limitless escalations. On October 15, ten thousand Berkeley demonstrators were stopped by police at the Oakland city line when they tried to march to the Oakland Induction Center. In Ann

Arbor, Michigan, demonstrators were arrested for trespass when they tried to apply the sit-in technique at a draft board.

The administration's response merely fueled the protest. Attorney General Katzenbach charged that the antiwar movement was Communist-infiltrated. President Johnson accused those attacking his policy with encouraging the enemy and prolonging the war. General Hershey instructed draft boards to induct them immediately.[4]

As sit-ins and other protests employing civil disobedience increased in frequency, it became obvious that the civil rights struggle had been a training ground for many in the budding antiwar movement. David Miller, who had been arrested in September 1963, after participating in several CORE demonstrations, came forward at a demonstration in front of the Whitehall Induction Center on the same day as the 1965 Oakland march, and set fire to his draft card, saying simply: "I believe the napalming of villages is an immoral act. I hope this will be a significant political act, so here goes."[5] It was a costly act. He was arrested two days later and sentenced to two and a half years in prison. Proof of the political significance of this first violation of the new law came slowly.

In March 1966, David O'Brien stood on the steps of a Boston courthouse with two young men about to go to trial for their part in a sit-in demonstration at the Boston Army Base. Both had just been reclassified 1-A because of their participation in antiwar protests. All three burned their cards and were imprisoned. O'Brien's case went to the Supreme Court. O'Brien argued that the purpose of the new law was at war with the spirit of the First Amendment, that its purpose was to outlaw a symbolic expression of dissent. The Court neatly sidestepped that argument, affirmed the conviction, and upheld the law on the ground that Congress had the power to ensure the smooth functioning of the draft system by requiring draftable men to carry ready proof of their status.[6]

By early 1967, well over a thousand draft-age men had signed pledges to refuse to fight in Vietnam. Some, however, were aware that a *pledge* of civil disobedience doesn't count for much in the political arena. In March, five members of a "We Won't Go!" group at Cornell University circulated a letter proposing an escalation by a mass burning of draft cards to invite criminal prosecutions. On April 15, while 125,000 persons came together in New York for the first massive protest march against the war, between 120 and 150 young men stood in a circle in Central Park and burned their draft cards. A new cycle of mass civil disobedience and repression, this time by the federal government, was under way.

The problem, as some of the student leaders saw it, was to find a way to make disobedience politically effective. Mass burning of draft cards could make protest highly visible, but it also destroyed the evidence of disobedience and gave the administration an easy way out: the administration was not yet seeking a risky courtroom confrontation with what still appeared to be a politically insignificant minority. Most of those who were ready to join a draft-resistance movement held deferments as students, ministers, or conscientious objectors. If they provoked their boards to reclassify them and order them to report for induction, they would be called up one by one with no opportunity to disobey *en masse*. Some already had refused induction and gone to prison, but theirs was a costly protest, hidden by the steel doors of army induction centers, and not the sort of civil disobedience which had galvanized the civil rights movement.

In February 1967, David Harris resigned as student body president at Stanford, and, with a few friends, began organizing a new national political organization designed to take the initiative away from the administration and the draft boards. They called themselves, rather grandly, *The Resistance*, and they set October 16 for massive civil disobedience.

As the war escalated through the summer, organizers crisscrossed the country, leaving Resistance groups behind them like so many Johnny Appleseeds. The groups focused on finding as many as possible who would agree to turn back their draft cards to the government simultaneously, thereby sealing publicly their mutual pledge to disobey orders to report for induction; to refuse, in fact, any further cooperation with the Selective Service System.

The philosophy of the Resistance led one member into an early confrontation with the law. Rick Boardman was a Quaker, and his draft board had classified him as a conscientious objector. He had, personally, nothing to worry about. On April 24, he returned his draft card to his board with the explanation that he felt obliged to refuse to cooperate further in *any* way. His reasons were, he wrote, "both idealistic and very practical, religious and political."

[T]o accept any classification is to tacitly accept the legitimacy of the system of conscription and the military for which conscription exists. . . .

I believe wholeheartedly that ends and means are inseparable: that, as Gandhi said, "the means is the end in the making." For this reason violence can never be successful in bringing about peace: coercion and tyranny will never work successfully in the "defense of freedom," and any contribution that one may make to supporting or cooperating with the system of organized violence we call "the military" will be directly opposing the human values, relationships, and social structures that men hope to develop in the world.

The weapons that one must use in the defense of freedom, or with which to build a better world, are the weapons that are commensurate with the ends they are used to achieve.

These are the weapons of truth, of love, of charity, of understanding, of community.[7]

Boardman's letter was an eloquent restatement of the
position of the Quakers in their Revolutionary War travails, but with a difference. The pacifist view was updated
with the nonviolent civil disobedience theorizing of Thoreau, Gandhi, and King, and it was intended to have wider
political repercussions than an isolated act of conscience: "I
hope that you will recognize," Boardman wrote to his
board, "the power that my example may have."

Rick Boardman was indicted, convicted and sentenced to
three years in prison. His rejection of a draft deferment and
the rather optimistic political view with which he accepted
imprisonment were duplicated by other civil disobedients
all across the country, not in great numbers, but in numbers great enough to have an impact on the complacent
attitudes of middle-gray America.

Political power in the United States resides somewhere
between the heart and the pocketbook of the very families
whose sons formed the core of the Resistance. The
disobedience of draft resisters could not really shut down
the draft or stop the war, but their display of political
courage and their powerful symbolic argument could, and
eventually did, provide the political preconditions for me
and for others looking for conventional ways to force the
Executive Branch to a public accounting in its policy of
continued war.

On October 16, almost twelve hundred draft cards were
turned in at Resistance rallies in cities scattered across the
country. The biggest Resistance demonstration was in Boston, where Michael Ferber and other members of the New
England Resistance arranged to use the Arlington Street
Church, a site of Abolitionist rallies in the 1860s. It took
only twenty minutes for sixty resisters to burn their cards

at a candle and for two hundred to hand theirs over to be returned to the government and used as evidence against them. FBI agents began to visit each Arlington Street draft-card returner. Theirs had been classic civil disobedience: public, nonviolent, conscientious disobedience, publicly explained.

On the West Coast, October 16 opened "Stop the Draft Week," a series of antiwar demonstrations time to generate support for the Resistance. Two thousand gathered at the Oakland Induction Center on that Monday to try to prevent the arrival of buses loaded with draftees. At a sit-in blocking the entrance, police arrested one hundred nineteen. A five-hour rally that night at the Berkeley campus brought three thousand demonstrators to the induction center on Tuesday. Police attacked quickly and mercilessly with billyclubs and chemical Mace to clear a path for the buses; two hundred protesters were hospitalized and twenty were arrested. On Friday, October 20, two thousand police were summoned to Oakland from thirteen cities, the National Guard was alerted, and ten thousand demonstrators, angered by Tuesday's carnage, milled about in the street to make arrests difficult, built barricades against police attacks, and, before the day was over, abandoned nonviolence and fought back. It was the first serious street fighting in the antiwar campaign.

Seven organizers of Stop the Draft Week were charged with a felony, not for having had any part in Friday's violence, but for planning the Tuesday demonstration. The Oakland Seven were charged with *conspiracy* to commit two misdemeanors, trespass and resisting arrest. The indictment alleged that they had committed "overt acts" in furtherance of this conspiracy: chartering buses, transporting loudspeaker equipment, making speeches, distributing leaflets, opening a Stop the Draft Week bank account, and acting as monitors at the Tuesday protest. In short, they were charged with having planned a political demonstration.

The trial, the first of a series of conspiracy trials involving leaders of antiwar protests, lasted three months. The climax of the prosecutor's case was a tape recording of the Monday night rally on the Berkeley campus. The tape played back for the jury all the political frustration, soul-searching, fear, and bravado of those who had taken part in the peaceful demonstration the next day. The prosecutor evidently felt the jury would be swayed to convict by hearing what seemed to him to be intemperate political rhetoric; but the jury, transported to a political happening, could not miss the spontaneity which proved an absence of conspiratorial planning. And by openly politicizing the trial, the prosecutor gave the Oakland Seven an unusual opportunity to use the courtroom as a political forum. The thrust of their defense was that two opposed political visions, not two misdemeanors, had resulted in the charges against them. After three and a half days of deliberations, the jury returned its verdict—outright acquittal for the Oakland Seven.[8]

Five days after the October 16 rallies, one hundred thousand people marched on the Pentagon. Hundreds were arrested when they refused to obey police orders to disperse. As evening fell, and the rest of the march retired a few yards to face the soldiers on the Pentagon steps for the night, the largest mass draft-card burning of them all erupted in a spontaneous disobedient protest. On the eve of that march, at about the time that the street fighting erupted in Oakland, Reverend Sloane Coffin was entering the Justice Department with Dr. Spock, Mitchell Goodman, Marcus Raskin, and others, to turn over the thousand draft cards that had been collected. On the steps he announced:

> We hereby publicly counsel these young men to continue
> in their refusal to serve in the armed forces so long as the war
> in Vietnam continues, and we pledge ourselves to aid and
> abet them in all the ways we can. This means that if they are
> now arrested for failing to comply with a law that violates
> their consciences, we too must be arrested, for in the sight
> of that law we are now as guilty as they.[9]

Coffin, Spock, Goodman, and Raskin were brought to
trial, along with Michael Ferber, not for "counselling, aiding or abetting" violation of the draft laws, but for *conspiracy*. Except for receiving the draft cards and turning
that evidence over to the Justice Department, purposefully
public actions, the "overt acts" of which they were accused
consisted entirely of published and publicly spoken words.

By the end of the *Spock* trial, some twenty-eight thousand
others had signed a "statement of complicity" to express
their agreement with the views of the Boston Five. But by
July 1968, when four of the Five were convicted of conspiracy and sentenced to two years imprisonment ("treason," the judge hinted darkly), the antiwar movement had
moved into conventional political channels with Senator
Eugene McCarthy's abortive run at the presidency and was
about to emerge again into myriad entanglements with the
criminal process. McCarthy's moment was made possible
by the same wave of revulsion against Johnson's Vietnam
policy, but the campaign sapped the strength of the Resistance as a political movement.

The Resistance probably would have died anyway, for
the number willing to place the perquisites of conventional
life in jeopardy by courting trial and long prison terms was
soon exhausted. Although as many as five thousand had
returned their draft cards by late 1968, the numbers never
snowballed. The appeal of their form of civil disobedience
further dimmed when, month after month, they sat

through legal and political hell. Most were declared "delinquents" and ordered to report for induction on an accelerated basis under Hershey's directive. Many avoided both the military and prison when they won a legal battle: the Supreme Court declared Hershey's punitive use of the draft procedures "a type of administrative absolutism not congenial to our law-making traditions."[10] Most who went to prison, on sentences as long as five years, went alone. Their trials and their travails went unremarked by most of the citizens whose political awareness they had sparked. In prison, a distressing number were plagued by a sense of having spent their liberty needlessly.[11]

The political process came unstrung in 1968. After President Johnson declared he would not seek renomination, Martin Luther King was assassinated, riots erupted throughout the nation's ghettos, the "Rap Brown Amendment" nearly outlawed interstate travel by political activists, Robert Kennedy was assassinated at the peak of his bid for the presidency, and a still-hawkish Hubert Humphrey became the alternative to an always-hawkish Richard Nixon.

The youths who flooded Chicago for the Democratic National Convention in August had pretty clearly given up on conventional political action. They were bent on protesting the war, protesting the unresponsive political system, and venting their anger. A good number wanted proof from the system that mass political protest in America is inevitably met by brutal repression. There was a lot of inflammatory rhetoric in Lincoln Park and Grant Park and a lot of deliberate provocation of the police, most of it verbal and symbolic; but Chicago's political authorities made the protesters' mere presence in the parks illegal by refusing permits, and they seemed bent, themselves, on proving the Establishment's intolerance of dissent. The resulting spectacle was accurately termed, by a report of the National Commission on the Causes and Prevention of Violence *(The Walker Report)*, a "police riot."[12]

The Democrats' inability to keep the American political process orderly, even at their own National Convention, cost Humphrey the election. It gave the administration a powerful motive to try to punish the demonstrators, but Attorney General Ramsay Clark resisted the pressure. From his point of view, the problem was one for local authorities. If a demonstrator had been identified in an act of violence or a policeman caught in criminal overreaction, there were local laws aplenty under which they could be prosecuted.

When the Nixon Administration took office, it quickly demonstrated a different view of the proper use of the criminal process. The Justice Department tried to draw together the threads of dissent and alienation—all the political, ethical, and cultural challenges to its values and its authority—and to weave them together in an indictment identifying a grand conspiracy at the root of America's unrest. The Chicago Eight were indicted under the "Rap Brown Amendment" for *conspiring* to come to Chicago with the intent of provoking a riot. The prosecution artificially forced into a partnership of sorts some very disparate and conflicting political factions: David Dellinger, the radical Christian Socialist and pacifist; Renne Davis and Tom Hayden, the ideologists of the New Left; Abbie Hoffman and Jerry Rubin, the hyperbolic showmen of the nonideological political Yippies; Lee Weiner and John Froines, politically obscure academic types, caught up in the protest and made prominent only by being included in the group; and Bobby Seale, black militant, Black Panther, and accomplished rhetoritician. Seale's place on a conspiracy indictment made the least sense: he had not met any of the others, except Jerry Rubin, until the trial; and although his speeches in Grant Park were among the most inflammatory, he had flown into Chicago for one day only as a last-minute speaking replacement for Eldridge Cleaver.

The real purpose of the Chicago Eight trial was not to mete out punishment for crimes, but to prove a political thesis, to discredit what the prosecutor Thomas Foran called "the freaking fag revolution,"[13] and to put it behind bars. Federal Judge Julius Hoffman attempted to help him do this, politicizing the trial even further and discrediting the judicial process beyond the wildest imaginings of the radicals who had already given up our system of government as a fraud. The result? When the verdicts came down, a series of disorderly protests around the country led to other political trials under the same repressive statute.

After the Chicago trial failed to identify a conspiratorial group as the cause of our country's obvious troubles, the Nixon Administration turned the disruptive 1971 Mayday antiwar demonstrations into another opportunity to do so. Prosecutors from the Special Litigation Section of the Justice Department's Internal Security Division transmogrified the American grand jury into an inquisitor of freedom of speech and freedom of association. Working closely with FBI intelligence agents, they directed a series of subpoenas at the loose and shifting network of friends and acquaintances which is persistently characterized as the "New Left." Behind the closed doors of grand jury hearing rooms, the Justice Department probed for the details of their personal relationships and their political beliefs, hoping (in vain) to emerge with the blueprint of a conspiracy that could be brought to trial and imprisoned at last.

Meanwhile, a whole new style in civil disobedience and a whole new breed of political prisoners had been conceived a few days after the climax of the Resistance in 1967. On October 27, Father Philip Berrigan and three others launched the "Ultra-Resistance"[14] when they walked into draft board offices in the Baltimore Customs House, poured blood over Selective Service records, and waited quietly for arresting officers. They were convicted of damaging government property, mutilating government records, and interfering with the functioning of the Selective Service System.

There is a tendency to lionize our Berrigans and Martin Luther Kings for originating novel forms of politically effective protest. And, indeed, their civil disobedience was creative. By framing "direct action" in suitable rituals and appropriate symbols, they were able to transform expressions of personal outrage and political frustration into communications which penetrated the conscience of others who were not yet in agreement with them. But the spadework for the Ultra-Resistance was done by one Barry Bondhus of Big Lake, Minnesota, who devised a very basic bit of direct action in the spring of 1966. Bondhus received an eighteen-month sentence when he broke into his local draft board and dumped a two-week accumulation of his large family's feces over several hundred I-A files. The protest was effective, but in only one dimension. No one could mistake what Barry Bondhus thought of the draft, but for others the symbol he chose could not be pried from its vulgarity to yield a moral insight on the evil of the Vietnam war. The Berrigans' symbolism was wholly different.

In May 1968, Father Daniel Berrigan joined his brother and seven others in destroying 378 draft files with napalm they had manufactured from a formula in the *Special Forces Handbook*. The destruction of property involved in this, and in the Baltimore raid, was disobedience of a particularly shocking kind. As the Berrigans themselves liked to point out, the American public had become so inured to the napalming of Vietnamese civilians that they could not at first see the awful irony of their outrage at the burning of paper. But just as the draft-card actions had worked a gradual shift in American attitudes, the persistence of the Ultra-Resistance was rewarded in the end. As Catholic priests and nuns filed through courtrooms and into jail cells, they were joined by others who were attracted to the limiting and focusing symbolism of this brand of civil disobedience, and as the initial shock wore off, public attitudes about the war shifted a bit further.

A sense of the scope of this development can be gleaned from a simple list of some of the Ultra-Resisters: the Boston Two, the Milwaukee Fourteen, the D.C. Nine, the Pasadena Three, the Silver Springs Three, the Chicago Fifteen, the New York Eight, the Akron Two, the Boston Eight, and the Camden Twenty-Eight. The Camden case was a special one. The man who planned the raid, who taught the others how to execute the plan, and who encouraged them to break the law when their courage failed them, was an FBI informer.

On the day that the FBI's *agent provocateur* in the Camden case blew his cover, another FBI informer was testifying in Harrisburg, Pennsylvania. The Harrisburg Seven were brought to trial after J. Edgar Hoover rolled out the conspiracy weapon once again, to accuse the Berrigan brothers and other Ultra-Resisters of plotting to kidnap Henry Kissinger and to blow up steam tunnels in Washington. The jury did not convict them, but the "plot" was a myth from the beginning. The Berrigans abhor anything involving physical violence to human beings. The ethical principle that drives them to extreme political conclusions about America's preoccupation with war and our development of ever more deadly weapon systems is the same principle that makes the method of a protest extremely important to them. It is ironic that the Berrigans' search for a protest with sufficient shock impact to penetrate American consciousness is made more difficult for them precisely because they accept social values generally more honored in the breach than in the observance by society.

Neither the Resistance nor the Ultra-Resistance brought an end to the war in Vietnam. Their followers' choice of prison, however, posed a moral issue that American politics could not easily evade. I know that it was a significant part of my own education. At the very point when the American public swung away from unquestioning support of our aggressive foreign policy, opposition to the war at home was met with repression. Vietnamization was not a new policy. For the past twenty years our leaders had been talking about training and equipping the South Vietnamese to fight for themselves. Vietnamizing the war was a token recognition of the sentiments expressed in every measure of public opinion. The deeper moral issue posed by the resisters was never rooted in American casualties or dollars diverted from other needs. It relates to what we do to other people, and to ourselves in the process. That issue still haunts America.

10

Criminalizing the Political Process--
A View from Inside

[T]he dangers of exclusive and unwarranted concealment of pertinent facts far outweigh the dangers which are cited to justify it. . . . No President should fear scrutiny of his program. For from that scrutiny comes understanding; and from that understanding comes support or opposition. And both are necessary. . . . I have complete confidence in the response and dedication of our citizens whenever they are fully informed. . . . [G]overnment at all levels must meet its obligation to provide you with the fullest possible information outside the narrowest limits of national security.
                                   —President John F. Kennedy,
                                   April 27, 1961

The Ellsberg case is a political prosecution of a very particular kind, and the first of its kind. In it, the Nixon Administration seeks, by making Ellsberg a criminal, to exert a tremendous power over governmental and nongovernmental employees who play an important part in our political process by keeping the public informed. If Ellsberg is convicted, the government will establish a power to imprison

143

persons using information "tinged with a governmental interest."

The forgotten figure in the case is Tony Russo, indicted along with Ellsberg and charged with having received such information from him. If he is convicted, no newsman desiring to continue to ply his trade outside of prison can feel safe in looking to his confidential sources within the vast federal bureaucracy for news of what our government is actually up to.

Today, in our complex society, self-government rests on more than the protection of all colorations of opinion. Government itself has become a major producer of information and disseminator of opinions. The information produced by government belongs to the people. If the nation is to be guided by the will of a knowledgeable electorate, government must accept a positive obligation, unless there is an *overriding* need for secrecy, to give the people maximum access to the information in its possession.

Very few people would deny the government's need to have some secrets. Congress, however, has never directly authorized a classification system and has never attempted by law to prescribe the limits of secrecy in matters affecting diplomacy or the national defense. In the early days of the Republic, the military and the president, as Commander-in-Chief, apparently assumed the authority to keep certain military secrets. Classification procedures were erratic, *ad hoc*, and informal.

The evolution of the classification system is a fascinating story, but not relevant here. Suffice to say that from 1953 to 1972, information "related to the national defense" was classified Top Secret, Secret, or Confidential by a limited number of government officials under the authority of President Eisenhower's Executive Order 10,501. Over the years many proposals have been made for an Official Secrets Act which would make unauthorized release of classified information a criminal offense, but Congress has refused to take that step. The thought of large numbers of federal bureaucrats stamping their mistakes Top Secret was too much for Congress. In addition, everyone in Washington is aware that the overwhelming majority of documents bearing a security stamp contain no information that should now be secret.

The first stated purpose of Executive Order 10,501 was to make as much information available to the American people as possible, consistent with national security. Although the Order contains explicit directions for declassification, in fact officials almost never remove classification stamps from documents. The formal process for declassifying documents is constipated, while declassification of *information* is near diarrhetic. No official with access to classified documents hesitates to reveal the information in them when it suits his purposes. As a result, the federal government is bloated with documents bearing classification stamps that contain no legitimately sensitive information. The secrecy machine runs out of control, nobody knows how to stop it, and the public gets only sanitized information.

It is in this context that we must view the Ellsberg case of 1972. The documents that have come to be known as *The Pentagon Papers* were routinely stamped Top Secret. They contain a history of how this country slid into an undeclared war in Vietnam, beginning with our aid to the French in Indochina from 1940 to 1950 and ending with the failures at negotiation from 1964 to 1968. The papers contain no military or diplomatic information that could conceivably be of use to the other side.

Dr. Daniel Ellsberg had been one of Secretary of Defense McNamara's "whiz kids" in the Pentagon and, in that job, he had contributed to the policies that led us into the war. He held virtually all of the highest clearances known to the

Pentagon. By 1967, however, Ellsberg had concluded that we were not going to succeed in Vietnam and he worked actively thereafter to end our involvement. Secretary McNamara was apparently having some doubts at about the same time, for it was in 1967 that he ordered the study that ultimately became the 7,000 page *Pentagon Papers*. Ellsberg himself worked on the study.

Late in 1968 as the newly elected Nixon Administration prepared to take office, Henry Kissinger asked Ellsberg to draft a series of probing questions about Vietnam which he submitted to all the appropriate agencies. When Ellsberg received the answers, he compiled a summary for President Nixon and Kissinger. It was from this material that seven options were offered to the president for his Vietnam policy. One of the options was complete unilateral withdrawal, which, incidentally, Nixon ordered dropped from the list at the outset.

When *The Pentagon Papers* were completed in the late spring of 1969, Secretary of Defense Laird had copies sent to nine or ten former Johnson Administration officials, none of whom were still occupying any official position. Though the papers were stamped Top Secret, absolutely no copies were sent to anyone with official responsibility in the new administration. After a portion of *The Pentagon Papers* was published by *The New York Times*, in June of 1971, Secretary of State Rogers had to call the former Secretary of State, Nicholas Katzenbach, to get a copy of them. No administration would handle information justifiably stamped Top Secret in such a way.

In 1969, Daniel Ellsberg still retained his Top Secret security clearance as a consultant to the Rand Corporation. It was in that capacity that he was given authorized access to *The Pentagon Papers*. He read them. The realization grew upon him that this information confirmed all the doubts, all the instinctive resistance to the war in Vietnam that had been constantly answered with the less than reassuring words: "The president is the only one who has all the facts." The critics, the protesters, and the civil disobedients had been right; presidents had been wrong. Worse than that, presidents had been given all the facts necessary to know that they were wrong.

The American people, however, had very few of those facts, except through leaks and through publications that had been either denied or ignored. Official statements continued to spread the myths that contradicted the truth. Why shouldn't members of Congress have this information? Perhaps, if they knew for a certainty what they felt in their loins, they would end the war in Vietnam.

It was in this frame of mind and with this hope that Ellsberg set about copying the seven thousand pages. He took them to Senator Fulbright. He took them to other members of Congress. All of this copying and most of the carrying occurred between the fall of 1969 and the spring of 1970. The FBI knew about it; they questioned Ellsberg's former wife in early 1970 about his xeroxing of *The Pentagon Papers.* But no grand jury was summoned, and no one thought to bring any charges.

Almost a year and a half later, in June of 1971, *The New York Times* began publishing *The Pentagon Papers.* The administration brought a suit to prevent further publication, and the day before the United States Supreme Court was to hear this civil case, the administration suddenly leveled a criminal complaint at Daniel Ellsberg. Federal cases usually begin by indictment, but the U.S. Attorney in Los Angeles resisted the Justice Department's decision and refused to sign an indictment against Ellsberg. Three days after the initial complaint, a grand jury *did* indict him.

What were the charges? That Ellsberg gave the documents to *The New York Times* or the *Washington Post?* No. He was accused of espionage, spying, for having enlisted friends to help him xerox the papers when he was trying to get a copy to the Congress of the United States a year and a half before the newspapers began publishing them.

The criminal charges were brought against Daniel Ellsberg for political reasons. Nobody in government really cared about his copying the papers. That happens all the time. But publication by *The New York Times* was exceedingly embarrassing. Why? Because *The Pentagon Papers* were irrefutable proof that government leaders, well-intentioned or not, had lied to us.

Many people ask why Nixon should be so concerned about revelations of the failings and deceptions of the Johnson Administration. It is a good question. One answer is that, although Nixon had made very significant decisions to limit the Johnson commitment, he had, nonetheless, accepted a view of our prospective role in Vietnam that had already been rejected by the best experts in government. Worse yet, *The Pentagon Papers* made it "perfectly clear" that our new president was deceiving us about Vietnam in the same ways that Johnson had deceived us.

There was no specific provision of law making a crime of the simple act of giving the American people information from documents bearing a security stamp applied by some bureaucrat. Government attorneys had therefore hastily thrown together a one-count indictment against Ellsberg for espionage. Six months later they developed the best approach that good legal minds could come up with for making Ellsberg's act a federal crime. They brought a new fifteen-count indictment, which charged essentially three things:

1. Conspiracy to defraud the United States Government of its lawful function of controlling the dissemination of classified studies.
2. Converting, embezzling or stealing the studies.

3. Giving documents related to the national defense to a person not entitled to receive them. [These are the words of the espionage law, stripped of the two elements most people and courts have always assumed were an essential part of the charge: involvement with a foreign agent and reason to believe that the information would injure the United States or aid a foreign nation.]

These charges were wrapped in the now all too familiar package of conspiracy.

Never before had anyone been charged under these laws, as interpreted by the government, for violation of security. Without arguing the legal issues, which are most interesting, let it simply be said that the government took a novel approach to the criminal law in order to *get* Daniel Ellsberg.

If Daniel Ellsberg goes to jail, he will be a political prisoner. He was not prosecuted because he violated a law that was understood to make his actions a crime or because others had been prosecuted for the same actions. Nor can the prosecution be justified as necessary to discourage others from doing the same thing. The security system has survived for years without a single such criminal prosecution. Security regulations have been adequately enforced by the demotion, transfer, reprimand, or discharge of the violator. A strong deterrent is the possible loss of future access to classified material. Often a clearance for access to such material is vital to a person's job or his professional work.

If Congress had wished to enforce the classification system with criminal sanctions, it could of course have done so. It has not. It is disgraceful when the government tries to stretch and distort provisions of criminal law to cover a political situation for which those laws were never intended and have never before been applied.

The criminal charges against Ellsberg were inextricably tied to the civil action brought by the government against *The New York Times* and the *Washington Post*. In each case, the Government was taking unprecedented action to prevent the free flow of information to the people under an exceedingly broad interpretation of what kind of information the government has the right to control. At one point, in the closed door proceedings against the newspapers, the government solemnly intoned that certain information about to be printed from *The Pentagon Papers* was of such great sensitivity that its publication would cause the gravest injury to the United States. An alert *Washington Post* reporter, admitted to the secret session as a consultant, was sure he'd seen the material somewhere before. Within minutes he was able to produce a print of hearings of the Senate Foreign Relations Committee that contained the exact material referred to by the government. It had been the subject of public testimony by an administration spokesman.

That was not an isolated incident. Although the time pressures were excruciating, the *Times* and *Post* reporters were able in a single night to produce the books, newspapers, or other publications in which most of the material listed by the government as the most highly sensitive and potentially injurious had been previously printed. In the Ellsberg case, the government took the position that the fact that classified information had already been printed and was in the public domain was not a defense!

At the very least it must be said that those who decided to bring Ellsberg and the *Times* to court were callous and insensitive to the public's right, and the public's need, to know.

Another revealing aspect of the Ellsberg case deserves mention in this respect. Four of the volumes that Ellsberg copied covered details of secret negotiations to end the war between 1964 and 1968. Although Ellsberg did not think the release of those papers would injure the United States, he did not want to do anything that might conceivably complicate any current efforts to negotiate a settlement. The negotiation volumes were, therefore, withheld from the newspapers and given only to Senator Fulbright. The government's indictment, however, includes those negotiation volumes. At the time they are put into evidence by the government, as they must be if they are to remain a basis for the charges, they become public property and are effectively declassified in their entirety. The government is thus in the position of contending that something horrendous will happen if someone else tells the public about these things, but that if the government does it no harm will come!

This kind of hypocrisy should have no place in the American system of justice. When columnist Jack Anderson got hold of the four negotiation volumes from some other source and released them in July 1972, there was no prosecution and no apparent injury to anyone. On the contrary, as President Kennedy said of presidential policies, "from their scrutiny comes understanding; and from that understanding comes support or opposition."

If Daniel Ellsberg broke any law in trying to get *The Pentagon Papers* to the Congress of the United States, he can be classified as a civil disobedient. Acts of civil disobedience, acts of protest, and vehement public demonstrations are unsettling and disturbing things. Often their very success depends upon their arousing the wrath of significant segments of the population. I dislike such activities but I dislike more the conditions that make them necessary.

The two and a half years that I served in the United States Senate were certainly among the most tempestuous in our history. Disruptive public meetings were the rule rather than the exception. Most of the demonstrations in which I participated were inspirational, but they were always unsettling and vulnerable to the erratic exploits of a few.

Americans will not soon forget the siege at Cornell University in the spring of 1969 which ended when black students emerged bearing arms. Three weeks before that drama, I was invited by students to attend a mass meeting on the Cornell campus. There was no speech. Four student leaders were chosen to question me at the outset, and thereafter there was a free-for-all debate. And debate it was. The questions were each preceded by an exposition of strong opinions, including harsh and ugly ones about the junior senator from New York. My frequent attempts to defend the American system in one respect or another were greeted with hoots and boos. When I asked the students to give Nixon six months more to end the war, the place almost broke up. It was the kind of clamorous and tumultuous session that politicians frequently had to face in that period. With the intellectual certitude so common to youth, the Cornell students condemned "the system" and sanctified all who opposed it, at home or abroad. They had no interest in trying to persuade a United States senator of anything. By their definition, I was beyond the pale of understanding. Their alienation was a repugnant thing and my reaction to them was totally negative, as they seemed to want it to be.

Later I came to understand that their unreasoning vehemence and their arrogance was born of helplessness and frustration. The war in Vietnam was so totally indefensible and the hope of ending it so seemingly remote, that no moderate protest within the system could be adequate for them. The phenomenon has been repeated many times in world history and in American history. The only counsel those Cornell students accepted from me that day was to keep our session nonviolent.

By the summer of 1969 the student Moratorium was born and with it came enough hope to change the nature and tone of the protest. Student leaders advocating retributive violence against society were no longer popular. There was a noticeable softening and gentling of the antiwar movement as it hardened its resolve to persuade middle America. In September, six months after the Cornell confrontation, I proposed the first bill in Congress to legislate an end to the war by cutting off all funds to support it after a fixed date in the future. Overnight I became one of those consulted by insiders in the peace movement (though any politician was consulted with understandable suspicion).

The first one-day Moratorium on October 15, 1969, was overwhelming. National in scope, it attracted large numbers of adults and was a model of peaceful protest. A follow-up November Moratorium was planned. It was to last for two days and there was great expectation that a tidal wave of revulsion against the war was imminent. Senator Fulbright had tentatively scheduled hearings on my bill, S. 3000, for early November. President Nixon announced that he would address the nation on the war on November 3.

It was then that I became aware that older antiwar activists were planning a massive march on Washington for November 15. They were a divided movement that embraced spokesmen for many segments of disaffected America. Reports of their meetings were hard to evaluate, but it was obvious that a titanic and confusing struggle was underway among those advocating varying degrees of violence, those addicted to abusive rhetoric, and those determined to launch an earnest appeal to middle America.

In late October, the Senate Foreign Relations Committee voted to postpone hearings on my bill to end the war because they wanted to hear what the president had to say in his speech before proceeding. More important I think, they feared that the march on Washington would be violent.

They did not want to give even the impression that they were contributing to such an eventuality. Their fears were not without foundation.

At first, word emanated from the leadership meetings for the march that they wanted no participation by politicians. George McGovern and I conferred frequently, sharing our concern that a violent march could be a disastrous setback for the peace movement. We agreed to act in concert and to support the nonviolent forces in the march leadership. It was our impression from the outside that the young people from the Moratorium were a crucial factor in swinging the pendulum toward nonviolence. When they decided to join the march, they pressed their less careful elders for decisions on the myriad details that are indispensable to an orderly demonstration of that size, and they maintained a liaison with those of us in Congress who were willing to help.

Gradually, the reports reaching McGovern and me began to indicate a trend toward nonviolence developing within the leadership councils for the march. An invitation was extended to each of us to speak from a platform at the Washington Monument. George McGovern was preparing to run for the presidency. He had little to gain and a great deal to lose by identification with the march, even if there was absolutely no violence. We jointly replied that we would not participate unless there was a unanimous pledge of nonviolence from the council leaders and realistic arrangements were made to control fringe militants.

The Nixon Administration was issuing ominous warnings of planned violence on a major scale and was refusing a parade permit. Nixon's speech of November 3 used the word "peace" thirty-nine times, which infuriated the peace movement by its cliché-ridden repetition of all the same shibboleths that had kept us at war. Washington was a high-tension city and the mood of the multifaceted movement was volatile. No other national politicians would endorse the march or pledge participation.

By this time we were being told by the march leaders that our participation would substantially increase the chances for a peaceful, orderly demonstration. We were the only politicians acceptable as speakers to those militants who were edgily threatening violence. We were told that nonviolent, adult, middle America, which had thronged to the October 15 demonstrations across the country, was awaiting such a signal that the march would not be a brawl. Their participation was essential as a restraint upon the others. On the other hand, if we refused, it would confirm the ultramilitants' conviction that there was no way to move the Establishment, and quite possibly it would throw control of the march to them. Although perhaps somewhat hyperbolic, these were the persuasive arguments presented to two reluctant United States senators.

George McGovern faced one of the most difficult decisions of his political life. Soon after the Nixon speech, I told McGovern privately that I had decided to participate in the march, but would withhold any definite commitment until his decision was made. It was obvious that if our participation was to have the desired effect, the decision would have to be announced very soon.

Since I was not privy to the process, I refrain from any attempt to describe what was transpiring in the leadership councils of the march. From our viewpoint, there were unsung heroes who patiently, persistently, and persuasively moved the group in a responsible direction. Their efforts were seriously complicated by the insensitive and simplistic mumblings that emanated regularly from a Justice Department obsessed with conspiratorial nightmares of communist subversion. Government officials seemed to have no notion that the violence-prone among the march leadership were the nonidealogues who disdained and ridiculed communism as much as they did the Establishment. If it had not been so dangerous, the bumbling efforts of a blind Justice Department to cope with a situation they totally misunderstood would have been laughable. A complex convergence of militant forces, almost entirely domestic in origin, were tentatively and mistrustfully united on only one thing: there should be a massive march in Washington to demonstrate opposition to government policies. Although the war was the dominant theme, more than twenty issues, ranging from welfare to women's rights, had spokesmen demanding a place in the march. These disparate and decidedly independent home-grown radicals were about as far as you could get from a disciplined international communist conspiracy. As always, however, the ineffectual and irrelevant involvement of a few communists was enough to loose the incubus that haunted J. Edgar Hoover: if communists were involved, they had to be dominant and the cause had to be wrong.

The history of communist movements in the United States is ample proof of how wrong American communists usually are about tactics. When Americans launch an indigenous protest in order to achieve what they conceive as greater justice, it is ridiculous to characterize it as international subversion just because it wins the support of a few tired and feckless American communists.

That, however, was the way the Justice Department characterized the November 1969 march. The march was ominously portrayed by the FBI as the product of secret plots hatched abroad and conceived in Moscow. Officials of the Justice Department warned that this was likely to be the most violent and bloody demonstration in the history of the nation's capital, because communists had planned it that way. George McGovern and I knew that violence was a good possibility, not because of any communist involvement, but because of the almost uncontainable explosive forces that our own society was producing. We also knew that we might contribute something to containing and controlling those forces.

The possibility of violence was greatly enhanced as the Justice Department interposed, each day, some new objection to the granting of a parade permit down Pennsylvania Avenue. Those in the march leadership who insisted that a peaceful and orderly march could reach the people and move the system, returned regularly to the leadership meetings with this evidence of a totally impenetrable system that would not even allow them to march in the nation's capital. I intervened with Attorney General Mitchell and Deputy Attorney General Kleindienst. After repeated and sometimes heated conversations back and forth over several days, they began to loosen. As the press began to report that the government might be willing to grant a permit for some alternative route which would avoid bringing the marchers into close proximity to the White House, it became obvious to the march leaders that there was hope for a reasonable accommodation.

Then time began to run out. Unless the parade permit issue could be resolved, the whole thing would come unglued and the government's predictions of violence might become a self-fulfilling prophecy. I told Kleindienst, for the last time, that his briefings were distorting the real situation. Our conversation ended with my comment: "The way this is being handled, some of the blood will be on your hands, if violence happens." The administration ultimately took the lesser risk and a parade permit was granted.

McGovern and I were informed that Coretta King would participate in the march only if we would. The widow of the nonviolent King, with all her dignity and grace, would be an awesome symbol to those who might be tempted to violence. We made our decision. We participated.

As it turned out, the total nonviolence of the November 15 march on Washington was marred only by two episodes independent of the march itself. A small group tried to get to the South Vietnamese embassy near Dupont Circle the night before, and another small number tried to storm the Justice Department after the march. Both incidents were easily contained. In contrast, three to five hundred thousand people marched and listened all day without a single serious disorder of any kind.

The television media, still reeling from Vice-President Agnew's attacks, virtually ignored the largest assemblage of American people ever to petition for redress of grievances in the nation's capital. Even the local stations carried re-run movies and other replaceable programs. Evening newscasts spotlighted the incidental violence before and after, while passing quickly over the massive peacefulness of the march itself.

As McGovern, Coretta King, and I led the march down Pennsylvania Avenue, Mrs. King turned to say: "This is the most impressive march I've ever participated in, and I've been in a lot. The people are all so committed—so peaceful and gentle." It was the ultimate attempt of people to change policies that they despised, without breaking the law.

As we stood on the platform, a sea of citizenry undulated before us, stretching to the left toward the White House and to the right toward the Washington Monument and the Capitol. The entire sweep of terrain was occupied for eight hours by people in gentle protest. Viet Cong flags waved here and there, but American flags seemed to wave everywhere. I was surprised as I walked through the crowd that the young were outnumbered by middle-gray America. Many of them even looked a little uncomfortable: they had never done anything quite like this before. Everywhere there was relief that it was working out so nicely. Then Pete Seeger began the plaintive cry, and it slowly grew and stayed, as the crowd swayed and sang: "All we are asking, is give peace a chance."

From the early sixties through the early seventies, the

United States was at war. At first there was almost no opposition; at the end almost all Americans were convinced the Vietnam war was a mistake. In the span of one decade, a nation was converted. Those first lonely dissenters and civil disobedients, and the millions who finally followed them into the streets, were proven right. Their stubborn resistance against the popular will was vindicated.

Working within the system is the only way to work for most of us, most of the time. What happened this time? Young men protested a war—fathers waved the flag and tried to reclaim their past honor with recessive patriotism. Politicians proclaimed their commitment to peace, people said yes—and we got more war. Computered men finally said no to the print-out of war—the undeclared Congress only listened. While people who cared about peace marched, a president who cared about football, watched. Working within the system didn't seem to work so well.

These confrontations are not new to our history. A government with enough power can resist dissent by ignoring it, but when it does, the system begins to crack. The cracks widen dangerously when the criminal process is used to suppress political dissent. The dissenters may well be wrong. Often they are. But the best things happen only because sometimes they are right.

If we as a people absorb the lessons of our history of resistance and civil disobedience, we will hereafter respond more quickly and in fairer measure to the small voices of dissent. When the tumult rises and society shakes with dissension, government may still have to be unyielding but it need not overreact. It should at least be responsive enough to understand what is going on and deal respectfully with the resistance, whose spokesmen will doubtless be disrespectful. As we fail in this regard, the choice increasingly becomes either total destabilization or repression. It's a bad choice.

Part II

HOW DOES
REPRESSION
SURVIVE
IN AMERICA?

It is by the goodness of God that in our country we have those three unspeakably precious things: Freedom of speech, freedom of conscience, and the prudence never to practice either of them.

—Mark Twain

11

The Urge to Repress Dissent

> I will begin at the beginning, and ask what is the accusation given rise to the slander of me . . . and I will sum it up in an affidavit: "Socrates is an evil doer, and a curious person, who searches into things under the earth and in heaven, and he makes the worse appear the better cause; and he teaches the aforesaid doctrines to others.
>
> —Socrates, addressing his jury in
> 399 B.C.

Socrates, perhaps the first victim of repression in a democracy, was convicted for "impiety" for not worshiping the gods officially designated by the political authorities of Athens and introducing new divinities of his own, and he was sentenced to death by a jury of fellow Athenians. It was the second count of the indictment against him which revealed why the philosopher was singled out for prosecution on a charge seldom used in the Athenian court of his day. Socrates, it said, "corrupted the youth" of Athens by encouraging them to question the accepted truths of their elders.

In Socrates' day, as in ours, the stress of war and its

aftermath generated an excessive zeal for orthodoxy. In such times, anyone casting doubt on generally accepted certainties risks being silenced by the overreaction of public authorities. Socrates' real offense was his irreverent attitude toward the political leaders of the city. They had been elected to office by lot, and he doubted their qualification for public office. The philosopher believed in government by the well-educated and well-informed.

There was no persuasive evidence of Socrates' criminality. His accusers resorted to the self-serving and time-honored device of politically motivated prosecutors everywhere: they argued to the jury that he would not have been prosecuted in the first place if he were not guilty. Socrates refused to abide by the demeaning convention of the Athenian criminal process; he refused to legitimize his accusers by begging for mercy. He mocked the court, chided the jury, and risked his life to speak an important political truth:

> The state is a great and noble steed who is tardy in his motions owing to his very size, and requires to be stirred into life. I am that gadfly which God has attached to the state, and all day long and in all places am always fastening upon you, arousing and persuading and reproaching you.

The wisdom of this argument for tolerating dissent was lost on his jury, which found him guilty by a vote of 281 to 220.

When his accusers gave him an opportunity to recommend his own punishment, they hoped he would suggest a convenient exile; Socrates further mocked the proceedings to make his point. His dissent had so well served the real interests of Athens, he suggested, that he deserved no less than the recognition accorded Olympic victors and other heroes—free board for life in the town hall. This disrespect for the judicial proceedings probably cost Socrates his life, as his jury voted for the death penalty by an even greater margin. Chained in a prison cell for thirty days, he refused to cooperate in the escape plans hatched by friends and, on the appointed day, drained the cup of hemlock as if it were somehow final proof that he was a citizen and not a criminal.[1]

The Athenian rulers knew what they wanted, and went about it as openly as their law permitted. We do not punish heretics so openly, so clumsily, or so cruelly as they did; but our authorities share with the ancient Greeks a need for political conformity. They have devised methods for achieving it which are more suited to our traditions.

Perhaps the most celebrated political trial of all time took place in 30 A.D. in the court of Pontius Pilate. Since none of the guarantees of fair trial existing under Roman law were applied in Jesus' case, the proceeding was short and to the point.

The Sadduccees, who did not believe in the Messiah concept, were the entrenched religious power in Palestine. Anyone claiming to be the Messiah would clearly undermine their authority and incur their wrath, but Jesus was a special danger. He attacked them for their hypocrisy and corruption while expressing disdain for the ritual law by which the Sadduccees exercised pre-eminent authority over the Jewish people. There also was a growing conviction among the people that he really was the Messiah. He had to go.

Although Jesus had committed various minor "offenses" under religious law, such as overturning the money-changers' tables and saying that he would destroy the handmade temple in order to build a new one without hands, the seventy-one member Sanhedrin was unable to find him technically guilty of blasphemy, heresy, or sorcery—the religious offenses which could have justified the death penalty they thought he so richly deserved. Furthermore, the elimination of one so politically popular as Jesus posed a delicate problem for those in power.

Their solution was to have him taken into custody at night, when he was apart from the throngs of his supporters, and to deliver him to Pilate to be condemned and executed under Roman law. Fortunately for the chief priests, a potential Messiah was considered under Roman law so serious a threat to law and order as to be guilty of treason. The accounts rendered in the Gospels suggest some surprising reluctance on the part of Pontius Pilate. Perhaps he suspected he was being used by the Jewish leaders to advance their own political and religious power. In any event, the prosecution of Jesus was actuated by religious and political motives, but he was convicted of treason, the ultimate political crime.

Jesus' crime was what he said, not what he did. It is interesting to speculate on the possibility that had Jesus lived in America in the early days of our Republic and spoken words that frightened the Federalists one-half as much as his words threatened the powers that be in 30 A.D., he would have been convicted for violating the Sedition Act. Perhaps if he flew into Washington in 1972 and applied for a parade permit to preach the Sermon on the Mount, the powers that be would have prosecuted him for "conspiracy to defraud the United States Government of its lawful function to control dissemination of information to the public."

In each society, in every era, the critical social and political problem is how to deal with dissent, to provide for needed change while preserving order. In the present era, change itself has become the most commonly encountered phenomenon. Each of us is relieved by some changes and distressed by others. But no one can doubt that change and the passion with which it is sought and resisted can be disruptive of the peace which makes life in the modern world possible.

A society can choose any one of a number of methods to deal with dissenting minorities and to balance stasis and change. Some societies have devised political systems to eradicate differences and to maintain control by force. Dissent from orthodox values or from an established rate and direction of change *can* be repressed if authorities are equipped with and willing to use sufficient force. In our society, we have made a choice against repression and, at least in principle, we build our hopes for long-term stability on the openness of dissent itself.

The most obvious reason why we abjure repression as a basis for our political system is that, as Supreme Court Justice Robert Jackson put it, "Those who begin coercive elimination of dissent soon find themselves exterminating dissenters. Compulsory unification of opinion achieves only the unanimity of the graveyard."[2] In some systems, men with authority over the institutions of government are expected to use that power to control and guide public opinion, but our Constitution is grounded in the principle that public opinion should control authority. No public official in America has the right to enforce his view of what should be orthodox in politics.

Our system assumes that the government, in controlling its citizens, acts as the agent of the majority of the people. But if American self-government is to survive, a minority, even of one person, must have the right to assail whatever course is chosen by the majority. Each of us is in a minority, on at least some issues, most of the time; majorities coalesce and dissolve constantly as the interests at issue and the dominant philosophy shift about. It is central to the success of a scheme of government like ours that any temporarily cohesive majority, no matter how large, be denied the power to bring about what Justice Louis Brandeis called "silence coerced by law—the argument of force in its worst form."[3]

Yet, when social tensions run high and many time-honored values are assailed, we can lose sight of the reasons for preventing those with political power from using the criminal process to control the expression of unpopular ideas and criticisms. The rationale for the First Amendment is not *merely* that we fear doing to others what we do not want them to do to us. Neither is it that we expect the rude agitation of *every* aggrieved minority to promote goals beneficial to the whole society, although this is very often the result.

The most important reason to protect all forms of political expression is that repression tends to obscure the problems actually facing the society and it diverts attention from real political issues to specious "law and order" ones. When this happens, and the grievances which are the real cause of irritation are neglected, the position of each interested group hardens and the kind of compromises that keep the system in balance become unattainable. And when repression drives opposition underground, it is likely to reemerge in forms much more destabilizing and destructive of our tranquillity than verbal strife.

Stripped of the argument of history and shorn of romantic libertarian rhetoric about the power of truth *always* to prevail over falsehood in the marketplace of ideas, our system of freedom of expression "provides a framework in which the conflict necessary to the progress of a society can take place without destroying the society."[4]

The basic hypotheses of the American system have not been proven wrong, nor are they likely to be. Yet the system has often suffered repressive distortions, and "the argument of force" regularly yields political prisoners. The reason for the contradiction is that the men we empower to administer our laws are also entrusted with preserving freedom of expression, even for those who oppose them. They sometimes yield to the strong temptation to use their power to eliminate the irritants.

Spiro Agnew's attack on dissenters as "home front snipers" and "the glib, activist element who would tell us our values are lies," is a recent example of the reflex response of those with power when their authority is challenged. It is a modern version of the attack on Socrates launched by the political leaders of Athens, the repression of Jeffersonians by the Federalists, and the repression of Federalists by the Jeffersonians. The certainty that he is right led Nixon's vice-president to acknowledge his desire to annihilate opponents, "to separate them from our society with no more regret than we should feel over discarding rotten apples from a barrel."

It is easy to be too harsh on Agnew for what is, after all, a very human reaction to certain dissenters who tried very hard to be offensive. William F. Buckley, a far more thoughtful man than Agnew and a distinguished writer and thinker on the conservative side of politics, is reported to have stated that a "premonitory sniff of repression would be salutary in these times."[5] And it should not be forgotten that Thomas Jefferson, perhaps our most eloquent spokesman for freedom of expression and a man who was deeply committed to liberty, came to believe, once he was in the presidency, that "a few prosecutions" of his most prominent critics in the press "would have a wholesome effect."

"Persecution for expression of opinions seems to me perfectly logical," Justice Oliver Wendell Holmes observed. "If you have no doubt of your premises or your power and want a certain result with all your heart you naturally express your wishes in law and sweep away all opposition."[6] Coupled with this is a natural tendency in all of us to think that whatever we dislike very much must also be illegal or even unconstitutional. And there has been much to dislike in the opposition. Dissent has seldom been polite or calm. Those who seek fundamental changes, having no doubt of *their* premises, but lacking the power to implement them, tend to cast their dissent in raw and unconventional terms. They often deeply shock and antagonize those who will not, or who do not yet, share their interests. The reaction is predictable: some form of an angry call for "law and order," with all its mighty delusions.

When political leaders use the prestige of office to cast lawful opposition as crime and to label their critics as "anarchists," they seem to be offering the American people a choice between repression and anarchy. And when the American people are given this unrealistically narrow choice, they will choose repression every time. Yet, the more strongly citizens feel about an issue, and the more excited and offensive they become in urging their view of it, the more the long-term stability of our society *requires* that the substance of their message not be obscured by politically motivated criminal charges.

We have become familiar with the phenomenon even when dissent is expressed in the most formal and legitimate ways. When I introduced bill S. 3000, President Nixon and those who supported his war policy began to understand that a determined effort to force an end to the war had a chance of success if a sufficient number of senators and congressmen would support an "Amendment to End the War." The reaction from the White House was not a reasoned defense of the war, but accusations that came unpleasantly close to charging me with treason—the most emotion-laden criminal charge of all. The demeaning spectacle was repeated when the 1972 Democratic primaries got underway and H.R. Haldeman, the president's White House chief of staff, went on national television to charge that the Democratic contenders' criticism of the Nixon war policy was "consciously aiding and abetting the enemy," which is the constitutional definition of treason.

Although many of those who have most strenuously tested the promise of the First Amendment have ended up in prison, what strikes me as most remarkable about the history of political prisoners in America is not that repression has been so frequent, but that it has been such a failure in what it was expected to accomplish. Individual political nonconformists who committed dangerous or violent political acts—Benedict Arnold, John Wilkes Booth, Sirhan Sirhan—were quite adequately punished in the course of ordinary criminal prosecutions.

On the other hand, when a significant portion of our society became irreconcilably disaffected and had sufficient power actually to launch a challenge by force and violence to the government's authority, we had a Civil War. That conflict and its attendant suffering could not have been forestalled by repression, even if we had been willing to devote a major portion of our resources to the effort. Will anyone seriously contend that the Civil War could have been avoided by subjecting the leading advocates of slavery and secession to a few "wholesome" prosecutions?

Repression *did* have a part in wiping out the Wobblies and their later cousins, the Black Panthers—groups whose condonation of violence made them easy targets for overreaction. With hindsight, we can see that the danger of spreading social disintegration which was feared from the activities of these groups was largely a fantasy. And it's fair to say, I think, that most of their potential for political violence did not flow from their ideas, but was provoked by the indiscriminate repression itself. Certainly it was the Wobblies' free-speech fights and the vicious police campaign against the Panther's political organization which won these groups such sizable followings, causing the fears which fueled further repression against them. Left alone in the marketplace of ideas, the programs they advocated probably would have fallen of their own bombastic weight.

Repression is most likely to seem successful when the political threat is largely imagined. It is almost certain to fail when the ideas repressed enjoy a genuine popular appeal and their advocates therefore pose a real threat to those whose power is dependent on the status quo. Repression in these circumstances has generally accelerated the spread of the feared doctrines, ensured the victims a helpful notoriety, and succeeded only in bringing the criminal process into unnecessary disrepute.

But what I believe is most disturbing about repeated and continuing abuse of the criminal process to control dissent is that, with no apparent gain to *any* interest, our criminal and political systems are ominously distorted. We rely on our criminal system to protect us from attacks on person and property. When the criminal process is used to coerce political conformity, the victims are not just the political prisoners. We are all victims. In the long run, law protects us only as long as most individuals overwhelmingly agree to condemn what the law condemns. The criminal law can serve its purpose when it punishes acts which genuinely threaten others. When the process is subverted, when ideas, attitudes, and personal life-styles are subjected to legal sanction, the criminal law is stripped of its integrity and the label "crime" loses its power to educate citizens about what is and what is not acceptable conduct.

When dissent is made criminal and when respected spokesmen for political minorities are punished because of what they stand for, ordinary lawbreakers will portray their crimes as dissent and will become spokesmen justifying crime. And, when repression is a fact of life, such actual wrongdoers are likely to get a sympathetic hearing. Even if repression worked better than it does to purge loathesome ideas, no one's interests are served when its subversion of the criminal process exposes us to a very real danger —a growing disrespect for indispensable laws.

"The dictum that truth always triumphs over persecution," wrote John Stuart Mill, "is one of those pleasant falsehoods which men repeat after one another till they pass into commonplaces, but which all experience refutes." The cost of repressive prosecutions is greater than the loss of liberty for individual political prisoners. A system of free and open debate does not *guarantee* the victory of truth in the marketplace of ideas, but it is an important check against error. Our national policies tend to go awesomely awry when they are formulated in secrecy and presented to an uncritical public. When the flow of relevant information to the people is controlled by the policy makers themselves, and when potential "gadflies" are made too fearful to stir us to life, costly errors result.

12

Fiddling with the First Amendment

> As to freedom of conscience, I meddle with no man's con-
> science; but if you mean by that, liberty to celebrate the
> mass, I would have you understand that in no place where
> the power of the Parliament of England prevails shall that
> be permitted.
>
> —Oliver Cromwell

The linchpin of our political system is the First Amendment to the Constitution, by which Congress is prohibited,
among other things, from making any law "abridging the
freedom of speech, or of the press; or of the right of the
people peaceably to assemble, and to petition the Government for a redress of grievances."

Throughout our history, those in authority have violated
this fundamental rule, producing political prisoners. Only
through a long and labored process have we reached an
interpretation of the First Amendment, which, in theory at
least, approximates what most Americans have always assumed: "We can say what we please!"

In the beginning of our Republic it was not even clear
who was to interpret and enforce our right to freedom of

speech. Since that time we have learned to rely on the federal courts, particularly on the Supreme Court, to make the promise of the First Amendment a reality. The experience of many contemporary critics of the Vietnam war, however, shows that judicial diligence in restricting those in power to the letter of the First Amendment does not alone guarantee the proper functioning of our system. Those charged with making and enforcing the ordinary criminal law tend to treat Supreme Court opinions in specific situations merely as limitations on how far a government may go in suppressing speech. The First Amendment is far more than that. It is a broad mandate which, together with the Declaration of Independence, sets forth the working principles of representative democracy.

The First Amendment is a declaration to all branches of government, covering all exercise of power, of what the Supreme Court recently called our "profound national commitment to the principle that debate on public issues should be uninhibited, robust, and wide-open, and that it may well include vehement, caustic, and sometimes unpleasantly sharp attacks on government and public officials."[1]

Relying on the Supreme Court to set aside repressive convictions has proved to be a slow and cumbersome way to implement the First Amendment. More important, the patchwork of rulings and guidelines developed along the way seem never adequately to anticipate the next fissure in the dike.

Sedition statutes were, for a long time, the favored device of those bent on repression, because they permitted the *direct* prohibition of remarks critical of existing conditions or authorities. The theory of sedition was that such expression, because it *tends* to spread disrespect for the government, *may* lead some who hear it to violate the government's laws. The Sedition Act of 1798, the Espionage and

Sedition Acts of 1917 and 1918, and the score or more state "criminal syndicalism" and "Red Flag" laws made no distinction between agitation for political change and direct incitement or solicitation to commit crime.

Without such a distinction, authorities were free to use the law to punish any social criticism or advocacy of political change which they believed had an "evil tendency." When those in political power exercise such discretion, the words of the First Amendment, with reference to freedom of speech, guarantee nothing.

The development of a First Amendment doctrine which would actually protect freedom of expression did not even begin until 1919, when Justice Oliver Wendell Holmes wrote his famous opinion in the *Schenck* case. Holmes emphasized that freedom of speech does not permit a man to falsely shout fire in a crowded theater and cause a panic, nor to utter "words that may have all the effect of force." Government can, he wrote, restrict freedom of speech only when the words create "a clear and present danger" that something will happen that government has a right to prevent.[2]

It seems reasonable to hold the government to such a standard, and for half a century, Holmes's catchy phrase served as convenient, but misleading, shorthand for what would justify the punishment of political expression. "Clear and present danger" is far too ambiguous a phrase to block the urge to repress dissent. Holmes had, after all, devised the standard in the *Schenck* case to justify one of the many World War I convictions based on pamphlets denouncing the draft law and questioning the motives of those who backed the war effort.

When the conviction of Eugene Debs came to the Supreme Court, Justice Holmes applied his "clear and present danger" standard to what Debs had said, and again he upheld the conviction. He focused his attention on the "probable effect" of the speech Debs had delivered, not on the clarity or imminence with which the country could be endangered by an aging Socialist's expression of opposition to the war.[3] It was already evident that the "clear and present danger" standard had become, even in the hands of its creator, a misleading justification for punishing the imagined "evil tendency" of disfavored political ideas.

If the First Amendment was to protect the expression of unpopular ideas, if it was to serve as a bar to political imprisonment, a more exacting standard would have to be devised. Holmes himself realized this when the *Whitney* case came before the Court in 1927.[4] Anita Whitney, the niece of a former justice of the Supreme Court, was a member of the Socialist Party in 1919 when the party split into militant and moderate factions. Miss Whitney labored in vain to prevent her own branch from adopting the Wobbly-like program of the Communist Workers Party. Despite her moderate views, she was convicted, under California's Criminal Syndicalism Act, for organizing and being a member of a group pursuing political change by unlawful methods. When she appealed to the Supreme Court, a majority of the justices affirmed her conviction, ruling that government may punish expression *"tending* to incite to crime, disturb the public peace, or endanger the foundations of organized government."[5]

Holmes refused to go along, and he joined Justice Brandeis in an eloquent opinion which has since become the most authoritative exposition of the meaning of the First Amendment:

> Those who won our independence . . . valued liberty both as an end and as a means. They believed that . . . freedom to think as you will and to speak as you think are means indispensable to the discovery and spread of political truth; that . . . discussion affords ordinarily adequate protection against

the dissemination of noxious doctrine; that the greatest menace to freedom is an inert people; that public discussion is a political duty; and that this should be a fundamental principle of the American government. They recognized the risks to which all human institutions are subject. But they knew . . . that it is hazardous to discourage thought, hope and imagination; that fear breeds repression; that repression breeds hate; that hate menaces stable government; that the path of safety lies in the opportunity to discuss freely supposed grievances and proposed remedies; and that the fitting remedy for evil counsels is good ones. . . .

Fear of serious injury cannot alone justify suppression of free speech and assembly. Men feared witches and burnt women. It is the function of speech to free men from the bondage of irrational fears. . . . *Every denunciation of existing law tends in some measure to increase the probability that there will be a violation of it.* . . . *But advocacy of violation, however reprehensible morally, is not a justification for denying free speech where the advocacy falls short of incitement and there is nothing to indicate that the advocacy would be immediately acted on.*

Although the Holmes–Brandeis opinion expressed the view of a minority of the Court, it had a powerful influence on development of First Amendment principles for the next forty-two years. In 1969 it was adopted by a unanimous Supreme Court, but a great many people went to jail in the interim for expressing themselves in ways that Holmes and Brandeis would have permitted.

On the same day in 1927 that the Court affirmed Anita Whitney's conviction, it held for the first time that the First Amendment prohibits state government, as well as Congress, from abridging freedom of speech. Up to that point in our history, the states had the power to punish speakers without restriction from the Federal Constitution.

Following the appointment of Charles Evans Hughes as Chief Justice in 1930, the Supreme Court began to slice away at the corners of state sedition laws. It insisted that laws be drafted with a sharp focus on illegal conduct so as not to sweep legitimate political expression within their prohibitions.[6] The Court also refused to attribute the conduct of some members of a political group to other members of the group.[7]

A premonition of the demise of sedition laws, and of their "evil intent" and "bad tendency" standards for permissible speech, came in the 1950s when the Supreme Court reviewed the convictions of Communist Party leaders under the Smith Act. That law was yet another variation on the sedition theme, punishing individuals who expressed the desirability or necessity of "overthrowing or destroying the government by force or violence." It also punished anyone who belonged to an organization that taught these things.

Communist ideology is based on assumptions antithetical to the principles that underlie representative democracy and freedom of expression. The unpopularity of communist ideas in this country rather obviously barred them from becoming a "clear and present danger." The offensiveness of what communists said, however, particularly aroused those who were too fearful of change to rely on freedom of expression to protect us from the "noxious doctrine."

Chief Justice Vinson's opinion upholding the convictions of leading communists in the 1951 *Dennis* case again distorted the meaning of "clear and present danger" beyond recognition. The jury had found that the communists "intended to overthrow the Government . . . as speedily as circumstances would permit." In the Chief Justice's view, such a political stance can be punished, despite the First Amendment, because "the gravity of the 'evil,' discounted by its improbability, justifies such invasion of freedom of speech as is necessary to avoid the danger."[8] In truth, the fear of revolution has always been the "grave evil" which those in power have used to justify invasions of the freedom of speech, no matter how much the danger of it is based on fear alone. Vinson's opinion left the door wide open for the punishment of opinions and ideas which, as Justice Douglas put it, were "made serious only by judges so wedded to the status quo that critical analysis made them nervous."[9]

Even at the time, the *Dennis* case did not leave the justices entirely happy. Justice Frankfurter voted to uphold the communist convictions, but conceded that "suppressing advocates of overthrow inevitably will also silence critics who do not advocate overthrow but fear that their criticism may be so construed."[10] Justice Douglas, in a strongly worded dissent, pointed to the absurdity of finding, in 1951, that the ideas on trial in 1948 had actually posed a "clear and present" danger of overthrowing the government:

> Communism has been so thoroughly exposed in this country that it has been crippled as a political force. Free speech has destroyed it as an effective political party. It is inconceivable that those who went up and down this country preaching the doctrine of revolution which [they] espouse would have any success.
>
> How it can be said that there is a clear and present danger that this advocacy will succeed is, therefore, a mystery . . . . [I]n America, [communists] are miserable merchants of unwanted ideas; their wares remain unsold. The fact that their ideas are abhorrent does not make them powerful.
>
> [T]he invisible army of the American Communist Party is the best known, the most beset, and the least thriving of any fifth column in history. Only those held by fear and panic could think otherwise.[11]

In 1957, the Court reviewed the convictions of second-level communist leaders based upon virtually identical evidence of the Party's doctrine. It concluded, in the *Yates* case, that there was nothing to indicate that the communists were even planning to call for revolutionary action, either then or in the future. The justices used that finding to reverse the convictions and to try to restore some substance to Holmes's fluid phrase, "clear and present danger"; they ruled that the expression of political ideas cannot be made a crime unless the listeners are urged to commit illegal action in language that is likely to incite them to do it.[12] Although the Court suggested, by using the word "incite," that the danger must be a "present" one, it expressly left standing the peculiar notion that political rhetoric uttered in the present can be punished for its feared tendency to incite *future* action. We have seen again and again how biased authorities can be in attempting to predict the consequences of dissent, and the *Yates* case still left lawmakers free to gut the First Amendment by acting on their fear that vigorous opposition to government policy tends to undermine the nation's security.

A perfect example of this absurdity was the *Spock* case. When the Boston Five appealed their convictions, the Circuit Court of Appeals found no First Amendment problem preventing the conviction of antiwar and antidraft critics for their admittedly gentle rhetoric. "What is effective persuasion," wrote the judges, "must depend on the circumstances [of] a large number of young men, perhaps impressionable, and in any event oriented [toward the Resistance] by natural self-interest. . . . In this context the 'soft sell' may be the most telling."[13]

Until 1969 the power of the First Amendment to prevent political imprisonment was sapped by the "bad tendency" standard set forth in the majority opinion in the 1927 *Whitney* case. Finally, the Court was presented with a case involving punishment of right-wing political rhetoric. In 1967, a national TV audience watched a group of men and women, carrying guns and garbed in full Ku Klux Klan regalia, gather around a large wooden cross somewhere in Ohio and set it aflame. Clarence Brandenburg, the leader of this particular Klavern, spoke into the cameras:

> The Klan has more members in the State of Ohio than does any other organization. We're not a revengent organization, but if our President, our Congress, our Supreme Court, continues to suppress the white, Caucasian race, it's possible that there might have to be some revengeance taken.

The implied threat was coupled with his announcement of a Fourth of July march on Washington. He was sentenced to up to ten years in prison for violating the Ohio Criminal Syndicalism Statute, a law like that under which Anita Whitney had been convicted, dating from the Red Scare period and prohibiting "advocacy" of unlawful methods of political change. When Brandenburg's case reached the Supreme Court in 1969, his conviction was unanimously reversed and the Court settled the meaning of the First Amendment for the foreseeable future with an opinion that spoke for every justice on the Court:

> [W]hitney has been discredited by later decisions [which] have fashioned the principle that the constitutional guarantees of free speech and free press do not permit a State to forbid or proscribe advocacy of the use of force or of law violation except where [it] is directed to inciting or producing *imminent* lawless action and is likely to incite or produce such action.[14]

The Supreme Court had finally changed its mind and adopted the minority view so eloquently expressed by the Holmes–Brandeis opinion in *Whitney*. A person may no longer be prohibited by antisedition laws from vigorously castigating policies or laws, or for advancing an unpopular view; he may not be imprisoned even if he urges that a law should be violated or that force should be used, unless he wants it to happen immediately and, by the way he urges it, he is likely to make it happen right away. "Incitement" and "imminence" are words which may restore to the First Amendment its power to prevent authorities from outlawing opposition on the ground of its "evil intent" and imprisoning critics for the "bad tendency" of their remarks.

Although the *Brandenberg* opinion seems finally to have deprived lawmakers of the handy subjectivity of antisedition laws, it carefully left intact their power to punish politically motivated "expression" that has all the effect of criminal conduct, such as instructing followers to bomb buildings or shouting "Off the pigs" to a militant who holds a machine gun on a squad of policemen. No system could tolerate such abuses of freedom of expression.

The development of First Amendment doctrine is a significant gain. But if sedition is dead, repression is not. Antisedition laws represent only one of the many devices for generating political prisoners. The patchwork system of Supreme Court rulings has slowly reached and contained the discretion of those who make our laws, but not those who enforce them. Frustrated at one point in the criminal process, the urge to repress dissent has merely been diverted to flow more strongly through less direct, less visible, and less easily contained channels. Those whose political beliefs and activities are "protected" by the First Amendment are being imprisoned still.

13

Abuse of Discretion--
The "Stretch Points" of Liberty

The Queen said: "Here is the King's messenger. He is in
prison now being punished and the trial does not even begin
until next Wednesday, and of course the crime comes last of
all."

"But suppose he never commits the crime?" asked Alice.

"That would be all the better, wouldn't it?" the Queen
responded.

—Lewis Carroll,
Alice in Wonderland

Today, after years of slow and complicated litigation, our
Constitution and our judiciary have established fairly effective checks against the enactment of repressive laws. But
enactment of a law is only the first step in the process
which can land a citizen in prison. The power to use the
criminal process to punish advocates of unpopular ideas is
not the lawmakers' power alone. Throughout the country,
on the federal as well as the state level, thousands of individuals wield wide discretion in deciding which laws to

enforce against which individuals, which citizens' lives to scrutinize for evidence of criminality, whom to question, whom to indict and on what charge, what evidence to present, what sentence to impose, whether or not to grant parole, and on what conditions parole will be granted.

It is a matter of some pride to most Americans that we are governed by a "system of laws, not men." But there is more play in the joints of our system, more opportunities for officials to make decisions wholly within their discretion, than in most European systems. The fabric of our criminal process is tailored by the discretion of the men who run it. Those men are politicians, their appointees, and governmental employees who share and respond to the accepted values and political prejudices of the day.

All those charged with enforcing the criminal law wield discretionary power, within a loosely woven system of rules, to punish whomever they choose. Ideally, their decisions should be made without regard to the legitimate political activity of the persons who become enmeshed in the criminal process. However, at any point in the step by step process, a citizen's political opinions can, and all too often do, make the difference against him. Any one of the key actors in the process may make a conscious or unconscious decision against a person, influenced by that person's political opinions and expression.

The First Amendment protects Americans against laws prohibiting opposition to the war in Vietnam, yet opponents of the war have been punished for making their views known. There is no law against adopting a life-style or appearance that expresses a rejection of orthodox customs and habits, yet anyone challenging authority in this indirect way risks criminal sanctions. Black Americans are guaranteed the right to advocate Black Power, black pride, and community control of police and schools, yet such advocacy has been punished, and punished severely. This discretionary repression is of low visibility, but it cuts as effectively into the heart of our political system as repressive laws do.

There is so much stretch in the fabric of the American criminal process that we are in serious danger of having the First Amendment nullified by public officials (including highly placed officials of the Nixon Administration) bent on accomplishing indirectly what the First Amendment forbids doing directly. In the spring of 1971, Richard Kleindienst, then Nixon's Deputy Attorney General and later the Attorney General of the United States, was asked whether officials of the administration would ever consider suspending constitutional provisions protecting political freedom, if dissension seemed to them to be getting out of hand. Kleindienst's reassurances were disconcerting:

> In the first place, we wouldn't have to, because our existing laws—together with our surveillance and intelligence apparatus, which is the best in the world—are sufficient to cope with any situation. And in the second place we wouldn't be allowed to. There is enough play at the joints of our existing criminal law—enough flexibility—so that if we really felt that we had to pick up the leaders of a violent uprising we could. We would find some things to charge them with, and we would be able to hold them that way for a while.[1]

We all want the federal government to respond effectively to real threats of insurrection, but our own history teaches us that those with political power tend to find such threats behind every vigorous movement for political change. Our plan of government demands that when citizens are imprisoned, they be tried for offenses specifically prohibited by law, unless things have gotten so out of hand that the courts can no longer perform that function. The

Supreme Court so ruled, when it reviewed the excesses that followed Lincoln's suspension of *habeas corpus* even in those sections of the Union where the criminal process was unaffected by the Civil War.[2]

Attorney General Kleindienst's expansive view of his power is nevertheless widely shared. From the nation's top prosecutor to the policeman on his beat, America's law enforcement community feels justified in using discretionary powers, whether given to them inadvertently or for some particular purpose, for purposes of their own choosing. Too often the purpose is to repress dissent and too often the abuse does not even come to light. But when the authorities in Columbia, South Carolina, stretched the law to repress the antiwar movement, the abuses were visible, all along the line.

Congress would not be likely to pass a law prohibiting the operation of antiwar coffeehouses. Such a law would be so clearly unconstitutional that even those who wanted to see the "coffeehouse crowd" punished would shy away from supporting the measure. If it passed, it would soon be struck down by the courts. But on April 28, 1970, a judge in Columbia, South Carolina, punished three coffeehouse operators for their political intransigence by sentencing them each to six years in the state penitentiary. Herein is presented an interesting story of justice gone awry because of abuse of discretion by a community's most respected officials.

Early in 1968, antiwar activists transformed a seedy poolhall across from the city hall on Columbia's Main Street into the UFO Coffeehouse where antiwar soldiers and students could meet. Their mere presence was an affront to the local Establishment. Columbia is the state capital, proud of its past designations as an "all-American City," and it is wedded in interest to the huge army base at nearby Fort Jackson. The UFO, in business to spread opposition to American foreign policy and to the part played in it by the army, provoked a repressive reaction from the Establishment of the city.

The Chief of Detectives of Columbia's police department told reporters that he believed the UFO to be a communist front, and made it clear that the police shared the larger community's distaste for the politics, appearance, and interracial mingling of the UFO's staff and patrons. Even though the Constitution protected such conduct, the police, as guardians of community values, felt duty bound to shut the coffeehouse down.

When the city attorney told them that an ordinance banning the UFO simply "wouldn't hold water," the police were thrown back on their own resources. For two years, the UFO, its staff, and its patrons were subjected to relentless surveillance by uniformed patrolmen, plainclothes detectives, and the undercover agents of city, county, state, and military law-enforcement agencies. Unable to punish the UFO crowd for their real offense of dissent, they sought some other basis for a crackdown and administered a subtle form of punishment by harassment on a continuing basis. Sometimes the UFO's patrons were subjected to arbitrary and humiliating searches by officers determined to find evidence of crime. One plainclothes detective made over three hundred visits to the coffeehouse, and at least one patrolman made three or four stops at the UFO every night he was assigned to the beat. The police chief, explaining his discretionary allocation of manpower, told a reporter, "We check them every night to see if we can get something on them."

Despite the harassment, the UFO was packed regularly, and an antiwar movement was spawned on its premises. The surveillance and the searches failed to turn up evidence of a crime for which the UFO's operators could be punished. One GI who worked as an informer for the army and for the local sheriff was given ten dollars to purchase drugs at the coffeehouse. He later testified that although he made three to five visits each week for several months, he still had the money and had been unable to find evidence of drug traffic. The staff rigorously barred from the premises anyone they even suspected of using or dealing in any form of drugs, including alcohol.

Columbia's patience ran out in January 1970. The city prosecutor found a way to proceed against the UFO by digging in parts of the city where drug abuse was spreading, while the police concentrated on the coffeehouse. By offering them promises of immunity from prosecution for their own offenses, the prosecutor had little difficulty in rounding up confessed and convicted drug pushers to testify against the UFO. He agreed to let eleven notorious drug pushers go without punishment, and was thus able to get four of them to say, on the witness stand, that they had sold drugs at the UFO. Testimony rewarded by immunity is always questionable, and in this case the informers had an additional reason to oblige the prosecutor—each had been thrown out of the UFO at least once because the staff suspected they were there to sell dope. One of them held the staff responsible for his own arrest on a narcotics charge. However unreliable this testimony was, the prosecutor decided to use it. But he still had a problem: there was no testimony that members of the UFO staff had been party to drug transactions.

To match his evidence to his target, the prosecutor resurrected an ancient and seldom used catchall crime buried in the state's common law, "keeping and maintaining a public nuisance." The Richland County Grand Jury, as anxious as he was to find some way to punish the dissenters and to shut the place down, quickly obliged him with an indictment. The rambling indictment charged that the UFO operators kept a "common, disorderly, ill-governed place" where "rowdy persons, persons of evil name, fame and conversation, men as well as women, . . . come together," and where "persons did possess, sell, or use marijuana" and where were displayed, "pictures, paintings, magazines, newspapers, pamphlets, and posters which were obscene." The day after the indictment was handed down, the UFO staff was arrested. Two days later the coffeehouse was closed and padlocked by police, acting under a court order.

Judge E. Harry Agnew, who was presiding in Richland County's General Sessions Court when the UFO case came to trial on April 15, shared the desire of the police, the prosecutor, and the grand jurors to see the UFO staff pay for their dissent. He immediately used his discretion to punish them by requiring each to post bail of $7500, although a murder suspect in the same court had recently been released on $3000 bail.

Judge Agnew refused to admit evidence showing the prosecutor's bad faith and unconstitutional purpose in selecting the UFO for prosecution while bars, poolhalls, and brothels remained open. He rejected evidence of the widespread drug abuse and drug peddling in other parts of Columbia. He let the prosecutor create the impression that this was a routine nuisance prosecution, although only ten nuisance charges had been brought to trial in the county in the eighty years before the UFO case.

The prosecutor's evidence of "obscene" periodicals and pictures consisted of a copy of the *Berkeley Barb*, seized from the UFO by an undercover agent, and a poster taken from the coffeehouse window, showing four soldiers squatting in front of two beheaded bodies and bearing the slogan "The Army Can Really Fuck Over Your Mind." Judge Agnew refused to let the defendants introduce copies of *Gent, Sex Orgies,* and *Climax* which were displayed and openly purchased at the Capital News Stand. They would have shown the UFO's poster and the *Berkeley Barb* to be quite tame by community standards of what should be prosecuted.

After ruling irrelevant the evidence that the prosecutor had improperly singled out the UFO for prosecution, the judge then instructed the jurors in terms which left the defendants fully exposed to the community's political prejudice. They should convict, he told them, if they believed the UFO to be a "noisome and offensive" place, or "a public outrage against common decency or common morality."

The jury seized upon this as an unlimited license to punish antiwar activists, and quickly returned a guilty verdict. Judge Agnew announced that, because nuisance was a common-law offense and no sentence was set by statute, the punishment was discretionary. He condemned each defendant to six years in prison, and fined the UFO $10,000.

From 1890 to 1969, only one of the ten "maintaining a nuisance" cases brought to trial by the authorities of Richland County, South Carolina, resulted in a prison term. In that solitary case, an individual with extensive underworld connections and boasting a local and multistate arrest record received an eighteen-month sentence for operating a house of prostitution. Even if the UFO operators had been guilty of a crime which could have been defined, a six-year sentence for a misdemeanor is a shocking abuse of judicial discretion.

In his remarks at sentencing, Judge Agnew momentarily dropped the façade of the "nuisance" charge and revealed that he had not based the exercise of his sentencing discretion on evidence, but on what he believed to be the evil intent and bad tendency of the UFO's political conduct, conduct theoretically "protected" by the First Amendment:

Certainly they have a right to their own thoughts, their own beliefs, but . . . I think they had in mind a more destructive influence rather than constructive.

As I understand it, two of the defendants come from great distances to this community . . . I don't know that there is anything that will change the thinking of the small number of individuals who feel that they have a right to be critical and demanding of the other ninety-five per cent of the people who have to work for a living.

Agnew was not content with a courtroom confession of his improper purpose. He went on local television to explain that the root of the crime, as he saw it, was that South Carolinians had been "exposed to the teachings . . . of people from New York and San Francisco."[3]

Had the judge kept his repressive purposes to himself, or had he been content to send the staff off to jail for six months instead of six years, the abuses of the criminal process involved in repressing Columbia's antiwar movement would have gone unnoticed except by those caught up in it and by readers of the underground press. The political prisoner issue would have remained below the surface, as it does in numberless discriminatory prosecutions, but the six-year sentences drew heavy criticism from newspapers around the country. The *Wall Street Journal* commented, "This sort of thing could erode respect for the courts far more effectively than any radical onslaught." Indeed, when the Vietnam war expanded into Cambodia a few weeks later, one of the sparks igniting disorders on the University of South Carolina's Columbia campus was outrage at the outcome of the UFO trial.

The national criticism so stung South Carolina officialdom that the prosecutor agreed, months later, to reduce the punishment to a year of probation and a suspended sentence, a combination amounting to an enforceable order to get out of town. Although this turn of events was a bit of good fortune for a few citizens who had been sentenced to prison for taking their First Amendment rights seriously, the compromise could hardly vindicate the criminal system or restore a lost political opportunity. Repression can be diplomatic and still be effective. Columbia simply had no reason, by the spring of 1971, to push the UFO case any further. The coffeehouse never reopened after it was closed in January 1970. With its funds and energies sapped by the legal battle, the GI protest movement which it had served simply died out.

It is easy enough to be indignant about the abuses of discretion in the UFO case, but they are only the tip of an iceberg. In obscure courtrooms across the country, policemen, prosecutors, and judges go virtually unchecked in applying their discretionary power in ways that chill political dissent. "Ordinary" criminal charges and apparently "routine" discretionary decisions are a perfect cover for unconstitutional programs of repression—repression implemented by the very officials to whom we have entrusted the integrity of our legal process. It is as important, today, to fashion checks against repressive uses of discretionary power at the "stretch points" of the criminal process as it was two hundred years ago to block the power of lawmakers to make dissent a crime. A Constitutional amendment will not, however, serve our present purposes. It will take a lot of hard work by legislators, prosecutors, judges, and others familiar with the special dangers and special needs of each "stretch point" in the criminal process.

POLICE

If we were to start from scratch to build a system of laws and enforcement agencies to protect us from disorder and to keep our communities peaceful, we would not send almost half a million armed men out on the street with the power to determine, on their own, which of us deserves to be interrogated, searched, and arrested, or who should be punished and what for. Yet, this is approximately what we have done.

One job of the police is to see that the guilty go to jail. They probably do as good a job of this as we can expect. On the whole, they investigate violations of law, arrest suspects, testify truthfully at trial, and enforce the law as well as their training and resources permit. But policemen, like the rest of us, form their own ideas about who should be punished.

What too few of us realize—because we ourselves appear to the police to represent the very values they feel duty-bound to protect—is that the policeman often operates with virtually no guidelines from the legislature, the courts, or his superior. He must make selections among the many laws which he could enforce, and among the many violators who come to his attention. We have generated so many laws, sweeping so broadly over human activity, that full enforcement is impossible and policemen are, in fact, thrown back for guidance on their own views about who should be punished. Those views are unreviewed, and inherently unreviewable, by prosecutors and judges.

From their day-to-day experience, policemen learn to identify potential assailants and others whose criminal propensity they can predict with considerable accuracy. They make, or they try to make, arrests before serious crime is committed. As a sort of sixth sense, a policeman's ability to recognize and act against "symbolic assailants" is undoubtedly necessary to his survival and desirable from the point of view of the rest of us. Unhappily, a sort of mystique has grown up around this, and police are accustomed to having prosecutors, judges, and juries vindicate their on-the-spot discretionary decisions. If a policeman thinks a person needs to be punished, he can arrest him, design a plausible charge, and usually see the case through to conviction.

But dissenters, whose "symbolic assault" is not of a criminal kind and is protected by the First Amendment, also trigger the sixth sense of the police. Police are sometimes as angered by attacks on Establishment values and political orthodoxy as they are by attacks on person or property. Not only can, and do, policemen administer on-the-spot punishment for "protected" political activity, but they can, and do, protect themselves from legal retaliation by leveling criminal charges such as disorderly conduct, resisting arrest, or assault on an officer, against those they have already improperly punished.

A policeman's discretion to select among violators of laws which are commonly broken and the discretion inherent in the credibility accorded his testimony give him an extraordinary license to punish. With nothing to go on but his own value system, a policeman becomes a decision-maker on social policy, a lawmaker quite beyond the control of the First Amendment.

My guess is that this is, and probably always has been, the most common and least visible type of repression in America. The Black Panthers were a case in point. They triggered a massive police crackdown by their rhetoric, by patrolling police patrols, by carrying guns to back up demands for Constitutional rights, by agitating for community control of the police, and by an aggressive pride in a racial identity which most white policemen feared. Some of the Panthers who were arrested, tried, and imprisoned were guilty of crimes, some were even guilty of the crimes with which they were charged; many, however, were victims of the discretionary power of policemen to punish their "symbolic assailants."

Any doubt on this score vanished on September 5, 1968, when an organized gang of about one hundred off-duty policemen attacked and beat a handful of Panthers who were walking through the corridors of the New York City courthouse itself. The policemen's evident belief that their lawlessness was justified, even in the halls of justice, is impressive support for the Panthers' charge that, from 1967 on, a fair number of their members who were convicted across the country on the testimony of police officers were wrongly convicted. If so, they were certainly political prisoners.

In 1967, Martin Sostre, a reformed convict, was operating a bookstore in a Buffalo ghetto. After years in prison, he had come out a Muslim and political radical. His bookstore carried black nationalist, Black Panther, communist, and revolutionary works running the gamut from literature to propaganda. His politics were offensive to the Buffalo police department, but he was no criminal. In the summer of 1967 a riot swept through the Buffalo ghetto in the aftermath of Martin Luther King's assassination. Buffalo's chief of police later testified in Washington that Sostre was the "subversive" responsible for the explosion of black rage, and Sostre was charged with arson and riot. But his responsibility for the riot was unsupported by the facts, and a new charge was quickly substituted. He was arrested, tried, convicted, and sentenced to spend thirty to forty-one years in prison for possession and sale of heroin. Sostre was not into drugs, he was into politics. His lawyers convinced me that the drugs were planted on him by arresting officers and that he was framed.

Such flagrant abuses of police power as these are really beyond the stretch points of the law. The remedy is obvious, though obviously difficult. Policemen must be disciplined by their superiors, and by the wishes of an informed community, to obey the law. Much more difficult is finding a remedy for abuses of police discretion *within* the stretch points of the law itself. The fault here is not with the policeman so much as it is with the system. We have so overcriminalized human activity that the policeman has no choice but to make his own value-based selections. We encourage him to protect us from those who have not *yet* committed crimes. We provide him with virtually no guidelines, and those we do provide are often confusing and contradictory.

In one area there has been some progress made by the courts. Laws such as breach of the peace, disorderly conduct, loitering, and vagrancy are so vague that policemen clearly do decide, in each case, what constitutes the crime. The civil rights struggle in the South brought a number of these laws and a number of repressive enforcement decisions to the Supreme Court for review. The high-level judicial scrutiny led to the demise of vagrancy as a crime, and to a gradual tightening of definitions, with the result that politically motivated arrests and convictions under such laws are harder to obtain and harder to make stick on appeal. But these crimes remain very ill-defined in most jurisdictions and there is a vast reservoir of other equally vague offenses. Arrests which are abusive of the spirit of the First Amendment are made daily. Even where a conviction would be reversed if the victim had funds to pursue the point on appeal, or where the charges are thrown out when the case comes to trial, arrest is itself a considerable punishment for challenging a policeman's value system.

This is enough to suggest that if we are serious about trying to halt political imprisonments flowing from unfettered police discretion, we must look to the reform of laws which cannot be fully enforced or which are so generally violated that selection is inevitable. Responsibility to amend and repeal criminal laws that are ill-advised, obsolete, poorly defined, or too costly to enforce fully should not be delegated to policemen making their decisions as they go.

We must look for reforms in police department decision-making as well. Where policemen are given discretion by an overly broad or unrealistic law but are not given legislative guidelines on how to make enforcement selections, police departments themselves should publish standards by which that discretion is to be exercised to investigate and arrest. If the legislature or the community objects to the policies when they are thus made visible, then the law or the standards can be changed. In any case, once policy is formalized defendants can begin to hold police to the policy. It would be a way to start.

JUDGES

A trial judge has wide discretionary power in setting the amount of bail, admitting or excluding items of evidence, permitting or denying lawyers an opportunity to raise an argument, instructing the jury on its duties, and determining sentence. When a judge's discretion is informed by political bias, conscious or unconscious, instead of justice, he can punish those whose politics he hates.

A trial judge's discretionary decisions are more visible than a policeman's, but appellate judges have been understandably chary about limiting the power of their brothers on the trial bench. Legislatures, caught up for years in the liberal ideal of individualized justice, have gradually increased judicial discretion by giving judges an almost unlimited power to set sentences; but they have not established workable guidelines for the exercise of that power.

Heidi Ann Fletcher, a white girl who is the daughter of the former Deputy Mayor of Washington, D.C., drove the get-away car for her boyfriend and others who robbed a Washington bank. In the course of events a policeman was shot and killed. Nevertheless, Miss Fletcher was immediately released without bail. After pleading guilty to murder, armed robbery, and illegal possession of weapons, she was given a short sentence at a correctional facility where she could be near her family.

Angela Davis was arrested about the same time on suspicion of murder, kidnapping, and conspiracy in connection with the shoot-out at a San Marin courthouse in which a judge was killed. Angela, both black and a communist, was denied bail.

Upon arraignment, the evidence of Heidi Fletcher's guilt was overwhelming, while Angela Davis's guilt was conjectural at best. Angela Davis was finally acquitted on all counts by the jury. It may well be that in both cases, justice prevailed in the end, but Angela Davis was imprisoned for sixteen months, waiting for the wheels of justice to grind so exceedingly slow, because a white judge *in his discretion* denied her bail.[4]

Some twenty-four million Americans have smoked marijuana. Policemen have found it convenient in recent years to arrest politically active youths, to find or to plant a joint on them or among their possessions, and to stand them before judges for sentencing. In ordinary, nonpolitical cases, possession of marijuana usually results in a probationary sentence. John Sinclair, a radical poet and leader of the White Panther Party (now the Rainbow People's Party) in Michigan was sentenced to nine and one-half to ten years in prison for making the mistake of lighting up with two undercover police intelligence agents assigned to watch his political activities. Lee Otis Johnson, a black militant and antiwar organizer at Texas Southern University, got thirty years for giving a marijuana cigarette to an undercover officer who had posed as his friend. These were exceptional cases, of course. Defense committees were formed, and after long imprisonments, the sentences were struck down on appeal. Two of the six justices of the Michigan Supreme

Court called the Sinclair sentence "cruel and unusual punishment."

Blacks get longer sentences than whites; political draft resisters get longer sentences than those whose draft refusal is religiously motivated. Racial and political biases are clearly improper grounds for punishment, whether they are embodied in statutes or hidden in the recesses of a judge's mind. But it is rare indeed that a decision "within the judge's discretion" is overturned. One reason is that it is very difficult to articulate rational grounds for *any* sentencing decision. We must face the fact that no method exists for fixing a "reasonable" punishment except the most primitive kind of guesswork. Perhaps it is time to recognize that judges are no better than the rest of us at predicting human behavior or the consequences of administering punishment. Perhaps it is time to return to a sentencing structure set within very narrow limits by the statutes which define the conduct to be punished.

An intermediate remedy, one applicable to bail abuses as well as to sentencing abuses, would be to require judges to state the reasons for the decisions they make. A judge's biases can be checked by him or by a higher authority only if they are articulated. Precedents can be developed to guide and contain the exercise of judicial discretion in future cases only if we have something to go on.

We tend too readily to think of the judge as a man above politics, a man wise with experience, a man whose concern is evenhanded administration of the law, not the outcome of any particular political conflict. And, indeed, the American judiciary has protected our system well. There are many examples of outstanding judges setting aside their interests and their politics to protect the First Amendment rights of citizens brought before them. I think it not too harsh to say, however, that most judges, even some impeccably honest and well-respected judges, are influenced in subtle ways by being part of the complex Establishment which "runs things" and benefits from the status quo. They are believers in the system that has rewarded them, even if they are better than others at exercising their power without yielding to the urge to repress advocacy of fundamental political, economic, or cultural changes.

It can be said another way: those who dissent and want to work for fundamental changes are unlikely to become judges. Nor would the dissenters be likely to make better judges. By all indications, they would be more ready to yield to their biases and to their certitude that they are right than are those who presently occupy the bench. Counterrevolutionary heresies are generally given short shrift after revolutionaries take power. Yet, in no era is it sufficient to rely on judges alone to guard against repressive law enforcement.

PROSECUTORS

I have never been a policeman or a judge, but I prosecuted cases in the Air Force and I worked for two years in the Justice Department with the section that made the decisions on each request from the U.S. Attorneys to proceed with prosecutions in cases where authorization was required. I agree completely with the late Justice Jackson who remarked, when he was still Attorney General:

> The prosecutor has more control over life, liberty, and reputation than any other person in America. His discretion is tremendous. He can have citizens investigated and, if he is that kind of person, he can have this done to the tune of public statements and veiled or unveiled intimations. Or the prosecutor may choose a more subtle course and simply have a citizen's friends interviewed. . . . He may dismiss the case before trial, in which case the defense never has a chance to

be heard. . . . If the prosecutor is obliged to choose his cases, it follows that he can choose his defendants. . . . [A] prosecutor stands a fair chance of finding at least a technical violation of some act on the part of almost anyone. . . . It is in this realm—in which the prosecutor picks some person whom he dislikes or desires to embarrass, or selects some group of unpopular persons and then looks for an offense, that the greatest danger of abuse of prosecuting power lies.[5]

The prosecutor's power is literally "lawless," in that there is no provision in the law giving it to him or directing him in its use. He need not explain, and he need not be consistent. He can pile on charges or plea-bargain them away as he pleases. In deciding whether he has enough evidence to prosecute, he knows that he can almost always get a grand jury to oblige him with an indictment, particularly against politically unpopular individuals. His decision to go forward, and the imprimatur of an indictment from the grand jury, can sometimes be enough to sway a jury to convict on even the most questionable evidence.

A prosecutor's motives for setting the criminal process in motion against a particular person, against an antiwar protester, an advocate of abortion reform, or an opponent of school busing, for instance, are his own; and if he chooses to call a proceeding a "routine" matter, there is no review and usually no questions are asked.

Recently I was talking about the Ellsberg case, political trials, and civil liberties generally, with a friend who is a professor at Harvard Law School. I asked him: "What position would you like to occupy to try to change the way things are going, if you had a choice?" His unhesitating reply was "Prosecutor." He reasoned that a judge concerned about abuses of civil liberties must wait for a case which gives him an opportunity to devise a remedy; defense attorneys usually have to go through long trials and appeals to undo the results of any repressive decision made along the way; but a prosecutor each week makes hundreds of unreviewable, invisible decisions that go to the very heart of justice. A good prosecutor can do more than most to keep the political and criminal processes in their respective places.

On the other hand, it has proved impossible to devise workable protections, even mild restraints, against abuses of prosecutorial discretion. I can think of no better illustration than the prosecution of Daniel Ellsberg.

I have described earlier the various political considerations that must have led the government to bring the unique set of criminal charges against Ellsberg in the first place. No one else had ever been prosecuted, for doing what he did, under the laws he was charged with violating. It is difficult to imagine a more powerful case to justify dismissal of an indictment as discriminatory.

The impossibility of proving a prosecutor's improper purpose, except where he admits it, has left the law in an extremely primitive state: there is virtually no precedent.

The Constitution guarantees each citizen the "equal protection" of the law. This has meant, since 1896,[6] that prosecutors violate the Constitution if they single out, for an improper reason, a particular individual or group for prosecution while leaving other individuals, who they know have committed the same acts, untouched by the criminal process. But the few precedents indicate that improper government conduct of this sort will bar a prosecution only when the individual accused can prove a systematic or intentional pattern of discrimination which is not based on some "reasonable" law enforcement purpose. It is easy enough for prosecutors, and particularly for the Justice Department, to devise a "reasonable" ground, or one that no federal court will disbelieve, for whatever prosecution they choose to commence. The Constitutional prohibition against discriminatory prosecution is the law of the land, but it is about as enforceable as a law denying the power of rain to fall.

Ellsberg was faced with more than a lack of precedents in trying to base a defense on the ground of discriminatory prosecution. An attempt to prove discrimination is usually as exorbitantly expensive as it is difficult. Usually the only way is to show that there are many others who regularly do the very acts with which the defendant is charged, and that none of them has ever been prosecuted. Proving a negative is never easy.

A prosecutor, backed by the vast resources of government, has no problem getting research done, paying witnesses' expenses, paying for legal counsel, or making a living until the case is over. One reason why legal challenges are seldom raised to the prosecutor's exercise of discretion is that most defendants simply do not have the money to pay for what has to be done.

Although Ellsberg's defense was always short of money, the notoriety and importance of the case enabled him to raise, through public contributions, substantially more than could most defendants. The Chief Counsel, Leonard Boudin, and co-counsel, Charles Nesson, had been intensively engaged in preparing the defense before I joined them. As one of the defense counsel, I contacted more than 120 potential witnesses myself prior to the scheduled opening of the trial in early June of 1972. We were prepared to present the testimony of some twenty-three witnesses at a pre-trial hearing on the question of discriminatory prosecution.

The question might legitimately be asked: why so many? Sometimes lawyers are justifiably criticized for making everything too complicated and difficult. Not, I think, in this instance. It was our belief, and still is, that Daniel Ellsberg was singled out in order to punish and make an example of him because *The Pentagon Papers* he copied and tried to get to Congress were politically embarrassing when they were ultimately published by the newspapers. They are a dramatic revelation of dereliction, secrecy, and deceit by the Executive Branch, and they gave further support to the critics of the war in Vietnam.

It was necessary for the defense to show that government officials regularly handle classified material exactly the way Ellsberg had handled it in this case. Our witnesses were ready to testify that they themselves often copied classified material, removed classified material from government buildings where they worked, transferred such materials without formally logging them, disseminated classified materials to persons not formally authorized to receive them, retained certain classified material in their personal possession, and treated such material as their own personal property after leaving government. Since we had to show that such things were done as a general practice without criminal prosecution, we had to round up former high officials of government, Washington journalists who participated in these practices, and classification experts.

When the judge asked us what we could prove in a hearing, we were able overnight to present him with a summary of the anticipated testimony. That offer of proof remains the most devastating indictment ever presented of the security classification system, as it actually operates. Its impact upon the judge seemed apparent. He postponed a decision on our request for a hearing for over a month although at the time of the proof's submission his decision appeared imminent.

The problem for the judge was further complicated when, two weeks after our offer of proof, the Circuit Court of Appeals for his own Ninth Circuit demolished the government's position that the law provides no such defense as discriminatory prosecutions. The appellate court reversed the conviction of one Steele, an outspoken resister of the census who had been prosecuted for refusing to give census information, a favorite conservative cause. Steele showed that the government prosecuted him and three other census resisters who were speaking out on the census issue, while it had not prosecuted six more who had committed the same offense but were quiet about it. In a strong opinion, the court said: "Since Steele had presented evidence which created a strong inference of discriminatory prosecution, the government was required to explain it away, if possible, by showing the selection process actually rested upon some valid ground."

It appeared to us that the Ellsberg case was far stronger than Steele's. We could show nonprosecution of thousands of people, not just six, who had dealt with classified material as Ellsberg had. In the Defense Department alone, over the past four years there had been 1,966 investigations concerning improper physical protection of information with 2,372 administrative penalties imposed and *no* criminal prosecutions or recommendations for criminal prosecution.

Yet, we were ultimately denied a pre-trial hearing on the issue. The trial judge may have been right in his application of the law on this issue to the Ellsberg case. Right or wrong, it should be obvious from this recitation how difficult it is, once a discriminatory prosecution is under way, to undo it by relying on the right to "equal protection of the laws." When judges are reluctant to act, defendants victimized by this sort of low visibility repression must fall back on the jury's common sense and instinct for fair play; they must carry the monumental and very expensive burden of getting enough evidence before the jury on this complicated issue.

Judges usually prevent the juries from hearing any evidence of unfair discrimination by the prosecutor (Judge

Agnew's discretionary rulings against the UFO defendants were fairly typical), and they generally instruct jurors to ignore any evidence of this sort that chances to slip in. The political defendant can only hope that his jurors will read between the lines, exercise their instinct for fairness, and acquit him. It is a rather weak line of defense against repressive distortions of the American ideal of evenhanded justice.

If a politically active citizen commits a crime, we expect, and the integrity of our criminal process demands, that he be treated as any other suspect. He should be arrested, prosecuted, tried, and sentenced for what he has done in violation of our laws. When the men who administer the criminal process discriminate against an individual because of his political stature, views, or affiliations, they invite the victims to politicize the criminal process even further, and they invite a watchful citizenry to grow cynical about the rule of law and the liberty guaranteed by the First Amendment.

Virtually every reform of the American criminal process has entailed a grant of greater discretion to the men who administer it. This has proved an unfortunate method of disguising our failure to decide precisely what we expect our criminal process to do, and our failure to find and prove effective ways to do it. No system of government and no criminal process can operate without some flexibility. Every government, including our own, is a government of laws *and men*. We cannot eliminate discretion entirely, and to do so would create other injustices. But we must recognize the danger points of discretion, taking into account the human frailties of those we ask to exercise it, and we must learn to channel and inform its exercise so that discretionary power serves the system as a whole and the individuals on whom it falls.

14

What's Wrong with Conspiracy?

Was your applause merely perfunctory politeness . . . or did
you applaud in *agreement* with the position he was taking,
and in *advocacy* of the same position?
—Prosecutor John Wall, cross-
examining Mark Raskin

Our fear of conspiracies has been played upon by those
with political power ever since George Washington tried
to lump together the anti-Federalists, the Democratic Societies, and the Whiskey Rebels into one grand anti-Ameri-
can plot. Today, cynical use of the doctrines of conspiracy
law is a serious threat to the American system of government and law. What's wrong with conspiracy is that the
devices the law provides for punishing surreptitious criminal enterprises can be, and are being, used to punish open
statements of belief and expression of ideas, and to punish
unpopular dissidents for crimes they have not committed.
No other criminal charge gives a prosecutor as much discretionary power against the politically alienated.

Conspiracy, wrote Justice Jackson, "comes down to us

wrapped in vague but unpleasant connotations. It sounds historical undertones of treachery, secret plotting and violence on a scale that menaces social stability and the security of the state itself." But, he added, "Its history exemplifies the 'tendency of a principle to expand itself to the limit of its logic' " and it has evolved into such an "elastic, sprawling and pervasive offense . . . that it almost defies definition."[1]

If a Justice of the Supreme Court could not define the crime of conspiracy, neither can I. More importantly, neither can prosecutors, trial judges, nor the ordinary citizens who are expected to avoid it. As a result of its elusive quality, a prosecutor who is so inclined can secure a conspiracy indictment on no more than speculation and whim. A friend, reflecting recently on his years as a prosecutor with the Department of Justice, remarked, "It's disgracefully easy. You could walk into a grand jury room with a laundry list and walk out with a conspiracy indictment." Because it gives greater scope to prosecutorial discretion than any other weapon on the books, conspiracy law is strewn with opportunities for repression. Its doctrines are riddled with traps for even the most careful advocate of unpopular ideas.

Prosecutors have reached for the conspiracy indictment to squelch political opposition with such frequency in the last several years that it can now be said to pose a clear and present danger to the integrity of our criminal and political systems. The Oakland Seven, the Boston Five, the Chicago Eight, the Panther Thirteen, Angela Davis, the Harrisburg Seven, Daniel Ellsberg and Anthony Russo—the protesters, radicals, or critics who have been the targets of conspiracy indictments are too many to name. So far as I can tell, these trials have had only three results: individuals have been tried for expressing their political views; responsible citizens have been given reason to avoid associating with groups that plan for effective, collective political action (leaving protest to the spontaneous leadership of the less reflective); and judicial and prosecutorial energy is being consumed by political trials which may cost over $1 million and which disgrace the administration of justice, while legitimate law-enforcement activities go neglected.

Conspiracy is said to be the agreement among a number of individuals to accomplish some wrongful purpose, or some legitimate purpose by wrongful means. Their agreement need not be "treacherous" or even "secret" and it need not be real. In fact, neither the purpose nor the means has to be criminal. Even without any evidence of crime, individuals can be indicted, tried, and convicted of conspiracy although they do not know each other, or even know of each other.

Strangers or not, when they are seated together before a judge and charged with a felony, the "conspirators" have a very obvious common interest: to destroy the government's case and win an acquittal. Their very presence together at the defense table, and their efforts to extricate themselves from a dragnet accusation will often convince a jury of the existence of some common improper purpose.

The peculiar procedures governing conspiracy trials permit a prosecutor to convict one man for the wrongdoing of another. Each defendant can be made responsible for the acts and statements of the others, and all can be damned in the eyes of the public and before the jury by inflammatory hearsay evidence which is considered so unreliable it is barred from ordinary trials. A defendant in a conspiracy trial can be made responsible, not only for the acts and statements of his co-defendants, but also for those of persons named as "co-conspirators" who are not indicted, and those of persons alleged to be co-conspirators whose identity remains, as indictments put it, "unknown to the Grand Jury." A conspiracy indictment is, as Judge Learned Hand dubbed it, the "darling of the modern prosecutor's nursery."[2]

The vague dragnet offense seems oddly out of place among the neat prohibitions of our criminal law. The unifying threads in our system of justice are that guilt is personal and that what is prohibited must be clearly prohibited. How was the "darling of the modern prosecutor's nursery" conceived? Like so many of the law-enforcement tools which can be used to bend the law to repressive purposes, conspiracy doctrines were originally designed to *protect* the administration of justice from abuse. An English statute of 1305 made it a crime for two or more individuals to arrange a false indictment against another. To prove the conspiracy, however, the government had to show that the charge was actually false, that the victim of the plot had been tried and acquitted.

Three hundred years later, this narrowly defined statutory prohibition was radically broadened by the infamous Court of Star Chamber. A group of poulterers falsely accused one Stone of robbery. Stone was so manifestly innocent that he was not even brought to trial. Since his innocence had not been formally established, there appeared to be no way to prove the crime of conspiracy against his accusers. Star Chamber cured this problem by holding that there was no need to prove that the accusation against Stone was false, for the essence of the crime was the *agreement* to do him wrong. The doctrine of the *Poulterers Case* of 1611[3], that the agreement to do a wrong is punishable as a conspiracy whether or not it is carried forward to actual wrong-doing, became the core of the modern crime.

Later, conspiracy drifted still further from its original conception as a vehicle for punishing abuses of the criminal process, and grew to encompass the planning of any kind of crime. By the eighteenth century, "law and order" buffs were finding the already sprawling conspiracy doctrines ideal for enforcing the prevailing political morality: individuals could be indicted for criminal conspiracy even if the purpose of their coming together was merely antisocial and not illegal at all.

In 1806, when a group of journeymen cordwainers in Philadelphia refused to work except for higher wages, they were indicted and convicted of conspiracy. The judge conceded that there was nothing illegal in seeking higher wages or in withdrawing one's labor to combat employer intransigence. The prevailing morality, however, held it inherently evil for workers to frustrate the interests of their masters, and the cordwainers' *agreement* to do so became a criminal conspiracy.[4] A few years later, when journeymen shoemakers tried to have the conspiracy doctrine applied to punish combinations by employers who sought to depress their wages, the judge threw the case out of court on the basis of the same extra-legal morality of that class-conscious time. He found no "improper motive" in the employers' agreement and ruled that "when . . . the object to be attained is meritorious, combination is not conspiracy."[5] Until the New Deal brought collective bargaining within the rule of law by statute, this extraordinary common-law conspiracy doctrine was of use to those bent on repressing labor's attempts to organize to change the imbalance of economic power in our society.

The gist of the crime remains what Star Chamber said it was: an agreement. But because conspiracy is considered a clandestine offense, a prosecutor is not expected to prove it as he would an ordinary crime. The law permits a jury to infer an agreement from purely circumstantial evidence which even remotely tends to establish it. It may then infer, from very little more, the intention of any particular individual to further its criminal objectives.

The testimony of a paid informer or a secret police agent is enough to establish the connection, and in the federal system a conviction can hang on nothing more substantial than the uncorroborated and inherently unreliable testimony of such a witness. In political cases, where prosecutors and juries can be all too eager to have their worst conspiratorial fantasies borne out, informer testimony is particularly common and its injustice particularly acute. The 1969–70 indictment and trial of three New York Panthers for conspiracy to rob a hotel is a good example: the prosecution was based, from start to finish, on a plan conceived and carried forward by a New York City undercover policeman. His testimony about the defendants' expressions of intent to commit the robbery was marred, in the jury's eyes, only by his unnerving habit of reporting even the most hyperbolic political rhetoric as a sober expression of purpose.[6] In this case the defendants escaped the conspiracy tag; in others they did not.

The possibilities for injustice have been compounded through the application of conspiracy doctrines to twentieth-century corporate conspiracies to fix prices and to control markets illegally. Because of the obvious difficulty of proving any "agreement" between abstract corporate "persons," juries have been allowed to infer conspiratorial collusion from evidence showing only that companies pursued "substantially similar" courses of action. The gist of the crime has become a legal fiction, to which a defendant may be attached by an inference.

It is by yet another legal fiction that the jury is permitted to weigh against each alleged conspirator hearsay evidence of the acts and statements of others. The *theory* sounds all right: because conspirators are partners in crime, any one of them—whether indicted or not—is presumed to speak and act for the others. To take advantage of this extraordinary exception to the hearsay rule, all a prosecutor must do is offer some circumstantial evidence of the agreement.

There is a certain absurdity to treating the acts and statements of one "partner" as if they were another's, in cases where the "partnership" is itself a legal fiction and the existence of the agreement is the very question the jury is to resolve. This absurdity is compounded by another peculiarity of conspiracy trials: the prosecutor need not follow a logical order in presenting his case. The accusation is such a sprawling one that, as a practical matter, an accused is often confronted with a hodgepodge of acts and statements by others which he may not even know about, but which help persuade the jury that a conspiracy exists. As Justice Jackson put it, "A conspiracy often is proved by evidence that is admissible only upon the assumption that a conspiracy existed."[7]

The circularity of conspiracy definitions and rules places in a prosecutor's hands a weapon for punishing inferred intent—a weapon we need, it is said, to fight organized crime. Our ordinary criminal law does not punish an individual for what he merely *intends:* we wait at least until he is attempting to carry out his intention of committing a crime. Yet we undoubtedly need some method to detect and punish those responsible for masterminding criminal enterprises. When crime is plotted secretly by a coordinated group, it is hard to stop it before it gets beyond an attempt, and those truly responsible may absent themselves completely from implementing their plot. Joint planning bolsters the resolve of each person involved, making it more certain that the intention will ripen into bank robbery or kidnapping or some other serious crime. Without special procedures and rules of evidence, many crimes and those actually responsible for them would go unpunished.

Because of this very real threat, we have permitted prosecutors to pile inference upon hearsay upon inference upon legal fiction. Obviously, such a formless and flexible weapon is dangerous in the hands of a cynical or overzealous prosecutor. When he believes a group deserves to be punished, but is frustrated because there has been no crime committed, he will almost always be able to ride some theory of a conspiracy at least as far as trial. That alone can be quite punishing, but if a jury shares the prosecutor's belief that such a group *intends* some evil, they will infer the evil intent from whatever circumstances are presented to them, and the prosecutor will get the conviction as well.

If the almost limitless possibilities of apparently plausible conspiracy theories have a logical limit, perhaps it can be glimpsed from the aftermath of an incident in Appalachin, New York: On November 14, 1957, a policeman stumbled on an extraordinary council of top underworld figures in progress at the Appalachin home of reputed Mafia boss Joseph Barbara, Sr. The fifty-eight men identified leaving Barbara's property were interrogated no less than 133 times about their purpose in attending the meeting. A large number said they had simply dropped by to visit a sick friend. Barbara was indeed suffering from a heart ailment, of which he soon died. The police were unable to come up with a shred of evidence of any criminal purpose in the meeting.

Much as most of us would like to see the Mafia leaders get their comeuppance, what happened in the Appalachin case borders on the ridiculous. The government had no evidence of any criminal activity, so they could not make any direct charges. The government had no evidence to prove that the strikingly similar alibis given by Barbara's guests were false, so they couldn't charge them with perjury. The government, therefore, used the very absence of evidence to charge those in attendance with a *conspiracy* to commit perjury in order to conceal the evidence. According to the government, since they admitted no criminal purpose they must have conspired to conceal whatever criminal purpose they had. Twenty-seven were indicted and convicted. A judge handed out prison terms running from three to five years.

Criminal justice cannot be based on the notion that it's a good idea to convict "those people." Under certain political conditions, if the members of the Daughters of the American Revolution, the Kiwanis or, for that matter, a State Bar Association, should consistently maintain that they had no criminal purpose in meeting together, they could, under the logic of Appalachin, be indicted for conspiracy to tell the truth.

The Appalachin convictions were reversed on appeal, but reversing convictions that so egregiously abuse the conspiracy doctrines does nothing to prevent prosecutors from trying again, against some other group, to punish them for the "evil intent" which those who fear them will assume is at the root of any similarities in their conduct. As one of the appellate judges in the Appalachin case pointed out: "A prosecution framed on such doubtful basis should never have been initiated or allowed to proceed so far."[8] Yet there is no check on a prosecutor's use of the conspiracy law except his own self-restraint.

The Appalachin case reveals, as well as any, the power of prosecutors to secure convictions for conspiracy against unpopular groups, without presenting any evidence of an agreement or of an intent to commit an underlying crime. All they require is a popular prejudice which lumps the targeted individuals together. It is not hard to see why such a doctrine has long been a favorite of prosecutors bent on repressing political movements. The self-fulfilling dragnet conspiracy charge has been aimed at the anarchists, the Wobblies, the antiwar groups in World War I, the communists, and the Black Panthers.

The evidence against the New York Panther Thirteen consisted of undercover police agents' testimony about a plot which, as the jury saw it, never got past the fantasy stage. *Some* individual Panthers might have been properly indicted and convicted of illegal possession of explosives or weapons, and the law-enforcement authorities had a responsibility to protect New Yorkers against the criminally inclined among them. The conspiracy charge, however, was much better suited to the effort to turn the fantasies of the politically alienated into a felony and to put members of a lawful political organization behind bars on the basis of the unlawful proclivities of a few. The indictment charged a conspiracy to murder, dating from the founding of the New York Black Panther chapter. The indictment opened with the peculiar accusation: "During the course of the conspiracy the defendants were members of the Black Panther Party." The judge, explaining conspiracy law to the Panther Thirteen jury, put it this way:

> The Black Panther Party is not on trial in this case. The defendants are on trial for crimes . . . whether the conduct was engaged in as members of the Black Panther Party or not. . . .
> It is exactly like what we see in a play. We have actors with roles of varying importance. . . . It is not necessary to be a player that a person be the leading man or that he play an important role. If his or her part requires him or her to do no more than walk across the stage or calls for the utterance of but a single sentence, he or she is a player despite the unimportance of his or her role.[9]

The Manhattan jurors, however, were quite sophisticated by national standards. Among them were a graduate student in political science, an editor, and others whose background gave them a perspective on guilt by association which doomed the prosecution to failure. After acquitting the defendants on all counts, one juror explained that, despite the judge's instructions, they felt they could not convict on such slim evidence without setting a precedent which would endanger the freedom of everybody. Another juror's outrage came through clearly in his remark: "I began to realize that conspiracy law is a lasso . . . turned into a hangman's noose that fits everybody's collar size."[10]

The New York Times found it "reassuring" that in the face of governmental politicization of the conspiracy device, "a New York jury was willing to insist on evidence of wrongdoing rather than wrong-thinking."[11] Other newspapers and commentators were quick to express agreement with the *Times*' editors.

I cannot agree. The *Times* drew, from the jury's resistance to repression, the lesson that the integrity of the criminal process had been vindicated. This makes no more sense than the Weathermen's belief that a "prerevolutionary situation" arrived in the United States when the police rioted in Chicago. The Weathermen's subsequent trashing of Chicago failed to ignite any revolutionary kindling and their illusion was a dangerous one for all concerned. Similarly, *The New York Times*' conclusion is illusory. The Panther Thirteen jurors vindicated themselves, and vindicated the defendants (a point apparently lost on the editors) by condemning the law, the judge, the prosecutor, and the system which had kept the accused Panthers behind bars for two years. There are juries all over the country which could not acquit themselves so well. The federal system is the home ground for major political conspiracy trials, a trial can be brought wherever any of the alleged "overt acts" took place, and there are countless judicial districts where it is easier to win convictions, on baseless and abusive conspiracy charges, than in Manhattan.

Repressive abuse of conspiracy's dragnet features has been with us all along. Since the demise of antisedition laws, however, conspiracy has emerged as a substitute for them—a substitute which the First Amendment does not seem to reach. "Freedom of speech" requires the government to prove, when prosecuting a man for what he says, that there is an intimate connection between what is said and some great danger which is almost certain to follow from it. Conspiracy requires only that the government persuade a jury that what has been said implies an agreement to act on some wrongful intent: when applied to political rhetoric, it is the old "evil intent" standard unencumbered by even a requirement that the expression have a "bad tendency."

Citizens coming together for political or personal reasons, or pursuing independently some common political cause, can be cast as criminal conspirators should any of them express, in the language of the politically alienated, what a prosecutor can construe as an intent to act wrongfully. Ever since the Star Chamber set the outer limit of conspiracy doctrine in the *Poulterers Case*, an implied agreement can be punished whether or not there is anything resembling a "clear and present danger" that it will succeed. The result: cynical prosecutors can nullify two centuries of developing First Amendment principles.

Among the first to protest the Vietnam war by refusing induction were the members and officers of the Student Nonviolent Coordinating Committee. In January 1966, SNCC's national headquarters in Atlanta released a policy statement terming United States policy in Vietnam hypocritical, aggressive, murderous, and a violation of international law. The statement expressed "sympathy" and "support" for those who were "unwilling to respond to a military draft," and expressly committed SNCC to "encourage" and "urge" all Americans to do so, though "it may cost their lives." Julian Bond, the Director of Communications for SNCC, endorsed the statement and explained to reporters that he was "eager and anxious to encourage people not to participate in [the war] for any reason that they chose." Bond, who had been elected to the Georgia legislature, was then excluded from the Chamber by his fellow legislators on the ground that his statements gave aid and comfort to the enemy and violated the draft law's prohibition of counseling, aiding, and abetting resistance.

In December 1966, the Supreme Court ruled unanimously that the Georgia legislature had violated the Constitution's guarantee of free speech. An expression of support and approval of draft refusal as a political tactic, even a statement of an intent to "encourage" and "urge" it, were not, the Court held, the kind of "incitement" that government can forbid. It specifically stated that "Bond could not have been convicted under [the law] which punishes any person who 'counsels, aids, or abets another to refuse or evade registration.'"[12]

But on January 5, 1968, a federal grand jury in Boston issued an indictment charging Dr. Benjamin Spock, Reverend William Sloane Coffin, Mitchell Goodman, Michael Ferber, and Marcus Raskin—the Boston Five—with conspiring together "and with diverse other persons, some known and others unknown to the Grand Jury," to "counsel, aid and abet" various forms of draft resistance and to interfere with the administration of draft boards and induction centers across the country. The indictment was the work of John Van de Kamp, head of a special unit set up in the Department of Justice soon after the Resistance hit a peak on October 16, 1967. Jessica Mitford in her fine book, *The Trial of Dr. Spock*, reports the rather startling reason Van de Kamp gave her for leveling a conspiracy indictment at these five: "We wouldn't have indicted them except for the fact there was so much evidence available on film. They made no great secret about what they were doing."[13]

The conspiracy charge, suggesting a covert plot, was more than ironic: it was fashioned from a theory of conspiracy which cast the entire antiwar movement as a federal offense on the basis of evidence consisting of overt

political statements and rhetoric which were "protected"
by the First Amendment.

The ease with which the Justice Department made out
its case should outrage anyone who has participated in an
American political protest campaign. Van de Kamp subpoenaed the television industry's coverage of the preceding
months' political events. The films showed Raskin, Spock,
Coffin, and Goodman attending a press conference called
to publicize the "Call to Resist Illegitimate Authority" and
its impressive list of signers. Each participant used the
occasion to state his personal reasons for associating himself with the "Call," a document detailing constitutional
and moral objections to the war and the draft. Like the
SNCC statement endorsed by Julian Bond, the "Call"
pledged its signers' moral and financial support to the
young resisters who were raising these issues through civil
disobedience. The subpoenaed news films recorded the
speeches Coffin and Ferber had delivered at the Arlington
Street Church card-returning ceremony on October 16.
Ferber cautioned those about to return their draft cards to
consider the consequences carefully; Coffin traced the history of civil disobedience and discussed the responsibility
of the church toward conscientious resisters. The films
showed Coffin again, speaking at the October 20 demonstration on the steps of the Justice Department itself, before he
and seven others, picked from the crowd of five hundred at
the last minute, entered the building to hand over to the
authorities the draft cards collected around the country on
October 16.

Each of the filmed statements was a classic exercise of
First Amendment freedom; each was cited in Van de
Kamp's indictment, not as a crime, but as an "overt act"
committed in "furtherance" of a conspiracy. The irony of
this appellation is obvious: the "overt act" requirement was
added to federal conspiracy law to assure that no indict-

ment would be issued until, as Justice Oliver Wendell Holmes put it, "the conspiracy has passed beyond mere words."[14]

But even if he could characterize political speeches as "overt acts," where had Van de Kamp found the conspiracy itself? How did expressions, of personal commitment to the movement, "further" a criminal plot? Judge Ford gave the answer when he explained to the *Spock* jury that a conspiracy can be proved merely by evidence that each of the accused was working "for a common purpose or purposes."[15] All that was needed to transform their common commitment to ending the war into a crime was to show either that the goal they sought, or the means by which they intended to seek it, was wrongful.

Coffin supplied that item when, in his October 20 speech, he said: "We hereby publicly counsel these young men to continue in their refusal to serve in the armed forces as long as the war in Vietnam continues, and we pledge ourselves to aid and abet them in all the ways we can."[16]

Coffin was speaking to a group of draft-resisters who had *already* violated the law. If anyone of draft age who was there still possessed his draft card, it must have been an FBI agent taking down what Coffin said; there was certainly no clear and present danger that a G-man would join the movement on Coffin's tepid counseling. But Coffin's speech, taken as a literal expression of *intent*, became the nexus through which anyone who seemed to agree with him could be punished for sharing it.

The crime of conspiracy continues until its purpose is accomplished or abandoned. The Justice Department's theory was that the conspiracy in this case encompassed all twenty-eight thousand who signed the "Call," everyone who spoke out in support of the resisters, and everyone who expressed approval of the defendants. All who attended rallies and demonstrations were intentionally furthering the illegal aims of the agreement. Everyone, in short, whose conduct or expression implied sympathy with a civil disobedience tactic to end the war or the draft could be indicted. The lawyers for the Boston Five had to take care, therefore, that the conduct of the defense not become grounds for a new and even larger conspiracy indictment. During the trial, they felt they could not safely hold public forums to debate the political issues kept out of the case by the prosecution's choice of the conspiracy charge. Nor could they safely launch a program to educate the public on the government's abuse of the courts, nor freely seek widespread support for legal costs.

The government's conduct of the prosecution made it clear that the lawyers were not paranoid. Three months after the indictment, *Dr. Spock on Vietnam* was published. In it, Spock discussed the rationale of the "Call" and extolled the power of draft resistance to end the war. Van de Kamp acknowledged to Jessica Mitford that he thought he could indict the publishers of the book, and the booksellers as well, for conspiracy.

John Wall, cross-examining Raskin at the trial, elicited the fact that Dr. Spock, who had never said he would counsel, aid, and abet anyone, had *applauded* "for a long time" after Coffin spoke on the Justice Department steps. To drive the point home, Wall pressed Raskin about his own applause: "Was your applause merely perfunctory politeness to Mr. Coffin or did you applaud in *agreement* with the position he was taking, and in *advocacy* of the same position?"[17] The question was absurd. There were five hundred people there, and they all applauded. It was Appalachin all over again, in a political context.

Later in the trial Wall tried to sugar-coat the theory, objecting that he never said applause is proof of conspiracy. He had found it useful *evidence* of conspiracy, however, a difference which is not likely to matter much to anyone attending a political rally. It seems to me that it is entirely improper for a prosecutor to try to convince a jury that a citizen's applause at a public political event has any conspiratorial significance at all.

The Boston Five were charged with a single count of conspiracy, but the agreement alleged in that single count went beyond "counseling, aiding and abetting" draft resistance; it included a scheme to "interfere" with the administration of the Selective Service System. To back up the second accusation, the prosecution ran a film of Dr. Spock being arrested in a nonviolent sit-in before the Whitehall Induction Center in New York City on November 12, a month *after* the draft cards had been turned in.

Because the government's position was that this was all part of the same conspiracy, Spock was theoretically acting on behalf of his partners in crime, making them responsible for this act too. Presumably the government could have brought in any or all of the thousands who participated in nonviolent civil disobedient demonstrations around the country from 1965 on. In short, such a single count conspiracy indictment *could* be used to punish anyone who participated in, supported, approved, encouraged, applauded, or, perhaps, wrote about the antiwar movement.

This end run around the First Amendment had a ridiculous side. The defense called to the witness stand John Lindsay, Mayor of the City of New York, who implicated himself thoroughly in the conspiracy. He had, he testified, sought out Dr. Spock who had known nothing of the plans for the November 12 Whitehall demonstration. The Mayor testified that he invited Spock to his residence for a meeting with the demonstration's leaders. An agreement was reached *there* for the New York police to cooperate in a peaceful rally which would culminate in the arrest of Spock.

Several of the jurors thought the Boston Five were innocent of any wrongdoing, until Judge Ford instructed them on the complexities and abstractions of conspiracy doctrine. They then found four of the defendants guilty of conspiring to aid and abet draft resistance, but not guilty of conspiring to counsel it. The jury simply did not believe that the defendants had masterminded the Resistance, nor that they intended to persuade anyone to violate the law; but they felt compelled by the technicalities to convict all except Raskin simply for expressing approval of the civil disobedience of others—expression which, according to the *Bond* case, was "protected" by the First Amendment. One juror later explained their convoluted reasoning to Jessica Mitford: "You can 'aid' " he said, "by addressing yourself to that issue." Another juror was more frank about the confusion:

> The Saturday after the verdict I woke with a splitting headache, wondering if I did the right thing. The conspiracy law should be changed—technically you could call the Mayor of New York and thousands of his policemen conspirators. I can't fathom it out, it's beyond me.[18]

The convictions and two-year sentences were, of course, reviewed by the First Circuit Court of Appeals, and they were reversed because the judge had prejudiced the jurors' deliberations by asking them a series of specific questions which made acquittal almost impossible.[19] The enduring importance of the *Spock* case, however, was what the judges said about conspiracy.

The majority applied traditional doctrines and found "ample common purpose" among the defendants to establish a conspiracy. Conceding that an individual's expression of "sympathy and support" for draft resisters is protected by the First Amendment and cannot be criminal, they found it a different matter altogether—a criminal conspiracy—when that right is exercised by a number of individuals, each sharing a common purpose. Van de Kamp had chosen his weapon wisely: conspiracy law *can* make lawful protest criminal and nullify the First Amendment.

One of the appellate judges disagreed vehemently. "There is no legal precedent for applying the conspiracy theory," he wrote, "to a wholly open, amorphous and shifting association, having a broad focus of interest in changing public policy and encompassing a wide spectrum of purposes, legal and illegal." To permit prosecutors to establish the existence of a conspiracy and to link citizens to it on the basis of wholly legal acts and statements, wrote Judge Coffin, "would have . . . a pronounced chilling effect —indeed that of a sub-zero blast—on all kinds of efforts to sway public opinion."[20] But his was a minority view.

An individual now cannot know, at the time he signs a petition, expresses his opinion, or joins others in a lawful demonstration, whether or not he will later be linked, by that act, to a criminal conspiracy. The emergence of conspiracy law in this form at this time places an intolerable burden on our vulnerable system of freedom of expression. The right to express opposition to administration policy with impunity is meant to be the cornerstone of our form of government and the first freedom of our citizens. The president however, has far greater access to the ears of the people than any other individual. His cabinet and the other persons of rank and status who speak for him simply augment that advantage. Perhaps the greatest power accruing to one in public life derives from the increased opportunity to be heard. Anyone, from town councilman to senator to president, who speaks with the prestige of official position can deliver more words with more effect on more people than the ordinary citizen. This is a fact, not a criticism, but a fact that must not be overlooked when large issues affect small voices.

The only way ordinary citizens can even begin to balance the scales is to join their voices together in large numbers and demand attention. That is why the Supreme Court has held over and over again that freedom of expression and the right to petition for redress of grievances *necessarily imply* a third right, the right to associate freely with others.[21]

Unscrupulous application of conspiracy doctrines to prevent citizens from combining to advance their beliefs or to make the expression of their dissent heard may leave each individual's First Amendment freedom technically intact, but it will deprive our system of government of open and *fair* debate, our principle instrument for resolving conflicts peaceably.

The First Circuit Court of Appeals, in *Spock*, did make one potentially important concession to the mandate of the First Amendment. In ordinary criminal conspiracy cases, the jury is permitted to infer an individual's criminal intent from sparse and ambiguous evidence. The *Spock* court made a special rule for conspiracy cases in which the alleged "agreement" involves both legal and illegal elements and is "political within the shadow of the First Amendment." An individual can be punished for adhering to the disobedient portions of a protest movement's program only when *his own* acts or conduct show *unambiguously* that it was his "specific intent" to do so.[22] According to this doctrine, a citizen's participation cannot be made criminal by the conduct or statements of others in the movement— even if they are named "co-conspirators."

Despite the strict ring of the ruling, the *Spock* case will have almost no impact on prosecutors who choose to use the conspiracy weapon in political cases. In the first place, the "unambiguous" but perfectly lawful statements and acts of the sort connected with any political movement may be used to prove "specific intent," even if they are "protected" by the First Amendment. Rev. Coffin's speech is a good example.

Although an act like signing the ambiguous "Call" (the underlying "agreement" in the *Spock* case) would not prove a specific intent to further the civil disobedience of draft resisters, a signer could become a full-fledged criminal conspirator anyway, by some second "unambiguous" exercise of his First Amendment freedoms. Despite the court's effort, the chilling effect of the conspiracy weapon remains.

The *Spock* rule also leaves to juries the job of resolving the ambiguity inherent in all political rhetoric and action. Prosecutors retain the discretionary power to indict political activists for conspiracy and to take them through costly and lengthy trials on nothing more than a hope that a jury will decide their intent to be "unambiguous." And the prosecutor can count on the topsy-turvy rules of evidence and order of proof in conspiracy cases to make what is ambiguous seem crystal clear.

Moreover, only the judges of the First Circuit Court of Appeals know what they mean by a conspiracy case that is "political within the shadow of the First Amendment." The rule they devised to reconcile criminal conspiracy and political freedom is impossible to apply unless a usable concept of a "political trial" is worked into our law—an unlikely development in the foreseeable future.

The unworkability of the *Spock* "specific intent" safeguard became apparent, less than four months after it was announced, at the conspiracy trial of the Chicago Eight in the aftermath of the Chicago convention of the Democratic Party in 1968. That trial was as "political within the shadow of the First Amendment" as any of recent years. The *Spock* indictment cast the entire antiwar movement as a felony; but the Chicago case put a whole politically alienated generation on trial, and Judge Julius Hoffman simply refused to treat it as anything but a "routine" conspiracy case and refused to apply the *Spock* rule. Even before the prosecutor had finished presenting his case against what he termed the "freaking fag revolution," Judge Hoffman instructed the jury to consider evidence of criminal intent previously admitted against any one of the defendants as evidence against all of them. Up to that point in the trial, there had been *no* evidence of statements or acts unambiguously indicating the specific intent of any of them to "cross state lines with the intent to incite a riot." There had not even been evidence that they agreed on anything except the necessity for a demonstration at the 1968 Democratic National Convention. "Conspiracy, Hell," said Abbie Hoffman, "we couldn't even agree on lunch."

The effect of Hoffman's ruling was to make conviction certain. The prosecution's case consisted primarily of undercover police agents' reports of what had been said by unindicted and often unidentified demonstrators at the height of a *police riot*. Their acts and statements were relevant because the indictment of the Eight cast all the others in Chicago for the Convention as "co-conspirators." Even speeches castigating the defendants for timidity in the face of police attacks were used against them at trial to show the criminal purpose of the conspiracy which they were accused of masterminding. When the strange trial ended, the government had failed to persuade the jury that there had been a conspiracy at all—the very idea that the defendants had acted together at one point, with the intent to have a criminal intent at some later time, offended common sense.

The cumulative effect, however, of presenting to the jurors all the prejudicial and customarily inadmissible hearsay evidence of rabble-rousing and angry words by unidentified persons not on trial, was to persuade them that the defendants were *somehow* responsible for it all and should be punished. Thus, on the basis of evidence admitted *only* on a theory of conspiracy which the jury rejected, the jury convicted defendants for coming individually to Chicago with the intent of participating in and inciting a riot.

The Harrisburg Eight case ended in a similar affront to the integrity of the criminal law. The Harrisburg Eight were indicted for conspiracy to kidnap Henry Kissinger, to blow up steam tunnels in Washington, and to mastermind draft-board raids across the country. Among the "overt acts" was an exchange of personal correspondence between Sister McAlister and the already imprisoned Father Philip Berrigan, in which the merits and demerits of various forms of protest were discussed. A battery of the best political lawyers in the country prevented a conviction on the conspiracy count by persuading a few of the jurors that the accusation was outrageous, and that no criminal law ought to reach that far back into private thoughts and fantasies to make inferences of evil intent and agreement.

Although the government could not make the conspiracy charge stick, the indictment had also characterized the exchange of letters itself as a crime—smuggling contraband in and out of a federal prison. The jury, evidently persuaded that the massive prosecution would not have been launched unless there was *some* reason to mete out punishment, compromised by convicting for a crime they thought was minor. But the "contraband" charges, never before used where the contraband was merely correspondence, carried potential sentences of forty years for Phil Berrigan and thirty years for Sister McAlister. As in the Chicago case, a politically motivated and preposterous conspiracy charge made it possible to secure convictions on lesser offenses, convictions which may repress the targets as effectively as conspiracy convictions would have.

Repressive abuses of conspiracy doctrines came full circle when Daniel Ellsberg and Anthony Russo were brought to trial for "conspiracy to defraud the government of its lawful function of controlling the dissemination of classified studies." Had Ellsberg acted alone, he would not have exposed himself to such a strange-sounding charge. Disseminating classified studies, except those containing atomic secrets, is not expressly prohibited by any criminal law. Nowhere in the laws is the so-called "lawful function" of controlling classified information mentioned; the power to withhold and to release information is based entirely upon the "inherent powers" of the president. The Justice Department hopes to get a criminal conviction in the case by using the old Star Chamber conspiracy theory that it is the plan and not the execution of the plan which is punishable, and that a joint plan to do something legal can be punished if the object is somehow thought to be reprehensible. If the government succeeds on this count of the Ellsberg indictment, it will, in effect, have permitted the president to enforce his orders as if they were criminal statutes. Our form of government has always required that Congress decide what shall be a crime: allowing the president to make noncriminal conduct into a crime represents a vast and novel extension of his power. The development is ominous in light of our political system's reliance on coalitions of citizens, acting together, to bring democratic pressure to bear on the authorities.

Conspiracy indictments are more effective in repressing dissent than the old technique of charging sedition. They also present far more difficulties in devising remedies. I suggest the following restraints, as a beginning:

1. Under no circumstances should the "overt acts" or the evidence of a conspiracy be comprised of protected political expression.
2. Federal law should not permit indictment or conviction on uncorroborated accomplice testimony. (Most states already forbid this.)
3. The order of proof in conspiracy trials should be made

more rigid, to conform more closely to procedures in nonconspiracy cases.

4. When the defense in a conspiracy trial alleges that the case is "political within the shadow of the First Amendment," there should be a pre-trial hearing to determine if the *Spock* rule applies.

If we are to concede the legitimacy of conspiracy charges in certain instances, it is time the law developed effective restraints against their abuse.

The recent rash of conspiracy indictments and trials is really a confession by the administration that it has nothing substantive to prove and that it must take advantage of the scatter-gun techniques of conspiracy law in order to cast a mass of prejudice against political minorities in the form of a criminal prosecution. It is also an indication that the government wants us to believe—or is run by men who want to believe—that the nature of its political problems is really conspiratorial. For its effect, it calls upon lingering memories of the state of mind of the 1950s.

15

Where Did the Grand Jury Go?
"From a Legal to a Political Engine"

Describe for the grand jury every occasion during the year
1970, when you have been in contact with, attended meetings
which were conducted by, or attended by, or been any place
when any individual spoke whom you knew to be associated
with or affiliated with Students for a Democratic Society,
the Weathermen, the Communist Party or any other organization advocating revolutionary overthrow of the United
States, describing for the grand jury when these incidents
occurred, where they occurred, who was present and what
was said by all persons there and what you did at the time
you were in these meetings, groups, associations or conversations.

—Guy Goodwin, prosecutor,
Tucson Grand Jury, 1970

Meetings, groups, associations, and conversations are the
First Amendment building blocks of our political process.
Unless the government is engaged in a bona fide presenta-
tion of evidence of criminal activity to a grand jury, it has
no business probing into such activities, frightening citi-

233

zens away from them, or punishing people who resist revealing them to hostile authorities. Yet, for the past two years, Guy Goodwin and other "special prosecutors" from the Justice Department have been asking Kafkaesque questions, like the one above, of hundreds of citizens whom they force to appear before grand juries in cities scattered around the country. Citizens who don't cooperate face jail sentences.

The function of grand juries in our system is to sit in judgment on the exercise of discretion by prosecutors; to grand jurors we entrust the sensitive job of weighing whatever evidence a prosecutor has gathered, authorizing him or forbidding him to proceed further against individuals in a public trial. For this purpose we have given grand juries extraordinary powers to compel testimony and to punish recalcitrant witnesses. But, as the questions that are being asked in today's political grand juries indicate, federal prosecutors are using these powers to elicit political intelligence data on the administration's critics. They are not attempting to persuade these grand juries to authorize indictments, and the citizens who have been subjected to these improper and pernicious interrogations are, almost without exception, accused of no crime.

Not all the victims are suspected of radical political beliefs. Nuns, scholars, journalists, and other professionals have also been ordered to testify for political purposes unrelated to the prosecution of crime. The inquisitions are intended to punish and inhibit protected expression and political activity, and to break down the private and professional relationships of academic liberals and of political activists. This must be a matter of concern for all of us, because when the search for repressive devices reaches the grand jury it alters one of the basic institutions of the criminal process. The power to compel testimony behind the closed doors of grand jury rooms belongs to whatever political faction wins control of our institutions of government. Today the targets are liberals and radicals—tomorrow's victims may be the Daughters of the American Revolution or the Veterans of Foreign Wars.

Because the grand jury operates behind a cloak of secrecy intended to protect suspects from public condemnation, its powers, and their potential for abuse, have gone largely unnoticed. But in a criminal system which relies on due process and public scrutiny to safeguard the individual's rights and the system's integrity, the grand jury has always been an anomaly. Persons ordered to appear before it have no right to be told what crime, if any, is being investigated or whether they are being questioned as potential defendants or as mere witnesses. There are no rules of evidence restricting the scope of the prosecutor's inquiry. Unprotected by the presence of either a judge or legal counsel, witnesses face interrogation that can reach into virtually any corner of their lives. The prosecutor's unfettered discretion to issue subpoenas to anyone, anywhere, whom he wishes to interrogate is easily transformed into a power to intimidate and harass advocates of disfavored ideas. Most importantly, those who are subpoenaed can be jailed if they refuse to cooperate.

The grand jury has been a sort of time-bomb ticking away in the Anglo-American legal system for over eight hundred years. Occasionally it served the people well, particularly when it investigated the very authorities who ran the system and brought the corrupt and lawless among them to trial. But the effectiveness of the "people's panel" has always depended on its independence from authority. On several occasions in the past, a grand jury, jealous of its rights, actually excluded the prosecutor from its deliberations in order to be free from the biases and self-interest of those with political power. Over the years, however, the complexion of grand juries has changed, their antiauthoritarian tradition has been diluted, and they have become dependent on and subservient to the interests of the prosecuting authority over which they were assigned to watch.

Colonial panels twice refused, as we have seen, to indict John Peter Zenger. In 1765, a Boston grand jury, elected by the radical-controlled town meeting, refused to oblige Royal officials who wanted it to indict suspected leaders of the Stamp Act Riots. In 1768, another panel refused to indict editors of the *Boston Gazette* who were accused of libeling the Royal Governor.

The Constitution, when it went into effect in 1789, made no mention of grand juries. Several state-ratifying conventions expressed uneasiness that the new Constitution left citizens to rely on the unfettered discretion of federal authorities to protect them against repressive prosecutions; the Fifth Amendment was ratified in 1791 to eliminate that danger. It provided that "No person shall be held to answer for a capital, or otherwise infamous crime," unless a grand jury authorized the charge. The hopes of those who drafted the Fifth Amendment with activist pre-Revolutionary grand juries in mind, have been largely disappointed. Thomas Jefferson charged that by 1791 the Federalists had already transformed grand juries "from a legal to a political engine" by inviting them "to become inquisitors on the freedom of speech."[1]

Although their full repressive potential was not systematically exploited until 1970, American grand juries only occasionally served the antiauthoritarian purpose for which they were prized by the architects of our legal system. Many states have abandoned the people's panels altogether; in other states and in the federal system (where the Fifth Amendment stands as a bar to abolishing it) the grand jury and its procedures have evolved in unanticipated directions.

In the 1920s and 1930s the grand jury's power to compel testimony proved useful to prosecutors trying to unravel and expose complex corruption and illegality in municipal governments, prison administration, police departments, and organized crime. People all over the nation followed Thomas E. Dewey's racket-busting grand juries in the mid-thirties. At the time that grand juries were beginning to be used in this way, they had already become reliable "rubber-stamps" for the conclusions reached by prosecutors who merely borrowed the panels' power to conduct their investigations. F. Lee Bailey voiced the sentiments of many lawyers today when he called the modern grand jury "a flock of sheep led by the prosecutor across the meadows to the finding he wants."[2] From these two developments—the grand jurors' increasing tractability and the prosecutor's increasing dependence on the panel's investigative powers—evolved today's pattern of grand jury political investigations.

During the anti-Communist hysteria of the 1950s, a stream of suspected communists was brought before grand juries where federal prosecutors pressed inquiries into witnesses' political beliefs and affiliations, and those of their acquaintances. It was rarely made clear what crime, if any, was being investigated, and indictments were not forthcoming to justify the probes. Instead, witnesses were handed summary contempt sentences and reports were issued to pillory those who had been subpoenaed and those whose names had been mentioned in the secret testimony.

The politically targeted grand juries of the McCarthy era resemble nothing in American experience so much as the antisubversive congressional investigating committees of the same period. The Nixon Administration's fondness for the people's panel is rooted in this aberration of the fifties, not in the colonial grand juries and the tradition underlying the Fifth Amendment. In the 1970s, the grand jury has almost completely replaced the moribund and powerless antisubversive committees of the earlier era.

In the fall of 1970, a grand jury in Tucson, Arizona, was investigating the purchase of some dynamite by an alleged Weatherman who had driven away in a car registered to a woman in Los Angeles. The grand jury indicted the buyer for illegal interstate transportation of the explosives. For several months FBI agents conducted heavy surveillance of the car owner's home in an attempt to confirm their suspicions that a plot was brewing, but they found nothing. Case closed. At this point, *after* the grand jury had performed its proper function, Guy Goodwin flew to Tucson to reopen the investigation. Goodwin is a member of the Special Litigation Section of the Justice Department's Internal Security Division—a division that was relatively inactive since the McCarthy period, until it was revitalized in 1970. The Special Litigation Section takes responsibility for prosecuting political cases wherever they arise in the federal system.

Goodwin obtained subpoenas requiring five young people who lived at the California address on the car's registration to come to Tucson to testify. Although he asked them a few questions about the use of the car, his questions generally had no bearing on any legitimate area of grand-jury inquiry. For instance:

> Tell the grand jury every place you went after you returned to your apartment from Cuba, every city you visited, with whom and by what means of transportation you travelled, and who you visited at all of the places you went during the times of your travels after you left your apartment in Ann Arbor, Michigan, in May of 1970.[3]

Goodwin asked these questions of persons subpoenaed as *witnesses*. They were not, and were not to be, accused of any criminal activity.

When the witnesses refused even to try to detail the travels and habits of friends and political associates, they were given full immunity from prosecution and asked again, this time under threat of imprisonment if they refused. They chose jail in early December 1970, and there they remained until the expiration of that particular grand jury's term at the end of March 1971. They were the first of a new class of political prisoners. When they were finally released, each was greeted at the cell door with another subpoena to appear before yet another grand jury. Grand juries in the federal system have a life of eighteen months. Faced with Goodwin's persistence and a potentially endless string of eighteen-month jail sentences, three agreed to testify. But it was not for their part in any plot that Goodwin wanted their testimony: he never secured indictments in this investigation. He persisted, in each case, with his fishing expedition into their personal and political affairs.

With the methods he had refined in Tucson, Goodwin looked for a new angle of inquiry into the amorphous organizations and *ad hoc* coalescings of the New Left. On March 1 a bomb had exploded in the Capitol. In late April radical organizers converged on Washington to plan and execute a Mayday protest against continuation of the war in Vietnam. On April 27, FBI agents arrested nineteen-year-old Leslie Bacon. She was held on $100,000 bail as a material witness in the Capitol bombing and she was sensationally characterized to the press as a link between the bombers and the organizers of the imminent Mayday demonstrations. By September it became clear that the characterization was false; the Court of Appeals ruled that the FBI had acted arbitrarily and illegally in arresting her without sufficient evidence.

Even before the Mayday demonstrations began, however, Leslie Bacon was flown to Seattle and subjected to Guy Goodwin's questioning. In the three days before an experienced lawyer entered the case on her behalf, she answered over two hundred and fifty questions touching on nearly every aspect of her life for the previous six months.

She was cited for contempt and jailed when she refused to cooperate any further with Goodwin's probe. His persistence in pressing for her testimony cannot be explained by a need for information on the Capitol bombing; she had none, she was the only witness called in the investigation, and no one was indicted. He wanted raw data about radicals. The "independence" of the grand jury, its freedom from rules governing the scope or relevancy of interrogation, its secrecy—all invited him to abuse it.

In her three days of cooperation, Leslie Bacon supplied Goodwin with a great deal of the intelligence data he sought. She had traveled extensively throughout the United States and attended a number of radical conferences in the previous year. Her work on the Mayday demonstrations had put her in touch with still others about whom Goodwin wanted to know more. About a purely social visit to California, Goodwin asked her where she went and what she did, who she "saw, visited with, or stayed with," the names of those with whom she traveled, and "what were the conversations in the car during the 56-hour drive?"[5]

When he questioned her about the organizers of the Mayday demonstrations, he traced her every movement, asking how she traveled from one place to the next, who was present at all times, what was said by each person, and even who slept with whom in which rooms of what house.

Some of the questions strongly suggested that the Justice Department already knew the answers, from secret wiretaps. Goodwin seemed to be probing for identical data in a form he could use in court if he ever needed it. Most important, Leslie Bacon revealed enough names and information for him to launch grand jury investigations in New

York, Washington, and Detroit, which he subsequently did.

In New York Goodwin subpoenaed seven witnesses. The questions went into familiar Goodwin territory and only one of the seven would testify. In Washington, Goodwin subpoenaed three Mayday organizers. Two were sentenced for contempt for refusing to testify, but appealed and won release on the ground that the government could not refuse to disclose whether illegal wiretapping formed the basis for the questions. Goodwin was not willing to proceed if he would have to reveal the illegal activities of the FBI, so he moved on to Detroit. There he issued subpoenas to seven others connected by Leslie Bacon to the Mayday activities. One testified, but six refused, raising again the embarrassing question of governmental wiretaps.

The basic thrust of the Nixon Administration's plan for the people's panel is clear. From Leslie Bacon's initial Seattle testimony, Goodwin launched three grand juries and questioned a score of witnesses. If no limit is imposed upon or accepted by Goodwin and his superiors, the Justice Department can smother radical political dissent in this country with a blanket of special grand juries.

The Nixon Administration has also bent the grand jury's compulsory process in an attempt to turn newsmen and scholars into investigators for the FBI's political intelligence gathering effort. In Boston, where the Justice Department conducted an investigation purportedly aimed at uncovering the facts behind publication of *The Pentagon Papers,* a stream of scholars, journalists, and writers were subpoenaed and asked to identify the sources of their information and opinions about the Vietnam war. The effect of this probe, and its likely purpose, is to dry up the flow of information, not classified information but all government information, which contradicts the Nixon view of events in that ongoing tragedy in Indochina.

The grand jury earned its popular title, "the people's panel," when it served as an instrument of popular government and as the citizen's counterforce to the otherwise unlimited discretion of prosecutors and other officers of government. It was thought to be a crucial link in our system of checks and balances. In the hands of the Nixon Administration its powers have been loaned out to the FBI. The FBI has no authority to force citizens to disclose the details of their personal lives, their political beliefs or associations, their sources of information, their travels, or their conversations with others. The FBI, which got almost anything J. Edgar Hoover asked of Congress, was denied the subpoena power he requested to assist his men in gathering just such information. Now this important safeguard has been circumvented. By coupling the unique powers of the "people's panel" to the FBI's continuing surveillance of political dissenters, an institution designed to protect us from the dangers of a police state has been used to bring us still closer to one.

Little effort is made any more to disguise the extent to which the grand jury's function has been distorted. A Brooklyn grand jury recently was investigating an attempt to break into an FBI office in Long Island. Witnesses reported that while the jurors read magazines and newspapers, the Justice Department prosecutor regularly excused himself to confer with agents of the FBI. Over and over again he returned to ask the same questions that the FBI had been asking the same individuals in its own investigation. It is becoming increasingly clear that the FBI has simply donned the august mantle of our people's panel and seized its powers. This distresses me both because the FBI has concurrently assumed the nature of a political police and because these changes obviously have the approval of the highest Justice Department officers responsible for the conduct of the grand jury proceedings.

The same subpoena power that is being used to satisfy the FBI's curiosity is being used to harass and punish the politically unpopular. It is very intimidating to be hauled before a grand jury, denied a lawyer, and asked: "Who was at this meeting?" or "What was said?" or "Give me the names of everyone you spoke to in March." On the West Coast a grand jury showered over one hundred subpoenas on individuals engaged in antiwar activities there. No indictments *ever* issued from the proceedings.

There is more to back-door punishment by grand jury inquisition than a barrage of hostile questions. It is an expensive, time-consuming, and often terrifying experience. Federal prosecutors in Pennsylvania tried to use a grand jury there to snuff out a movement to raise money and organize support for Eldridge Cleaver when the California Adult Authority revoked his parole for improper political reasons. While Cleaver was back in jail, and before an appellate court released him, a group of prominent writers and editors ran an advertisement in *The New York Times* urging people to indicate disapproval of the abusive parole decision and soliciting contributions to pay for the ad. The secretary and treasurer of this *ad hoc* committee were subpoenaed and ordered to produce before the grand jury all their records, including correspondence with persons who responded to the advertisement. The pretext was an investigation of mail fraud; but no indictment issued and the nature of the fraud was never explained.

When J. Edgar Hoover attempted to discredit and smear the Catholic antiwar movement with his sensational charges of a bombing-kidnaping plot, he was immediately challenged to substantiate his charges. Hoover's superiors in the Justice Department viewed the speculative letters exchanged between Sister McAlister and Father Philip Berrigan, and the testimony of *agent provocateur* Boyd Douglas, insufficient to support a criminal charge. They had already refused even to convene a grand jury. But Hoover's public outburst forced his titular superiors to act. The sinister picture he painted was given an easy kind of legitimacy by indictments secured from an obedient federal grand jury in Harrisburg on the basis of the same testimony and letters that the Justice Department had already deemed insufficient. Almost eighteen months passed before a trial jury in Harrisburg vindicated those the FBI Director had accused by refusing to convict the defendants of anything except the technical offense of smuggling letters in and out of prison.

The Harrisburg grand jury served two other improper purposes. Over thirty persons, all closely connected with the antiwar movement, were subpoenaed in a belated effort to dredge up evidence to corroborate the unsubstantiated, politically motivated accusations already made publicly; and Guy Goodwin appeared, moving his own peculiar probe from the New Left to the Catholic Left.

The continuing investigation by the Harrisburg panel also created the impression of an even wider conspiracy than the one pictured by Hoover. This impression was compounded when witnesses were sentenced for refusing to respond to Guy Goodwin's fishing expeditions. Their refusal was not based on fear of prosecution—the noncooperators included those to whom Goodwin had granted immunity—but on principle and on law: the questions exceeded the proper scope of a grand jury's function; the prosecutors were seeking evidence, but the panel had already issued the indictment; and the evidence used to support the subpoenas was itself the product of the government's illegal wiretapping.

Objections to the scope of the inquiry and to its post-indictment purpose are fairly easy to understand. It is worth looking more closely at the wiretapping objection, not so much because it has halted a number of these probes, but because it reveals much about the kind of games Nixon's legal troops have played with our system of laws and the criminal process in particular.

The Omnibus Crime Control and Safe Streets Act of 1968 unequivocally prohibits prosecutors from asking questions of grand jury witnesses if the questions are derived from electronic surveillance conducted in the absence of a properly issued warrant. Congress made this law, in the words of the Act, "to protect effectively the privacy of wire and oral communications, [and] to protect the integrity of court and administrative proceedings." Of course, it is a rare case when a citizen knows that his conversations have been subjected to illegal surveillance. If there were no way to force the government to admit its wrongdoing, the privacy of citizens and the integrity of the courts would be at the mercy of prosecutorial whim.

One of the first witnesses subpoenaed, granted immunity, and compelled to testify before the Harrisburg grand jury was Sister Joques Egan. She was asked questions such as "Relate all conversations you have had in the past year with Sister Elizabeth McAlister." Minutes after she refused to answer questions that she claimed were based on illegal wiretapping, she was held in contempt and jailed. On her appeal the Justice Department did not deny the charge, but argued that she had no right to raise the issue at all!

The Court of Appeals brought the Justice Department up short, freed Sister Egan from the contempt judgment, and ordered a hearing to determine whether the questions *were* based on illegal wiretapping. The judges had a simple answer to the Department of Justice's objection that it would unreasonably delay grand jury deliberations if a witness could force a hearing merely by alleging she had been the target of illegal surveillance: "We assume that the Government will attempt to conduct surveillance within statutory and constitutional limits, and that . . . the Government will produce in court the warrant by which it proceeded, and a brief inquiry will demonstrate that the warrant was properly obtained and that the surveillance did not exceed the authority."[5]

The Justice Department didn't like the Court's common sense and appealed to the Supreme Court. In a five to four decision, with all four of Nixon's appointees dissenting, the Circuit Court was upheld. But even after the Circuit Court's decision in *Egan* was handed down and fully digested, the Justice Department revealed its propensity for bad faith by responding to wiretap challenges raised by scholars at the Boston *Pentagon Papers* grand jury with a series of ambiguous statements that the Court found to be "inadequate denials." So long as the Justice Department avoids the procedure outlined by *Egan*, we lose the one opportunity the much-abused political grand juries offer for uncovering illegal conduct, but the lawbreaking in question is the Justice Department's and the Justice Department controls the grand jury game.

The record of the Justice Department's use of the grand jury in the Ellsberg case is itself a catalogue of the abuses to which the people's panel has been subjected. After publication of *The Pentagon Papers*, federal investigators' harassment of Daniel Ellsberg and his neighbors, tradesmen, and acquaintances was supplemented by subpoenas summoning his family and friends to appear before secret grand jury proceedings. A subtle form of punishment, it reached a peak when Ellsberg's former wife was persuaded to testify by the promise that her son would then not have to appear; but a few days later, Ellsberg's fifteen-year-old son was served with a subpoena at 7:30 A.M., requiring his appearance before the grand jury just two hours later.

Can the abuse of the grand jury be stopped? The Nixon Administration's choice of our grand jury system as an instrument of repression is so dramatic a reversal of its intended purpose that everyone, including the courts, has been caught quite unprepared.

It overstates the case to argue, as some do, that the grand jury has only recently been politicized, or that it served its constitutional purpose of safeguarding the people from repressively motivated prosecutions until the Nixon Administration took it over. Cases in which grand juries actually exercised their inherent power to protect political minorities were important in our tradition, but were, in fact, rather rare. Grand juries have always served the interests of whichever political element could control them. Where, as in pre-Revolutionary Massachusetts, grand jurors' sympathies were with the patriot faction, they frustrated the Crown's efforts to punish radicals. In other colonies, where they were sympathetic to Royal officialdom, they served Royal interests well. The image of the grand jury as a shield, important though it was in the minds of the framers of our Constitution, was based on a mythology of sorts. The problem is not that the grand jury has ceased to be what it never consistently was. It is that prosecutors who have repressive purposes in mind are virtually unchecked in abusing the panels' compulsory process and its rule of secrecy.

Some lawyers argue that the grand jury is so prone to abuse that it should be abolished. Why not? It has become so dependent on the prosecutor that it no longer checks his power; nor is it likely on its own to launch investigations of corruption and crime in government. Its only remaining function seems to be to aid prosecutors in the investigation of crime. Federal prosecutors argue that even if grand jury power is abused by irresponsible prosecutors in some political cases, they would be unable to enforce the laws against environmental pollution, antitrust offenses, police corruption, narcotics smuggling, securities fraud, or organized crime if they could not subpoena books and records and compel the sworn testimony of witnesses. But if it *is* necessary for prosecutors to have or to borrow these powers, why must we have the expensive and cumbersome pretense of a people's panel? Half the states have abandoned the grand jury, and England, the land of its origin, has been operating without it since 1933.

A society plagued by complex and secretive criminal activity must have *some* form of compulsory process to aid investigation. We would gain nothing by abandoning the grand jury only to be subjected to widespread searches, with or without warrants, and more spies and informers. Nor do I think we would gain much by eliminating the people's panel and simply giving the prosecutor its powers. A large number of citizens looking over his shoulder, whatever their sympathies, must be some restraint on any prosecutor tempted to abuse the power. Would we prefer a solitary FBI agent as the only audience to an interrogation conducted in the prosecutor's private office?

The most serious obstacle to abolition of the grand jury is the Fifth Amendment itself, which requires indictment by grand jury in serious cases in the federal system. I think anyone who has read this far into the book will agree that this is not a good time in our history to invite a free-for-all over whether to retain which provisions of the Bill of Rights! But if we must retain the grand jury, it is essential that we find ways to stop the process which has made it a means of harassing and intimidating political activists. The people's panel has been trivialized by being made a sub-agency of the FBI. Increasingly this undermines the integrity of the rest of the criminal process. If we cannot reverse the trend, then a serious debate about abolishing the grand jury will be in order.

MORE INDEPENDENCE FOR THE PEOPLE'S PANEL?

Can the grand jury be made less subservient to prosecutors? Our political and legal process would be well served by an institution, responsive to broad community sentiment, that actually would scrutinize prosecutorial motives and weigh the sufficiency of evidence whenever authorities move to invoke serious criminal sanctions.

Yet true grand jury independence may be unattainable today. When grand jurors were presented with simple accusations rooted in the context of their own community life, they could, and sometimes did, launch their own investigations, independently judge the substance of the charge, and view critically the motivation of the prosecutor. Today, grand juries disagree with prosecutors in less than *2 or 3 percent* of the cases presented to them. An ability to act and think for itself was possible only so long as the grand jury could operate independently from the legal expertise of the prosecutor and the technological expertise of the FBI. Today, without investigators, stenographers, clerks, and legal experts of its own, the grand jury must rely, for the basis of an informed judgment, on the resources of the very same authorities whose judgment it might otherwise control.

An abundance of resources would not change grand jury behavior unless grand jurors were disposed to assert themselves. One of the most distressing aspects of today's panels is the apathy and lack of interest exhibited by the members, who have been seen reading newspapers, playing cards, and gossiping while prosecutors abuse their special prerogatives. Many grand jurors are simply unaware of their right to call witnesses and to ask questions on their own initiative. It would help if judges gave newly empaneled grand juries a better sense of their powers and duties. Peter Weiss of the Center for Constitutional Rights has suggested that grand jurors might be shown a training film of the kind used in industry and in the military. Such a film could depict grand jurors taking an active part in deliberations and questioning, and could demonstrate dramatically the kind of prosecutorial abuses that turn the grand jurors' power to repressive ends.

In New York, a pamphlet is given to each novice grand juror, telling him of his right to call witnesses and to ask relevant questions. But prosecutors can, and they often do, simply say that the request is irrelevant. They are considered to be the experts, and their decision, whatever its merits, is not taken to any higher authority for review.

Occasionally we get a hopeful sign of change. In California recently, as three grand jurors walked out to protest a prosecutor's behavior, they were cheered by some of their fellow panelists. One of the three told reporters:

> The grand jury did not objectively and thoroughly examine the charges made. We were unable to ask the proper questions of witnesses, unable to hear all the evidence we should have and did not deliberate the way we should . . . We did not act independently of the District Attorney.[6]

This panel had just returned a conspiracy indictment in the case of the slayings of guards and inmates during the attempted prison escape by George Jackson at San Quentin. The rebellious juror said he believed some prisoners should have been indicted, but that the "conspiracy indictments are very shabby instruments of justice." The prosecutor, he felt, used the conspiracy charge for no reason except to drag into the case prisoners against whom he had no real evidence. He complained that he and other grand jurors had been forced to haggle with the prosecutor over their right to ask their own questions, and that the prosecutor had declined at first to produce for them the wig under which he claimed George Jackson hid a pistol to make his escape attempt.

This sort of rebellion against prosecutorial highhandedness is unusual. The very composition of most panels ensures the prosecutor free reign. Although selection methods vary widely from jurisdiction to jurisdiction, they tend to result in uniformly middle-aged, middle-class, white grand juries. Grand jurors are often the friends and relatives of those who run the criminal process. In this California case, the selection method for grand jurors had just been changed. Previously, panels had been picked by local judges who tended to choose persons who shared their biases and who were unlikely to find fault with the judgment of any law enforcement authority. The rebellious grand jurors were selected under a new procedure which put the selection process in the hands of various civic organizations in the county.

Reform of the composition and selection of grand juries will not be easy. There has been some movement on the federal level: the Jury Selection and Service Act of 1968 requires random selection of grand jurors from voter lists. But many state grand jury lists are still made up by sheriffs, judges, and commissioners, and the panels they choose remain grossly unrepresentative of the community. Grand jury associations composed of past and present members meet regularly in many jurisdictions: they can be expected to battle any serious reform effort through their newspapers and lobbying efforts.

I think grand jury reform might be more profitably pursued piecemeal, in the courts, as the problems arise, by forcing a reexamination of the powers and procedures that lend themselves to rather effortless prosecutorial abuse.

SCOPE OF INQUIRY

Does the First Amendment protect political activists from harassment and intimidation by abuse of the subpoena power? Is there a First Amendment as well as a Fifth

Amendment privilege not to testify? If so, what is its extent?

The Supreme Court has recently rejected a journalist's effort to derive a privilege not to testify from the First Amendment's guarantee of freedom of the press.[7] If the panels continue to be used to probe the beliefs and associations of private citizens, however, the courts may begin to develop restrictions on the scope and nature of questioning, similar to those derived from the First Amendment to restrict the witch-hunting legislative investigating committees of the 1950s. There has already been some promising movement in this direction.[8]

Prosecutors must be prevented from using the panel's compulsory process to gather evidence and to interrogate increasingly remote associates and friends of those they have already indicted, even long after indictments have been handed down. The potential for political abuse in this practice is clear from the Harrisburg Grand Jury's investigation and the Boston and Los Angeles Grand Juries' investigations in the Ellsberg case. We cannot, I fear, rely on the good faith of the Justice Department to abandon this practice. In argument before the Boston Court of Appeals on Ellsberg's motion to close down the post-indictment grand jury investigation, lawyers from the Department of Justice argued that they were investigating other crimes, not Ellsberg's. Before the Supreme Court, however, the Solicitor General of the United States argued against delay of the Boston proceedings because the prosecution was gathering information for use in the upcoming Ellsberg trial!

We also need some rules of evidence to confine prosecutor's questions to legitimate areas of grand jury concern. It is because the prosecutor can cast his net so widely that he can probe innocent movements and conversations, make dissent and political organization seem criminal, and interfere with the privacy and confidentiality of the personal and professional relationships that are vital to the nation's political life. The prosecutor should at least be required to demonstrate, to a judge, that he has ground to believe the person he wants to question is in *some* way related to actual criminal activity. A prosecutor should not be allowed to go "fishing" in First Amendment waters unless he can show there is something there he needs. I do not believe such a requirement would hamstring legitimate grand jury investigations, where a crime has been committed.

We would be far better off if prosecutors were restrained by rules requiring relevancy in questioning. They need not be as stringent as the rules of evidence at trial, but a grand jury witness today is not even permitted to ask for an explanation of the relevancy of a question. This must change, as a first step. The grand jury's job is to evaluate the sufficiency of *evidence*. Hearsay cannot be used to convict anyone, but an indictment may be based entirely on it. So long as we permit this, it will be difficult to control the scope and relevancy of a prosecutor's interrogations. An anachronism stands in the way of reform: the original grand juries in England were called upon to help the King *because* they were familiar with local incidents, hearsay, and rumors.[9] But the grand jury today is no longer a group of neighbors pooling their personal information about the possible misdeeds of others. It should be permitted to indict only upon competent evidence, and the prosecutor's inquiry should be similarly restricted. When he seeks to invoke the court's power to put recalcitrant witnesses in jail, he should show that the information he seeks would be relevant and proper.

Perhaps we should require a prosecutor to defend his exercise of the subpoena power. Whether a subpoena is issued in the name of the convening court, the prosecutor, or the grand jury itself, present practice effectively makes its issuance a matter of the prosecutor's discretion. This has been transformed into a license to harass dissenters. Courts should require a prosecutor to show something like probable cause before permitting him to issue a subpoena. A subpoenaed witness should then be entitled to force the prosecutor to show that he is actually investigating the commission of some crime. It would help if a prosecutor were required to file a memorandum privately with the court, before launching a grand jury probe, setting forth what he is seeking and what he already knows. Such a document would be invaluable in helping a judge decide whether or not the prosecutor is abusing the people's panel when a witness balks at responding to a subpoena or to a question. As in other areas of the criminal process, the prosecutor's discretionary power must be controlled or it will be used illegitimately to single out the politically unpopular for abusive and repressive treatment.

16

The Dark at the End of the Tunnel--
A Police State?

HAMLET: Denmark's a prison.
ROSENCRANTZ: Then is the world one?
HAMLET: A goodly one; in which there are many confines,
wards, and dungeons, Denmark being one o' the worst.
ROSENCRANTZ: We think not so, my lord.
HAMLET: Why then 't is none to you; for there is nothing
either good or bad, but thinking makes it so: to me it is a
prison.

—Hamlet, 2.2

PRISONERS OF FEAR

A people remains self-governing by the exercise of freedom
of expression, not by a paper guarantee of it. Self-censor-
ship can close the marketplace of ideas just as decisively as
antisedition laws or repressive law-enforcement. In fact, to
the extent that a government succeeds in making people
afraid to dissent it has substantially less need to generate
political prisoners, to sully its courts, or to twist its laws.

255

In a police state, each potential political troublemaker is a prisoner of his own fear, believing that informers and microphones lurk everywhere, that all expression deviating from the dictated norms of social and political thought will be duly noted by "Big Brother" and stored for future use.

America is obviously not now a police state. No major American official in modern times has consciously sought to build a police state on these shores. It is just as obvious, however, that police state tactics are on the increase. Many of the incursions into our political liberties complained of today were hailed, during the Kennedy and Johnson Administrations, as answers to knotty law-enforcement problems. More extensive wiretapping was the answer to our growing organized crime and narcotics problems; blanket surveillance of dissidents became our early-warning system for the explosive ghettos. Officials are too often absorbed in midsummer dreams of "law and order" to be properly concerned about the winters of democracy that lie ahead. Much of what the Nixon Administration has done suggests that officials of our government are now willing to knock down the walls of our constitutional shelter, so laboriously put together brick by brick over the years. The effect may well be to obviate the need for political prisoners in a society at war with itself, by using the paraphernalia of the criminal process to create prisoners-at-large instead.

In a police state, the secret police use informers to break down the integrity of personal relationships; they use electronic surveillance to destroy the sense of privacy and the elbowroom that fosters spontaneous grass-roots political interaction. A police state attempts to deal with evil thinking by keeping alive in each man's thoughts the belief that his slightest indiscretion will find its way into a dossier from which it can be retrieved and used against him, formally or informally, should he incur the displeasure of political authorities.

Of course no society has the resources to have *every* citizen followed, listened to, photographed, and informed upon *all* the time. The critical ingredient of a police state system is paranoia, and the key to paranoia is secrecy. A certain amount of overt political surveillance will go a long way toward inducing a general belief that Big Brother is watching; a shroud of secrecy over the actual scope and nature of the police intelligence operation will prevent any particular individual from knowing whether his own telephone conversations are being typed up and filed, whether the man with the camera is a newspaper reporter or a cop, whether the friendly hippie offering to help plan a demonstration is a political ally or a political policeman. The point is that if you believe you are being watched, you will behave accordingly; the dossiers generated by a police state apparatus may be few, inaccurate, and incomplete, but the process of gathering them can crush dissent.

"AN FBI AGENT BEHIND EVERY MAILBOX"

In July 1970, there were widespread newspaper reports that federal agents were examining the circulation records of libraries to find out who was reading what they described as "militant" or "subversive" material.[1] If people come to believe that the government is monitoring their reading habits, they will, almost unconsciously, curb their intellectual curiosity by avoiding reading matter which might displease the government. This particular attempt at thought control was apparently halted after librarians in several cities publicly complained that the investigators threatened to subpoena their files if they did not turn them over voluntarily. Yet someone in the administration obviously thought 1984 was already at hand. Is it? Does America have a political police?

On August 17, 1970, a group with little in common but

their separate friendships with Father Daniel Berrigan came together for dinner in Weston, Connecticut, to talk about Berrigan's arrest six days earlier. They toyed with and discarded the idea of making a "citizen's arrest" of Henry Kissinger, a man as important to the Nixon Administration as Berrigan had been to the antiwar movement. Sister Elizabeth McAlister brought the idea up again a few days later in a letter to Daniel's brother: could the antiwar movement be reinvigorated by a nonviolent kidnaping of Kissinger?

Father Philip Berrigan was in Lewisburg penitentiary and the mail from Sister Elizabeth was smuggled to him by Boyd Douglas, a fellow prisoner with extensive extramural privileges. Douglas worked for the FBI. A few days later, Douglas smuggled out Philip's reply: the scenario was "too grandiose," wrote the priest. But in "trying to weave elements of modesty into it" Berrigan kept the idea alive. After xeroxing Berrigan's letter, and before sending it on to Sister Elizabeth, Douglas added his own note. Whatever Philip's reservations about the "scenario," Douglas was "delighted" about the "plan" and volunteered his services. Douglas's idea of "services" did not run along nonviolent lines. He was, after all, serving time at Lewisburg for assaulting an FBI agent with a pistol, among other things. It would, he wrote to the nun, be necessary to use a gun; he preferred a real gun to a fake; and he could furnish an untraceable weapon (presumably from the FBI's armory).

Sister Elizabeth recalls that, the minute she read Douglas's "pragmatic" letter, the kidnaping fantasy "was a closed book." Reading the note "was like holding something hot and horrible. I could hardly even bear to look at it." Douglas never got the opportunity to plant that gun, but J. Edgar Hoover had been stung by Daniel Berrigan's uncanny ability to evade platoons of his special agents for months. In an attempt to prove he had been dealing with a dangerous cabal, the FBI director made the extraordinary charge before a Senate subcommittee that the Berrigans were engaged in an ongoing and deadly serious "conspiracy to kidnap a top government official." The machinery was set in motion for a show trial of the "Harrisburg Seven."[2]

Whenever a political police expands a political surveillance program, a network of undercover informers expands with it. Almost inevitably some informers attempt to provoke the sort of conduct among the politically alienated which seems to justify their own role. When government attempts to brand dissenters as criminals and civil disobedients as anarchists, informers are sorely tempted to place in the hands of the individuals who have been targeted for surveillance the instruments of violence which make it possible for them to realize their revolutionary fantasies. Police states justify this conduct as "preventive." If the government has a hand in creating such an opportunity for criminal violence, they argue, the police can be on hand to make the arrest before the violence is committed. In recent years, undercover political informers in America have given angry citizens grenades, planned robberies and bombings, trained militants in handling firearms and explosives, thrown molotov cocktails, and precipitated attacks on police and national guardsmen at demonstrations—attacks which served to justify repressive crackdowns and arrests of the others in the resulting melee.[3]

Although it is impossible to know to what extent provocation by the political police forces in this country is the result of conscious policy decision, and to what extent it is the undesired excess inevitably accompanying rapid expansion of undercover surveillance operations, there are other political police practices quite clearly designed to repress dissent without resorting to the more visible methods of political trials and political imprisonment.

In August 1971, two hundred people attended a fund raising in Wellfleet, Massachusetts, for the Harrisburg Seven Defense Fund. Afterward, FBI agents began to interrogate a number of the guests. One reported that when he declined to speak with the agents, they threatened to call him before a grand jury. Hoover defended the investigation by claiming that the sole purpose was to determine whether Daniel Ellsberg had made any reference to *The Pentagon Papers* in his address to the gathering. But another of the guests said he was asked to give the FBI information on who was present, and what he knew about his host. He later recalled the psychological intimidation which is the consequence, probably the intended consequence, of all such "investigations": "The request that I disclose names of friends and acquaintances that were present was shocking and caused me to wonder about who 'informed' on me . . . it leaves me with just a little less freedom [than] I thought I had under the Constitution."[4]

When, in April 1971, the majority leader of the House of Representatives accused the FBI of tapping his telephone, J. Edgar Hoover and Attorney General John Mitchell were quick to deny the charge. Mitchell said the accusation was a new type of paranoia: "Tappanoia."

Mitchell's tone was glib, but in a widely read essay, "America Is Not a Repressive Society," Lewis Powell, formerly head of the American Bar Association and now a Supreme Court Justice, argued that the charge of repression in America is "standard leftist propaganda" and "a conspiracy to confuse the public." He labeled it "a cover for leftist-inspired violence . . . a propaganda line designed to undermine confidence in our free institutions, to brainwash the youth and ultimately to overthrow our democratic system." According to Powell, "there are only a few hundred wiretaps annually, and these are directed against people who seek to subvert our democratic form of government. Law abiding citizens have nothing to fear."[5]

I wonder. When I was in the United States Senate, a senate telephone employee reported a recent tap on my line. I had, it is true, strenuously opposed the war and voiced concern about the cavalier treatment given to privacy and civil liberties under the Nixon Administration. Perhaps this branded me as one seeking "to subvert our democratic form of government," one whose privacy must, in the Attorney General's view, give way to the Administration's "right of self-defense." In the fall of 1971, a conservative senator called me from his home, only to say, "You know I can't *talk* on this phone." He asked me to stop in to see him the next time I was in Washington. In a system which depends on a maximum openness of discussion, flow of information, and exchange of ideas, there is something terribly amiss when even the current administration's friends are afraid to express their reservations in private.

As it turned out, the chief source of "tappanoia" was not subversive leftists, but the FBI itself. On the night of March 8, 1971, more than one thousand documents were pilfered from the Bureau's office in Media, Pennsylvania, by the "Committee to Investigate the FBI." The bootlegged Media documents were embarrassing. They suggested that roughly 40 percent of the FBI's activity is political—aggressive surveillance of innocuous civil rights and antiwar groups.

As the Media documents trickled out through the press, it became obvious that the FBI was not just keeping tabs on persons suspected of committing crimes, or on those who could conceivably be thought to be threats to national security. One file was a lifetime profile of an antiwar activist who had committed no offense beyond a breach of the peace for which he had been fined $5 in 1954. The special agents of the FBI and the informers in their employ are policing all those whose conduct or political ideas are the least bit unorthodox.

But by far the most stunning find in the Media documents was a memorandum informing all agents that at a conference on the "New Left," held at FBI headquarters in September 1970, "there was a pretty general consensus [*sic*] that more interviews with these subjects and hangers-on are in order for plenty of reasons, chief of which are it will enhance the paranoia endemic in these circles and will further serve to get the point across there is an FBI agent behind every mailbox."[6] Paranoia is not a legitimate aim of a police force in a democratic society; it is the tool of social and political control favored by police states.

The growing power of political police forces on the federal and local level, their stimulation of tappanoia, their use of informers and wiretapping to build dossiers, and the inevitable appearance of *agents provacateurs* are more than disquieting. They are very real threats to our liberty. Though we see no signs of jackboot gestapo, concentration camps, torture, and the like, we should remember that a police state is characterized by the repressive purposes and techniques of its political police, not by their brutality. Historically, police states run the gamut from paternalistic to genocidal.[7]

A large number of Americans, both in the general populace and at the highest levels of government, are behaving as if we already had a police state in America. What we are witnessing is the development of a style of repression that is new to us, the establishment in this country of conditions —technological, psychological, and legal—making government by police state possible through an apparatus of total surveillance that seldom would need the reenforcement of a political trial.

THE PATHWAY TO A DOSSIER DICTATORSHIP

The greatest dangers to liberty lurk in the insidious en-
croachments by men of zeal, well-meaning, but without understanding.

—Supreme Court Justice Louis
Brandeis

The exponential growth of privacy-invading technology, a
nonpolitical "scientific" development, is whittling away
our privacy so rapidly that soon we may not be able to
prevent our government, employers, and others who pass
judgment upon us from knowing virtually everything
about us from the moment of birth to the date, amount,
purpose, and recipient of our last check. In this computer
age, virtually everywhere we go we leave electronic tracks
on somebody's computer. Not only computer technology,
but microfilm, laser beams, miniaturized photographic and
electronic recording-devices, and other innovations have
been adopted by a wide variety of public and private snoop-
ers, for good ends and for bad, to satisfy an insatiable appe-
tite for *potentially* useful information.

In the fall-out of the war in Vietnam, previously unima-
gined technological wonders are bringing us potentially
much closer to 1984 than the dozen years actually interven-
ing. Engineers are modifying the PPS-14 foliage-penetra-
tion surveillance radar to enable domestic police forces to
see through brick and cinderblock walls. The police can
already see in the dark, thanks to night vision devices also
developed for Vietnam.[8]

Computers can store an infinite number of informational
"bits" and can retrieve them at the rate of a few nanosec-
onds (billionths of a second) per bit. Computers can also
communicate directly with each other so that data can flow
in and out of separate systems. A properly designed computer program enables an investigator to push a button and

264 / *Political Prisoners in America*

get an instantaneous print-out presenting in various forms all the accessible information stored on an individual. Information and surveillance technologies have expanded far more rapidly than our ability to control them, and the resulting web of imperishable, instantaneously retrievable, noncontextual, often inaccurate, and often derogatory data lends itself to police state abuses.

One of the witnesses before Senator Sam Ervin's Subcommittee on Constitutional Rights made the chilling point that America is "on the pathway toward a dossier dictatorship." I think it is clear enough that we have not yet approached the end of that path. We are far from it. A police state does not rise from information and technology alone, but from the decision of those with the power to do so to put them to that purpose.

The promise of such power has not, however, been overlooked by the existing political intelligence network in this country. The amalgam of loosely coordinated military, federal, state, and municipal agencies with responsibility for law-enforcement, counterintelligence, and internal security has become a political surveillance network. The ordinary American will feel understandably inhibited if he comes to believe that by attending a meeting, by signing a petition, by receiving political literature, or by engaging in public and even private political discussion he becomes a "person of interest," a potential troublemaker, in the files of those monitoring the political life of the country.

There is ample evidence that this is happening. The police departments of most major cities have political units or "Red Squads"; some of them have been engaged in surveillance of lawful political activity since the Red Scare. Today they routinely photograph every "controversial" protest, identify the participants, open dossiers, and exchange the contents with other agencies interested in keeping tabs on the politically active.

Peaceful, moderate, lawful organizations have become intelligence targets on the theory that because of their dissent they are, or might become, dominated by communists or some other conspiratorial subversives more frightening still because unnamed. The domestic political intelligence community has proved unusually resistant to attempts to bring it within the constitutional framework. Investigation is not prosecution, surveillance is not punishment; the protections developed over two centuries of effort to bring the urge to repress dissent within constitutional control seem useless against this development. A powerful political argument also hampers attempts to restrict it. Frank Donner, a longtime student of police intelligence operations and the director of the ACLU Surveillance Project summed it up: "Few want to shackle the police in this hunt for wrongdoers, especially those who threaten the safety of the Republic. Why should one question a 'mere' investigation, even if tons of constitutional ore may have to be excavated in order to find a single subversive nugget?"[9]

"INHERENT POWER"

In January 1970, Christopher Pyle, an attorney and a former captain in the U.S. Army's intelligence branch, publicly accused the army of conducting a massive spying operation directed against civilians. Ever since World War II, the armed forces have played a part, albeit a minor one, in the domestic political intelligence network. But after the Newark and Detroit riots in 1967, he reported, the army deployed over one thousand military intelligence agents throughout the country in a full-fledged counterespionage effort to monitor all politically active persons who, by expressing dissatisfaction with administration policy and with the status quo, seemed to be potential troublemakers.

The intelligence net was thrown over critics and protesters of every stripe, newspaper reporters, university professors, businessmen, and local, state, and federal officials. For almost twenty months, Senator Ervin's Subcommittee on Constitutional Rights tried to discover the extent and basis of the army's covert monitoring and infiltration of civilian politics, to discover what was contained in the military intelligence dossiers, and to bring the program to a stop.

The Defense Department declassified and gave to the Subcommittee an army directive of May 1968, which ordered U.S.-based intelligence units to provide all information they could on the "well-springs of violence and the heart and nerve causes of chaos." But the Defense Department did not declassify and produce for the Subcommittee the superseding directive dated April 1969, after the Nixon Administration took over the helm of government. This document devoted three pages to a "partial list of organizations . . . of intelligence interest." The list covered the political spectrum from the American Nazi Party to the Black Panthers; but it also included the National Association for the Advancement of Colored People, the pacifist American Friends Service Committee, the American Civil Liberties Union, and the Americans for Democratic Action.

I was told that seven army agents kept me under surveillance while I, as a member of the United States Senate, was working quite openly to bring the Vietnam war to an end. I was particularly interested in a report which I understand was filed with Army Intelligence on what I supposedly said in a speech to the National Student Association in August of 1970 at St. Paul, Minnesota. As it happened, a last minute Senate vote forced me to cancel that speech. Perhaps we will be saved from repression by the ineptitude of the repressors, for the agent seems to have filed his report on the basis of the advance press release and gone to a bar for a few beers.

Not everyone who was caught up in the intelligence net, however, was so lucky. At a time when the number of Americans opposing the Vietnam war was approaching a majority, army intelligence agents were instructed to gather "full identifying data on individuals/groups who are engaged in . . . anti-war activities." There is simply no acceptable rationale for the sweep of this directive. Agents were instructed to gather data on "all persons involved or expected to be involved in protest activities."[10]

Senator Ervin asked the administration "whether the constitutional rights of individuals were violated by government surveillance in cases where there was not probable cause to believe that a particular individual had committed a crime." William Rehnquist was, at the time, Assistant Attorney General in the Office of General Counsel. As the lawyer for the president's lawyer, he told the Subcommittee that the Constitution (which directs the president to "take care that the Laws be faithfully executed") empowers him to prevent violation of law by maintaining surveillance of those who, in his opinion, *might* violate it.

It was an extraordinary claim of presidential power. It was the administration's view, Rehnquist went on to say, that even when it collects intelligence data which does *not* relate to this broad preventive purpose, and even when it disseminates derogatory data about individuals for wholly other purposes, it is not violating anyone's Constitutional rights. The administration would, he said, "vigorously oppose" any legislative or judicial supervision of its surveillance of American citizens.[11]

When Ervin was unable to get satisfactory information about military snooping or satisfactory assurances that the political data already gathered would be destroyed, he joined the ACLU in an attempt to bring the army to trial. They petitioned the court to rule on the constitutionality of the surveillance and to oversee destruction of the microfilm libraries, the blacklists, the indices, and the computer punch-cards and tapes in which so much derogatory information had been stored. The Supreme Court dismissed the suit by a vote of five to four—and William Rehnquist, by then an Associate Justice on the high court, cast the deciding vote.[12]

A great deal of what little information Ervin's Subcommittee did get to see remains classified. But Ervin reported that a print-out from the army's central computers might list as a "subversive" a citizen who had done no more than make an obscene remark about President Nixon, or subscribe to a newspaper that some soldier considered insufficiently patriotic. Lawrence Baskir, the Subcommittee's chief counsel, says a great deal of it concerns the "psychological aspects of people, and personal relationship and personal finances." Ex-intelligence officers appearing before the Subcommittee testified that much of the data was "unsubstantiated rumor" and "unusable misinformation" from "unreliable sources." But the army had simply transferred the hundreds of thousands of "bits" of raw material from notebooks, cameras, and tape recorders into the memory banks of computers at Fort Holabird, Maryland.

The best way to get rid of the misleading trivia and venomous mendacity that fills such "intelligence" files is to destroy them. But, as Senator Ervin was moved to remark when he heard some of the Keystone Kop stories from ex-military intelligence agents, "military intelligence is a contradiction of terms."

Apparently the army could not purge from its computers the derogatory data collected during four years of domestic spying. Lawrence Baskir reported that when information reached the Army Intelligence Command's headquarters at Fort Holabird, it merged with the computerized information system already carrying almost eight million dossiers compiled in the process of investigating people for security clearances. This computer now provides an instantaneous print-out of the rumors, gossip, and speculations about countless Americans whose perfectly lawful political activities were of "intelligence interest" to the military from 1967 to 1971, and perhaps beyond. This alone casts thousands of Americans as "security risks" and discolors their employment prospects. Not only was the data absorbed into the Investigative Records Repository, but, according to Baskir, once it got into the system, it "flowed like water, going everywhere and anywhere."

AN IDEOLOGICAL DICK TRACY

By the time Rehnquist testified about the Nixon Administration's view of its inherent power, full responsibility for the intelligence gathering system had been transferred to the Internal Security Division of the Justice Department. The same sort of data is now collected by the FBI and is fed into the central computer of the Justice Department's Interdivisional Intelligence Unit (IDIU)—an information storage and retrieval system more sophisticated than those at Fort Holabird and Fort Monroe. The FBI has been, for decades, the central and indispensable piece in the domestic political intelligence community. The FBI's intelligence techniques and the political philosophy of its late Director, J. Edgar Hoover, set the standard for all the others.

As the FBI is essentially a *secret* operation, it has always been particularly difficult, even for an attorney general, to study its workings. Hoover manipulated the surface of things so well for so many years that the American people were struck by a virtually flawless image of the FBI. Few men have been so highly regarded and few institutions have been so much admired as the Director and his FBI. Only after a series of unsquelchable embarrassments in the last few years of his life, particularly the revelations of the Media files and the fantastic charge that the Berrigans were about to become kidnapers, did his critics assemble enough negative information and interpretive material to begin to right the balance. By and large, I think it important to take the legend apart, if only to see how best to disassemble the elements of his "fiefdom" which smacked of the police state.

Hoover was a dedicated man, and an incorruptible one. His judgment was sterling in some areas, at least some of the time. One of my duties as an assistant in the office of the Deputy Attorney General in 1953 and 1954 was to get Hoover's views on proposals for new federal legislation. He consistently fought any expansion of federal criminal laws into areas traditionally handled by state and local police. He sincerely believed that it would be dangerous for the FBI to go around enforcing rules in the everyday lives of citizens. In that sense, he did not want the FBI to be a national police force, and he said so.

But Hoover had no qualms about the FBI's ever-expanding role as a national investigative and intelligence-gathering agency. He pursued a policy based on the obverse of the basic premise of our political system: he believed the marketplace of ideas was where bad ideas drive out the good. He consistently identified "national security" with the preservation of traditional political and social ideas; dissent was disloyalty. Anyone actively seeking change was a potential "subversive."

He thought preventive surveillance by the FBI was the nation's main defense against subversion, and that criticism of him or of his Bureau were attempts to undermine

America's defense. Another of the Director's theories, one reminiscent of the paternalistic thinking that gave rise to European police states, was that Americans, if left to themselves, were liable to be seduced or deceived by purveyors of false ideas. He assumed that any dissenting group would follow the lead of its most extreme members, that dangerous ideas were contagious, and that therefore anyone who associated with "subversives" should also be watched for signs of such diseased thinking. Surveillance of "subversives" was an endless chain potentially leading to every American's closet. It was his desire to protect us from evil thinking that led to most of Hoover's excesses.

There is a serious question, however, whether the FBI has authority to engage in political intelligence activity at all. Congress has never granted it such powers as it exercises. In 1919, Hoover was placed at the head of the newly created General Intelligence Division in the Justice Department and assigned the job of focusing on "alien agitators." The Palmer Raids on the night of January 2, 1920, were the result. With the raids fresh in his mind, Attorney General Harlan Stone reorganized the Bureau of Investigation in 1924. He spoke directly to the point:

> The Bureau of Investigation is not concerned with political or other opinions of individuals. It is concerned only with . . . such conduct as is forbidden by the laws of the United States. When a police system passes beyond these limits, it is dangerous to the proper administration of justice and to human liberty, which it should be our first concern to cherish.[13]

Hoover conceded at the time that the reorganization was intended to strip the FBI of all but a law-enforcement function. "The activities of Communists and other ultra-radicals have not up to the present time constituted a violation of the Federal statutes," he said, "and consequently, the Department of Justice, theoretically, has no right to investigate."[14]

Hoover's latter-day reputation as a sort of ideological Dick Tracy, and the enormous scope of the FBI's current political surveillance activity can be traced to an Executive Order issued by President Roosevelt on September 9, 1939. Nazi and Japanese spies were already operating in this country, and the president called on Hoover's FBI to investigate foreign espionage and sabotage. In dangerous and perhaps inadvertently broad language, he authorized the Bureau to investigate "subversive activities" in general.

With Germany's armies invading Poland and legitimate fears of a "Fifth Column" gripping the country, little attention was focused on whether the president actually had an "inherent power" to employ the national police in activities not mandated by criminal statute. At any rate, Hoover quickly responded by setting up a General Intelligence Division to take over where he had left off after the debacle of the Palmer Raids.

Hoover always claimed that the FBI's sole function in the political intelligence area was to collect information and pass it on to appropriate authorities. But there is no control over what the FBI is to collect, whom it is to watch, what is "relevant" and what is "reliable" information, and to whom it is to be disseminated. Given the potential for abusing these files Hoover was generally discreet in their dissemination. He was known, however, to entertain presidents, attorneys general, friendly congressmen and others with material from the FBI files. Much of the material is the unreliable product of ambitious agents or avaricious informers paid to find or fabricate the kind of intelligence data that seems to confirm Hoover's conspiratorial fantasies.

When I was in the Justice Department in 1953 and 1954,

I studied FBI reports on nominees for federal judgeships, U.S. attorneys, and federal marshals. The reports were full of the most damaging and unreliable kind of roughage. Agents had apparently conducted interviews with anyone they could find with a gripe against the nominees, and had written up the worst kind of rumors about them. There was often no effort made to check out derogatory items; in fact, the same report would contain conflicting derogatory information. It was all thrown together and the cumulative effect of some of these dossiers was devastating.

After reading the reports, it was my job to take them over to "Wild" Bill Langer, Chairman of the Senate Judiciary Committee. At one point Langer tried to pressure the administration to give a federal judgeship to a professionally unqualified friend of his; he kept saying there were "problems" raised by the FBI reports on a series of Eisenhower's appointees. I knew there were no real problems, but Langer was the only member of the Committee cleared to read the gossip. To the credit of Attorney General Brownell, he refused to cave in to Langer's blackmail. Nonetheless, the incident showed me how easily the very existence of a secret file on a man can damage his reputation.

He who seeks shall find, and Hoover sought hard to prove that every canker in the body politic was yet another eruption of the communist conspiracy on which he was so expert. In 1956, Hoover reported to the Cabinet that the Communist Party was planning to force Eisenhower "to take a stand on civil rights legislation," and to "embarrass the Administration and Dixiecrats who have supported it." To "illustrate the potency" of this subversion in Chicago, he cited only a leaflet calling on Eisenhower to dismiss the Attorney General for failing to bring to trial those who lynched Emmet Till, and a follow-up campaign to get the president and the Senate to act. "Mayor Richard J. Daley of Chicago . . . wired the President urging intervention,"

Hoover reported. "I hasten to say that Mayor Daley is not a Communist, but pressures engineered by the Communists were brought to bear upon him."[15]

The Bureau has been gathering what it calls "Racial Intelligence" for a long time. Like FBI surveillance of "subversives," its Racial Intelligence operation is "preventive," grounded on "inherent" powers of the Executive Branch, and only incidently serving any law-enforcement purposes. The "Racial Intelligence" has never been very good, perhaps partly because of the purity of the special agents' blood lines. When the Justice Department was finally persuaded to release FBI minority employment figures in 1971, it could report only fifty-one blacks among the special agents—less than ½ of 1 percent.

Years of devotion to the hunt for a communist conspiracy at the root of black unrest, and the dearth of blacks in its ranks of special agents, left the FBI unprepared for the spontaneous ghetto uprisings of the late 1960s. According to Jack Shaw, a special agent drummed out of the FBI's New York office for criticising the Director, his office responded to trouble in Harlem by dispatching carloads of conspicuously white sleuths equipped with nothing but mug shots taken of unidentified blacks at rallies.[16]

Hoover was not the only one responsible for the saturation surveillance that followed. After the 1967 Newark and Detroit uprisings, Attorney General Ramsey Clark called on the Bureau to supply whatever information would help predict and prevent riots. As no one knew then or knows now what really triggers such limitless mass rage, the ghetto intelligence assignment was impossibly broad. It was Clark, too, who set up the computerized IDIU in the Justice Department to turn into readily retrievable form the information flooding in on individual ghetto-dwellers, their organizations, attitudes, beliefs, and plans.

In documents stolen from the FBI's Media office, all

agents were instructed to initiate in "ghetto type areas" a "wide-spread grass-roots network of sources" to keep tabs on "attitudes and tensions" and on "individual troublemakers and rabble rousers." Ex-GI's, cab drivers, salesmen, and other reliable types were suggested as potential recruits. The informants were asked to identify "black extremist militants" and to "visit Afro-American type bookstores" and to "identify the owners, operators, and clientele of such stores" where "militant extremist literature is available." Files were to be opened on all individuals and organizations mentioned by the informers. Still hoping for that missing link, the Bureau wanted informers to "report on all indications of efforts by foreign powers to take over the Negro militant movement."[17]

The heart of the problem is that interpretation of such terms as "militant" or "extremist" was left to individual agents. In any political intelligence-gathering operation, there is a premium put on material seeming to document the notions of those who control it.

Robert Wall was a special agent for five years until April 1970. At one point he was assigned to investigate a children's school sponsored by a number of ghetto organizations including the Black Panthers. The Vice-President of the United States had already labeled the Panthers, *all* Panthers, a "completely irresponsible, anarchistic group of criminals." When Wall's supervisor began calling the ghetto school a "guerilla warfare training center," Wall put six informers on the payroll for six months to keep him abreast of developments. He finally reported back to his boss that the subversive institution was "nothing but a school"; but he was simply taken off the job and another special agent was assigned to conduct a whole new six-month probe.

The Bureau's Racial and Racial–Ghetto Intelligence assignments have expanded alongside a growing program aimed at the "New Left." The New Left, whatever else it is, is not a structured organization. Attempts to cast the amorphous "youth movement" as a conspiracy on the Old Left model have failed, notably in the Chicago Eight conspiracy trial. The difficulty this gives our political police is suggested by a Media document containing an informer's report that at a women's liberation meeting "where there appeared to be approximately eight females participating," one of the women "kept going in and out of the meeting to attend her small child who was in the kitchen." Observing "other rather hippie-type individuals" coming and going from the upper floors, the informer concluded that "it would appear that the three-story house is being operated as a commune." Copies of this report were routed to nine separate files, including a new one for the commune and an existing one on the women's liberation movement.

Evidently on the basis of such data, filtered through the IDIU computer at the Justice Department, an Assistant Director of the FBI reported in February 1970 that the New Left is "made up of over 200 committees, organizations and groups consisting of 15,000 to 20,000 activists, plus over 300,000 general supporters."[18]

The huge antiwar protest march on the White House in November 1969 was carefully planned in the best American traditions of free speech and assembly, and it provides a case study of the interference of our political police with the First Amendment activities of the public. Ex-agent Wall reports that his Washington, D.C., FBI intelligence squad

> ... addressed a letter to the leaders of the National Mobilization Committee which said that the blacks of Washington, D.C., would not support the upcoming rally unless a $20,000 "security bond" was paid to a black organization. ... At the same time we instructed some informants we had placed in

the black organization to suggest the idea of a security bond informally to [their] leaders.

The letter we composed was approved by the Bureau's counterintelligence desk and was signed with the forged signature of the leader of the black group.

Later, through informants, we learned that the letter had caused a great deal of confusion and had a significant effect on planning for the march.

"Preventive surveillance" was particularly open. Youngsters entering the offices of the New Mobilization Committee Against the War in Vietnam were stopped by agents and asked "Will you work for us?" No one could doubt that the whole operation was being watched. Robert Wall reports that some of his fellow-agents tried to confuse demonstrators by handing out leaflets with misleading information about the time and place of the march.[19]

Worse, in my estimation, was the way the Justice Department used the FBI and the IDIU files. On the basis of a secret memorandum, the Justice Department threatened to deny parade permits and issued chilling predictions of the worst violence in the history of the nation's capital. The memorandum was prepared by someone in the Internal Security Division who had gathered together an astonishing mix of outdated and largely irrelevant information and misinformation concerning the members of the New Mobe's Steering Committee.

Although indications of potential violence abounded in Washington in early November 1969, the secret memorandum's predictions of violence hung primarily on a thread tied to David Dellinger's trips to Hanoi in 1966 and 1967. It traced alleged contacts between other Steering Committee members and communists and suspected communists. To the memo's author, the "pro-revolutionary proclivity" indicated by this data gave the march an "extremely high" potential for "violence with resulting personal injuries and possible deaths." The unblinking identification of "communist" and "violent" seems anachronistic enough, but some of the crucial data was simply false, and the effect of the memo was to mislead the officers of our government as to the true nature of the danger.[20]

The ironic result of this "intelligence" operation was to increase the likelihood of violence. A provocative oversupply of troops was summoned to protect the city; the procedural delays frustrated people already very angry at their government on the substantive issue of the war; and the predictions of violence scared away from the march some of the more peaceably inclined while attracting to it the thrill-seekers who were the ones, all along, threatening to turn a political event of immense importance into a brawl.

"NONE OF YOU GUYS ARE GOING TO BELIEVE THIS, BUT . . . "

Of course, neither the mushrooming surveillance technology nor the FBI's aggressive intelligence gathering makes America a police state. The outcome depends on what the highest officials of the Executive Branch of our government choose to do with the potential for political control inherent in the apparatus. If they continue to yield to the urge to repress dissent, if they continue to reach for and exercise the "inherent powers" to suspend the Constitution whenever their own paranoia gets the better of them, then the possibility of a police state must be considered quite seriously.

In his eulogy at J. Edgar Hoover's funeral, President Nixon praised the late FBI Director "not only as the director of an institution, but as an institution in his own right." Many of Hoover's critics agree, so closely identified with its Director had the Bureau become. Hoover was a charis-

matic cop with a good nose for a headline, but the institution he bequeathed to America is a formidable institution
indeed: a secret political police operating nationwide.

Hoover's death was a unique opportunity to expose to
public and congressional scrutiny the practices of an
agency that has been operating for sixty-four years free
of democratic controls, the only governmental agency
never subjected to the kind of periodic public accounting where performance is measured against the norms
of the Constitution and the needs of our people. It was a
chance to reverse the practice of eight presidents, sixteen attorneys general, and thirty-two congresses which
had given the Bureau enormous power and little direction or control.

In 1968, Congress gave the Senate an advise-and-consent
power over the appointment of Hoover's successor. Senate
subcommittee hearings on a nominee might have been the
occasion for the first high-level review in our history of the
Bureau's effectiveness (in the neglected organized crime,
civil rights, and police brutality areas of law enforcement,
for instance); we might have determined the reliability of
the crime statistics the FBI uses to buttress its claims for
more funds and more power; questioning could have
focused on the actual practices that underlie the phoney
wiretap and bugging statistics which the Bureau uses to
reassure Congress that it exercises its extraordinary powers
with restraint. A congressional hearing would have been
an ideal forum to reevaluate the Bureau's domination of
local and state police policy across the country, its gathering of intelligence and building of dossiers beyond legitimate law-enforcement needs, its use of informers and its
policy toward provocation by undercover agents, and its
dissemination of derogatory and often inaccurate data to
public and private agencies. In short, America might have
had a chance at last to determine the propriety of a secret

police network which monitors and attempts to control our political life.

President Nixon dashed these hopes when he appointed a long-time personal and political friend, L. Patrick Gray III, as "acting director." Although Gray lacks any criminal law-enforcement experience, and although presidents, including Nixon, have often been surprised by the results when they appoint intelligent men to high office with the expectation of continued closeness in point of view, there are some signs already that Gray's managerial expertise is matched by a public relations genius as inspired as Hoover's.

In one of Gray's first attempts to increase FBI exposure to the public ("opening the window a little," as he called it), he told reporters: "None of you guys are going to believe it, but there are no dossiers or secret files. There are just general files . . . "

Now virtually *all* of the FBI's records are secret, by *law*. And the millions of investigative reports and intelligence summaries compiled over the years have certainly not been lost nor destroyed. It would run incredibly against the nature of *any* governmental agency, particularly a police agency, to discard potentially useful information. The FBI may not keep dossiers on every individual who comes to its attention; but all names in its intelligence reports are indexed and given reference numbers so that, by using carefully compiled and overlapping indices, the reports can be thoroughly combed whenever information on a particular individual is desired.

Perhaps Gray felt his statement was justified because the modern FBI doesn't use secret *files*. All the intelligence data and derogatory information received at Bureau headquarters in Washington can be conveniently stored on magnetic computer tape. Americans are accustomed to relying on the inefficiency of bureaucracies as one of the bulwarks of freedom. The computer print-out makes it possible for the FBI actually to *know* what is in its files. Within minutes an agent sitting at a simple computer console can have a report on the name, address, fingerprints, arrests, habits, attitudes, friends, and gossip about any one of millions of citizens who have done no more than speak out on a public issue, or attend a political meeting, or associate with those who have dared to do so. There is something intolerably cynical about telling the American public that the FBI has no secret dossiers while *not* telling them that it is now feasible with laser technology to store twenty-page dossiers for every single American on a strip of magnetic tape only a few thousand feet long.[21] Hoover may be gone, but the national political police network is with us still.

The "police state" issue may or may not be just another of the intermittent crises of civil liberties in the United States. In the past, the victims of the urge to repress dissent were adequate testimony to the danger emanating from some source of unfettered discretionary power within the system, and judges or legislators moved to strengthen and preserve our system of self-government by wide open and robust debate. Certainly no one can argue that the times are as grim today as they were during the Palmer Raids or that the quiescence of the body politic approaches that of the 1950s. And the constituent elements of a police state apparatus in this country have developed independently and for what appear to be inoffensive or even essential purposes. The Nixon Administration has *created* no more than its share. But we are beginning to see, I think, a systematic attempt to put these elements together, to weave the threats of national secret police, intelligence gathering, informers, electronic surveillance, and modern computer technology into a mechanism of social control that would be accepted practice only in a police state.

Government generally has become the victim of systematic planning, contingency planning, and technological quantum jumps. The war in Vietnam is but one example. In the 1970s, the comfortably diplomatic notion of "policy" has been shoved aside by a more martial and managerial term, "strategy." One peculiarity of the Nixon Administration has been its congruent set of such "strategies" for the control of foreign, domestic, and partisan political affairs. The president has pursued a Vietnam strategy, a global foreign policy strategy, a congressional strategy, a Southern strategy, a law-enforcement strategy, and a strategy for the control of dissent. Subversion of the grand jury and refinement of conspiracy as a substitute for unconstitutional antisedition laws are elements of the latter strategy. These developments can be resisted, assuming sufficient vigilance in the legislature and in the courts. But if the overall strategy for control of dissent encompasses—as it seems to—the more subtle devices peculiar to police states, resistance will be no easy matter.

17

Fighting Back --Five Days in the Life

Liberty has never come from the Government. Liberty has
always come from the subjects of it. The history of liberty
is a history of resistance.

—Woodrow Wilson

Civil liberties, particularly the liberty to think what you
will and say what you think, are the most fragile elements
of our political system, despite their central importance.
We rely on sensitive public officials to preserve them. In the
past when legislators or officials of the Executive Branch
have attempted to undermine them, courts have stepped in
to right the balance. But when civil liberty comes under a
sustained and systematic attack by the men whose sworn
duty is to protect it, and when an element of their strategy
is to avoid court rulings on their methods, then it becomes
an open question whether our political freedoms can be
protected. Certainly it is no easy task. When prosecution
gives way to "preventive surveillance" as the principle
method of stifling dissent, the technique only occasionally
comes to the attention of judges to be measured against
Constitutional standards.

There is no doubt that, on the record, the Nixon Administration has taken a harsh and hardened approach to the principles of an open society, creating an atmosphere stifling to civil liberties. The highest government officials persist in viewing the charter of our government as an obstruction to be overcome when it cannot simply be ignored or evaded. When courts have insisted on compliance, the Justice Department has considered itself bound only by the letter of the law. I do not think we are governed by cynical men; they really believe that to save our democratic form of government it is necessary to use totalitarian methods. They perceived a rising tide of protest and criticism not as a sign that their policies were out of line with public needs, but as a sign that the nation's security, its very survival, was endangered. Their argument against full freedom of expression is the argument of necessity, an argument which history has time and again proved groundless. We should be no more willing to allow our democracy to be wrenched from its still hopeful course by the imperatives of their paranoia than we are willing to let it be overwhelmed by the imperatives of revolutionary fantasy on the fringes of the Left.

Yet, at the very time when the political police in this country are encouraged to generate the raw material of tyranny, and when the highest political authorities in the land seem inclined to change the basic premises of our system, public opinion polls show that a substantial part of the American people approve of what they think the FBI has been up to and no longer know or cherish the Bill of Rights. Perhaps Jefferson was right when he said, "The natural progress of things is for liberty to yield and government to gain ground."[1] We have recovered from repressive periods in our past, and I do not doubt that we will recover from this one too; but we seem headed for some dark days.

Public apathy is only one of the difficulties. The legal

system, the preferred forum for resistance to repression, is an enormously complex and costly tool for those who do want to resist. The Justice Department not only seems bent on using police-state tactics, it seems determined to make it as difficult as possible to raise Constitutional challenges to its techniques in courts of law. So much in any legal battle hangs on fortuitous circumstance. I can think of no better illustration of the difficulties of resistance than the extraordinary way that the Department of Justice's illegal wiretapping came to light on the day before we were to go to trial in *The United States* v. *Daniel Ellsberg and Anthony Russo.*

One of the greatest dangers of widespread electronic surveillance by the government is the real possibility of interception of conversations in which an upcoming political trial is discussed. The government already has so many advantages in a political trial that the whole thing becomes a farce if the prosecutor can also monitor the struggle to build a defense.

In recent years it has become almost routine for lawyers approaching a political trial to file a motion requesting the judge to order the government to disclose whether or not it has intercepted this sort of communication. Because an individual is ordinarily not able to prove that he is being watched and listened to, the Supreme Court has interpreted the Sixth Amendment's "fair trial" guarantee to require the government to search its files and to divulge the existence of any electronic surveillance and its substance if it is illegal. Where a prosecutor discloses illegal wiretapping or eavesdropping (possibly even if the surveillance is legal) he must submit to a hearing in which the judge listens to both sides before deciding whether it taints the government's whole case. If it does, the trial is over right then and there.[2]

In January 1972, long before the Ellsberg trial was due to

begin, we made such a motion. The Justice Department replied at a leisurely pace in February with an unsworn statement denying that electronic or any other kind of surveillance had been used by the government in the case. As the Justice Department well knew from its unhappy previous experience in political cases, this reply was glaringly insufficient. The Justice Department is required to check with all agencies engaged in electronic surveillance, and to divulge the results in an affidavit sworn to and signed by the person making the survey.

On May 2, two months before the trial was scheduled to begin, Judge Byrne ordered the government to go back and try again. The transcript of his remarks shows that he told the prosecutor to produce "any and all logs, records and memoranda of any electronic or other surveillance" of conversations in which any "attorney, his agents, or employees were present." It was probably the broadest order ever handed down by a trial judge in a political case; but it was made necessary by the Justice Department's continuing use of the FBI and two grand juries, right up to the time of the trial, to hunt for evidence and to harass everyone even tangentially involved with Daniel Ellsberg.

Rather than comply, the Justice Department sought to keep to itself as much information as possible about the sweep of its electronic surveillance network. After a silence of almost three weeks, during which we went ahead with the preparations for trial, hoping that the government was studying its files and would disclose what it found, the Assistant U.S. Attorney David Nissen asked the judge to modify the order. The "burden" of checking the files for evidence of taps or bugs on the lawyers and their agents, he insisted, was simply too great. Nissen is a very competent prosecutor; it was clear that they were not even trying to come up with the information.

In the middle of June, Judge Byrne formally refused to

modify his order, and he told Nissen to have the files searched for surveillance of any of the attorneys and any six of our consultants we chose to name. Nissen's last gasp was to challenge the credentials of our consultants, but Byrne took a close look and found the consultants necessary. By the beginning of July we were bringing the government's silence to the judge's attention almost daily. Finally, on July 7, Judge Byrne put the May 2 order in writing so the prosecutor would be sure to understand it. Three days later Nissen produced an affidavit, by personnel in the Internal Security Division of the Justice Department, swearing that a check of the FBI, the Bureau of Narcotics and Dangerous Drugs, the Bureau of Customs, the Secret Service, the Internal Revenue Service, the State Department, the Defense Department, and the CIA had revealed no "electronic surveillance of the conversations of defendants" or "conversations occurring on their premises."

But Judge Byrne's order required much more than disclosure of surveillance on the defendants. What about the attorneys and our consultants? When we looked more closely at the affidavit, we saw that a Deputy Assistant Attorney General, Internal Security Division, had sworn to and signed it on June 8: Nissen had been sitting on the document for over a month. It was clear by this time, with the trial fast approaching, that he was going to give us as little as possible, as late as possible.

Ten days after the jury had been sworn in, and late in the afternoon of Friday, July 21, Nissen offered us an affidavit stating that there had been no electronic surveillance "directed against" the attorneys and consultants on our list, and that "none of the oral or wire communications of any of the individuals listed . . . have been overheard, except as may hereafter be disclosed."

Opening statements in the trial were slated for the following Tuesday. As we studied this peculiar document over the weekend, we became increasingly puzzled about its meaning. Had the government been listening to us or not? Almost three months after the judge ordered them to answer, we still did not know. Perhaps there had been an interception of conversations through a tap or bug "directed at" someone else. When Russo's attorney, Lennie Weinglass, was pointing out this ambiguity to the judge on Monday, Judge Byrne interrupted him and told us that on Friday afternoon, without notice to defendants, Nissen had given him surveillance logs concerning someone on our list. "Was it one of the lawyers?" we asked. "Can we have a hearing to determine whether the intercepted material is relevant to the trial?"

Byrne's silence was deafening. He postponed, for one more day, the opening statements to the jury, and set Tuesday down for legal arguments on our right to see what the government had overheard. At 4:30 Tuesday afternoon he denied our request for a hearing saying that, in his judgment, the intercepted message was not related to the trial and that therefore we had no standing to demand a hearing on its contents. The relevance of the contents is, however, the very issue that the Supreme Court had said must be determined in an open hearing, with the full and informed participation of the defendants.

Tuesday night the entire defense team met with Tony Russo and Dan Ellsberg to discuss the opening statement, scheduled for the next afternoon. Now we also had to decide what to do about the wiretap issue. We were furious, but it seemed that Nissen had boxed us in. Byrne's decision could not be appealed without delaying the trial, and *no* federal trial, within the memory of anyone in the room, had ever been "stayed" once the jury was selected and sworn. Equally discouraging, an application for a stay of the trial could not be easily produced overnight, several items still had to be argued and ruled upon in court, and Ellsberg's chief defense counsel, Leonard Boudin, needed the time to put the finishing touches on his opening statement. A persuasive argument was raised that we might have to go to the Ninth Circuit Court of Appeals several times during the trial and, since there was almost no chance of getting the trial stayed now that it had begun, we should not prejudice future applications by irritating the appellate judges on the wiretap issue.

Under ordinary circumstances these difficulties would have overwhelmed us but the prosecutor's cleverness in this case was undone by a coincidence. The Ninth Circuit Judges were holding their annual conference in Pasadena, just forty minutes from the Los Angeles Federal Court Building. Justice William O. Douglas, the Supreme Court Justice with jurisdiction over the Ninth Circuit, was there to meet with them and deliver the main address. It was just possible that we could get the application for a stay all the way to Justice Douglas, even if, as predicted, the Ninth Circuit turned us down. Lennie Weinglass and I agreed to take the responsibility for arguing the application, and Charlie Nesson, a Harvard law professor and Ellsberg co-counsel, agreed to argue final pre-trial matters in court the next morning. Sometime just before midnight, Leonard Boudin finally said, "Let's do it."

Without a highly talented team of young lawyers and a strongly motivated staff, it couldn't have happened. The lawyers went to work immediately, while secretaries and other staff who could type arranged to get up at 3:30 in the morning to produce the required multiple copies of what turned out to be a fifty-seven-page application for a stay of the trial. By 8:00 A.M. Wednesday, the paper task was finished. An hour later, Weinglass and I set forth for Pasadena, accompanied by Mark Rosenbaum, a bright second-year Harvard law student who had spent the night researching and helping to draft the application.

At 9:40 we reached the Sheraton Huntington Hotel in Pasadena where the judges were in conference. While Mark and I went in search of the senior Circuit Judge, Weinglass went in search of a men's room to shave and try to erase the signs of his sleepless night.

Fate was finally dealing us a good hand. The first person I saw in the lobby was Justice Douglas, who threw me off balance by welcoming me to the judicial conference. He apparently thought I was going to address the conference. After exchanging pleasantries, I seized the opportunity to explain to him my mission and hinted that we might well be seeking him out during the next few days if the Circuit Judge denied our application. He cordially replied, "Well, Mrs. Douglas and I will be here today and tomorrow. We leave at six o'clock Friday morning for Portland, Oregon, where I have some dental work to be done, and then on to Yakima, Washington, on Friday afternoon."

In a little over four hours the Ellsberg trial was to begin in Los Angeles. The Senior Circuit Judge had to be located, hear our application for a stay, rule on it, and, if he denied it, we would have to go back to Justice Douglas and try to get him to overrule the Circuit Judge. After opening statements by prosecutor and defense counsel, it would surely be impossible to delay the trial. If this long-shot effort was to have any chance of success, it would all have to be done in the next few hours. The proximity of an alerted Justice Douglas and the notoriety of the Ellsberg trial made it barely possible.

Senior Circuit Judge Ely emerged from the conference at 10:40 to meet with us. As we walked down the corridor looking for a suitably secluded setting, he gave me a sly look and said: "I've asked the Justice to sit in with us, so he doesn't give us any trouble later on." It took a moment for me to realize the import of that offhand statement. Douglas himself could immediately overrule a Circuit Court decision. We were, in effect, saving valuable time by skipping the conservative Circuit Court and presenting our application for a stay directly to Justice Douglas.

Two accommodating members of the conference staff vacated their working area to provide an improvised courtroom. Justice Douglas, flanked by Judge Ely and Judge Browning, seated himself on one side of a long folding table covered by one of hostelry's ubiquitous conference green tablecloths. Lennie, Mark, and I pulled up chairs facing them across the "bench." I briefly outlined the case and presented our request for a stay of the trial.

Weinglass and I then answered all the Judges' questions, except for one fielded smoothly by law student Mark. After about fifteen minutes, Judge Ely asked us to leave so that they could confer privately, but Douglas ignored the suggestion and plunged on with his questions: "Do you mean that you weren't even told what *type* of surveillance it was?" "Are you claiming both Sixth and Fourth Amendment violations?" "When did the Government inform you of the wiretaps?" "Was there a court order authorizing the wiretap?" "You say the jury was sworn before you were informed of the wiretap?" When Douglas had finished his grilling, he suggested that we give them a few minutes alone. Ten minutes later we had our stay.

We were embarrassed to note that, in our hasty overnight production, we had neglected to provide the judges with the usual proposed order for them to sign. The three judges had scrawled across our application the welcome words: "Further proceedings are stayed pending determination by the Court of the petition for mandamous." [*sic*] We were so elated that even Lennie Weinglass looked refreshed.

A combination of circumstances had produced the unusual result for us. Weinglass, one of the brightest and best in the legal profession and a veteran of political trials in America, was almost disbelieving as we moved over the Los Angeles freeways back to the political trial that was about to stop, at least temporarily. When we arrived at the court at about 11:45, it was in recess. As we handed the stay order to the court clerk, a tremendous stir spread from the defense table in to the press rows right behind, and to the spectators. It was the first event of any consequence in the whole pre-trial period that gave the defense a cause to celebrate, and it wasn't much.

At 2:30 a three-judge Circuit Court panel heard arguments on the wiretap issue for an hour. Within twenty-four hours they had denied our request for a hearing on the relevancy of the tap to our case. The stay was vacated. Our only recourse now was to apply for still another stay of the trial, not just for a few days this time, but until the Supreme Court returned from its summer recess in October. A new application was prepared while I set about trying to locate some judges.

Douglas was not in his hotel room. When I finally reached the Clerk of the Circuit Court, he informed me that all the judges were at the Universal Studios attending a reception. This public servant told us that there was no way to get anything accomplished that evening, and why hadn't we provided the Circuit Court with the required three copies of our first application? For a full three and a half minutes he hammered it home: if you are coming out here tonight, bring three copies!

The ever-alert press were in their cars, waiting with engines running when we set out for Pasadena at 5:30 with no idea how we were going to reach anybody. Douglas was to leave in twelve hours, but fate delivered the judges to us en bloc at an outdoor cocktail reception, with their ladies. We were seeking Senior Circuit Judge Ely, but the first person I spotted was the Clerk who had forgotten to tell me that the unreachable judges would all be back from Universal Studios for this occasion. "Judge Ely is right over there, in pink slacks you just can't miss," he volunteered. I missed them, but in the meanwhile I found Justice Douglas at the bar. "Hello, Senator, have a drink," he said warmly. I agreed, but the minute I made it clear that I was seeking him out professionally as a litigator, not socially as a former senator, a screen descended between us. We shared a bemused three minutes of chilly silence, neither of us volunteering to make small talk. As refilled glasses moved into his hands, he nodded and returned to his wife.

By this time, the others had finished meeting with Judges Ely and Browning in the lobby. We had been referred to Judge Merrill, who had presided over the three-judge panel of circuit judges the day before. I had a fix on the location of Judge and Mrs. Merrill, so Leonard Boudin and I honed in quickly. I delivered the shortest legal argument of my career. "Judge Merrill, this is the first time I've ever applied for a denial, but I believe the Circuit Court must deny our application for a stay of the Ellsberg trial before Justice Douglas can consider it." He laughed and said, "Yes, you may be right on that. Consider it denied."

Since Justice Douglas was aware of our presence, we now had only to await his pleasure; but we reminded him of our purpose by maintaining our presence about ten feet away from the group he had joined. In due time, the Justice invited us into the lobby. There, in front of the cigar stand and a few feet from the hovering press, we outlined the problem and requested a hearing. He expressed great reservations about stopping a trial in progress for what might be months, and he made it clear that he could do nothing that night, since he was to deliver the principal postprandial address to the conference. Obviously, said Douglas, both sides had to be heard on such a critical issue. We had notified Assistant U.S. Attorney Nissen of our plans, but he had not appeared. "You'll have to let the government

know that I'll hear the arguments at 4:30 tomorrow afternoon at the post office building in Yakima."

Yakima, Washington, was convenient for Douglas: it is
a few minutes from Goose Prairie where he goes to get
away from people. Nissen was able to fly there directly on
a navy plane, but Boudin and Weinglass, who left Los
Angeles at 9:00 A.M., did not get there until 3:30 after numer-
ous stops and layovers. Still, Boudin is probably the best
appellate attorney in the land, and he was quite at home
arguing precedents and hypotheticals before Douglas, who
has a quick mind and an encyclopedic knowledge of the
cases. Nissen, for the first time, was a little overawed. Unable to evade a direct question from a Justice of the Supreme Court, he finally admitted that the material he had
filed secretly with Judge Byrne concerned a wiretap for
which the Justice Department had not secured a warrant.
Just before it recessed for the summer, the Supreme Court
had unanimously ruled against the Nixon Administration
on just this point. According to that *Eastern District Court
of Michigan* case, the President and his Attorney General do
not actually have the "inherent power" they had claimed
to suspend Constitutional safeguards; they too are bound,
by the Fourth Amendment, to secure a warrant before
listening in on those whose views they think endanger
national security. "But *this* warrantless tap," said Nissen,
"is not of that kind. It is for gathering *foreign*, not domestic
intelligence."

Everyone came back to Los Angeles but Justice Douglas.
Sometime the next morning he stepped into a public telephone booth, called the Clerk of the Supreme Court in
Washington, and dictated his opinion. Douglas was not
worried about a tap on his home phone, he just doesn't have
one in Goose Prairie. Before noon on that Saturday, we
were on the phone to the Supreme Court too, and our
efforts over the preceding five frenetic days were rewarded
with these words from Douglas's opinion:

[T]his application for a stay raises a profoundly important constitutional question. . . .

The electronic surveillance used by the government was represented to me on oral argument as being in the "foreign" field. No warrant, as required by the Fourth Amendment and by our decisions, was obtained, only the authorization by the Attorney General. Such authorization was held insufficient in our recent decision. . . . It is argued [by Nissen] that that case involved "domestic" surveillance, but the Fourth Amendment and our prior decisions, to date at least, draw no distinction between "foreign" and "domestic" surveillance. . . . Moreover, in the light of the casual way in which "foreign" as distinguished from "domestic" surveillance was used on oral argument it may be that we are dealing with a question of semantics.

Defendants' telephonic conversations, it seems, were not tapped, nor were those of their attorneys or consultants. But a conversation or several conversations of counsel for defendants were intercepted. . . .

[T]he right to counsel guaranteed by the Sixth Amendment . . . obviously involves the right to keep the confidences of the client from the ear of the government, which these days seeks to learn more and more of the affairs of men. The constitutional right of the client, of course, extends only to his case, not to the other concerns of his attorney. But unless he can be granted [a hearing] to determine whether his confidences have been disclosed to the powerful electronic ear of the government the constitutional fences protective of privacy are broken down.

I am exceedingly reluctant to grant a stay where the case in a federal court is barely under way. But . . . if the law under which we live and which controls every federal trial in the land is the Constitution and the Bill of Rights, the prosecution, as well as the accused, must submit to that law.

Those were words we wanted to hear. Under any circumstances but the very peculiar ones of this case, the Justice Department would have succeeded in blocking *any* timely judicial scrutiny of its wiretapping practices and deceptive trial tactics. No one on our side of the case, however, was really happy to have the trial delayed. The administration should never have accused Ellsberg and Russo of espionage for what was, in essence, taking the truth and giving it to the public. But if there was to be a trial, we wanted to present *The Pentagon Papers* and our experts' testimony about the shocking contents both to the jury and to the American people at a time when it might hasten the end of the war. In the end, the Supreme Court deferred decision on the merits and permitted the trial to continue. The delay hurt most of all because it costs a small fortune every day to keep a defense team in readiness for a major political trial, and we had already spent more than what had come in from contributions.

Nonetheless, our efforts had won us more than another one of Justice Douglas's moving opinions. When individuals are willing to face the expense and frustrations of challenging police state tactics on the occasions when they come to light, even a comprehensive strategy for repression is a failure. A people can only free itself from the effects of governmental intimidation and deception—just as an individual does—by the very process of fighting against it.

Part III

LIVING WITH CIVIL DISOBEDIENTS

I've never felt more a partner in the making of American law than when I was in jail for breaking one.
—Dr. Martin Luther King, Jr.

18

Civil Disobedience – Politics between the Ballot and the Bomb

Under a government which imprisons any unjustly, the true place for a just man is also in prison.

—Henry David Thoreau

For almost two decades America has been buffeted by two simultaneous political upheavals: a widespread and impassioned resistance to the war in Indochina and a seemingly endless revolution in the relationship between races. Either of these might have shredded less resilient political systems; there has been resultant repression, but there has been less during this period than in some other, less turbulent, eras.

Despite the repression, and despite occasional outbreaks of insurrectionary violence, this country is far from coming apart at the seams. Does this considerable success of our political and legal institutions mean that civil disobedience is never called for? Let us not forget that much of the credit for our movement forward belongs to yesterday's civil disobedients—citizens passionately opposed to what seemed to be intolerable moral and political evils. They abjured revolutionary violence against the state, but nevertheless violated the law in order to make their protest effective.

Civil disobedience is as much a part of the American system, as much responsible for its successes, as trial by jury and presidential elections every four years. At the pivotal points in our history, marking virtually every important step forward, politically motivated lawbreaking provided a significant push.

Dr. Martin Luther King spoke for an important American tradition when he said that he never felt more a partner in the making of American law than when he was in jail for breaking the law. What I find remarkable is that after two hundred years of this sort of partnership, we have not made room for civil disobedience in our conventional political and legal theory. Our institutions are consequently out of touch with reality in important and dangerous respects.

A citizen has the raw power to choose whether or not to obey the law, whether to comply or risk punishment. Ordinarily, his approval of the law or his fear of punishment will secure his obedience. But what is there to guide his discretion if he believes that a law is unjust, or that only disobedience can influence the political process?

Sometimes politically motivated lawbreaking serves our long-term interests; sometimes it is a dangerously destabilizing influence, and nothing more. Civil disobedience must be recognized, however, as an integral part of our system of government. We should seek a role in guiding its impact and in keeping it within bounds likely to serve, rather than destroy, our deepest values. We must develop principles by which to gauge our response to its regular reappearance.

Since there is nothing comparable to the Bill of Rights which tells us when political disobedience is justified, we must look for guidance to various types of civil disobedience: how they have actually functioned in the political process, and what are the arguments advanced by supporters and detractors of the method.

Civil disobedience is a deliberate violation of law by an individual, in his political capacity as a citizen, to express his objection and opposition to some governmental activity. It may be intended to provoke major changes of law, policy, or social structure, but it is "civil" only if it seeks to do so within the general constitutional framework. An individual who tries to solve his financial problems by theft acts as a criminal. One who, by sitting-in at a construction site, tries to eliminate the job discrimination that keeps him impoverished, acts as a citizen. He openly violates the letter of the law in an attempt to preserve the spirit of social justice which should inform all laws.

The civil disobedient acknowledges his ordinary duty to obey law. He disobeys because he believes that the particular law or a particular political policy contradicts in a fundamental way the ethical basis of his citizenship obligations. His violation of law is conscientious, motivated by the obligations imposed on him by his conscience to pursue right and avoid wrong.

DIRECT CIVIL DISOBEDIENCE

Whatever the moral standards by which a citizen of a democracy concludes that his obedience to a particular law would work an injustice, he is faced with a dilemma. Henry David Thoreau, who coined the phrase "civil disobedience," in his famous essay, put it this way:

> Unjust laws exist: shall we be content to obey them, or shall we endeavor to amend them, and obey them until we have succeeded, or shall we transgress them at once?

Many citizens with a strong sense of right and wrong have agreed with Thoreau that "What I have to do is see, at any rate, that I do not lend myself to the wrong which I condemn." He counseled direct disobedience of any law that "is of such a nature that it requires you to be the agent of injustice to another."

A major provocation of this sort of disobedience has been laws which work as an injustice to racial minorities. When Ralph Waldo Emerson read the Fugitive Slave Law of 1850, the immediate reflex of his conscience was: "By God, I will not obey it." Martin Luther King, in "Letter From Birmingham City Jail," wrote that "segregation is not only politically, economically and sociologically unsound, but it is morally wrong and sinful."

An equally persistent motive for direct civil disobedience has been the conflict between the general moral obligation not to take the life of another, and the laws by which the government conscripts manpower for the "legal" killing of war. "Conscientious objectors" are not civil disobedients; they are granted an exemption from combat under the draft laws which defer to the scruples of their consciences.*

---

*In 1863, the first federal draft law made no mention of "conscientious objectors," but it did permit an individual to procure a substitute or to pay the War Department $300 to do this for him. This obvious injustice led, in part, to the Draft Riots in New York and elsewhere and to a new Draft Act in 1864. The steady pressure of disobedient protest directed at the provisions of successive conscription laws has provoked increasingly generous attempts to accommodate the obligations of conscience with the obligations of citizenship. The new law in 1864, for example, exempted persons "conscientiously opposed" to bearing arms because of the prohibitions of their "religious denominations." Those exempted were required either to perform hospital duty or to pay $300 for the benefit of sick and wounded soldiers.

But in all our wars, and particularly during the Vietnam war, a significant number of persons who would have qualified as conscientious objectors under the law at the time, chose to disobey even the provisions of the draft law by which they might secure exemption. For these absolutists, *any* cooperation with the government's institution for organizing men to kill others is morally repugnant. Even registering for the draft as conscientious objectors, they feel, would lend them to the wrong they condemn.

War produces other kinds of direct civil disobedience. There are those conscientiously opposed, not to war in general, but to some particular piece of killing. This group, too, has been particularly large in recent years. Many Americans, ultimately a majority, were simply not persuaded that our national security was sufficiently threatened by the "enemy" in Indochina to override our ordinary abhorrence of inflicting death and destruction on fellow men.

Others chose to disobey directly when the dictates of conscience could not countenance a particular military order. Captain Howard Levy refused to train Green Berets because he felt, as a doctor, that he could not lend himself to the atrocities of which he believed the Special Forces

---

Although it permitted a much more equitable accommodation of conscience, the 1864 law introduced a concept quite alien to our political system by conditioning conscientious exemption on religious affiliation. As a secular state, America is committed to the principle that religious beliefs should not affect the distribution of privileges and burdens among her citizens. In 1940, the concept of conscientious objection expanded, but it still legitimized only those pacifist scruples rooted in "religious training and belief." The provision remained an oddity in our law until the Supreme Court, in the face of mounting protest, struck it out in 1965. *United States* v. *Seeger*, 380 U.S. 163 (1965).

Obviously, a great many potential conscientious objectors became direct civil disobedients because, through the world wars and a good part of the Vietnam conflict, our law recognized an individual's conscientious opposition to participation in war only when it was grounded in beliefs, about a Supreme Being, programmed into him by a religious sect.

culpable. Less well known is the case of Staff Sergeant Herschel Poplin. He was assigned to the army's Psychological Operations Unit in Okinawa where his duty was to write material for use in the army's "psy-war" effort. The order Poplin refused to obey is classified, its exact nature unknown; but we do know that in November 1970, he refused to prepare a pamphlet to be dropped over North Korea for the edification of survivers in the event that our country dropped a weapon of mass destruction there. It was only "contingency planning," but Poplin was horrified at the possibility that to obey would, if the contingency arose, make him responsible for aiding and abetting a war crime.[1]

When a citizen goes to prison to point to the gap he perceives between legal duty and morality, the rest of us are forced to reexamine the accuracy with which our law reflects our own values. When an act of direct disobedience touches upon a common chord of conscience in the nation, it can work a shift in political attitudes which makes possible a degree of social change beyond the power of mere law reform to evoke. Segregation ordinances have disappeared and the draft law has changed under the pressure of direct civil disobedience, but more remarkable is the quickening of the American conscience regarding racism and war.

Direct civil disobedience may, however, involve more than an appeal to the national conscience; it may be an appeal to the Constitution itself. Some 86 federal laws, and over 700 state and municipal enactments have been declared unconstitutional by the United States Supreme Court.[2] In many cases the process of conforming law to the Constitution has depended on some citizen's deliberate disobedience; in some cases it is the *only* way, in our system, to get a ruling. We are accustomed to acknowledging this when a protest is provoked by laws restricting freedom of speech or by laws designed to preserve racial discrimination. But the law-testing function of direct civil disobedience goes well beyond such familiar ground. In 1961, for instance, Planned Parenthood made birth-control information and contraceptive devices available in New Haven in a deliberate attempt to test the constitutionality of Connecticut's law prohibiting it. The case reached the Supreme Court in 1965, and the law was struck down.[3]

Of course, appeals to the Constitution by civil disobedients are not always successful. A number of the draft resisters and soldiers who disobeyed orders to report for induction or to report to Vietnam hoped that their protest would be the occasion for the Supreme Court to rule the war unconstitutional. But the Supreme Court, in at least a dozen cases since 1967, has refused even to consider the issue, treating it as a "political question." In lower court cases where it was considered, the constitutionality of the war was upheld.

INDIRECT CIVIL DISOBEDIENCE

Political consequences become a central consideration of civil disobedience when it is indirect, when there is a violation of a morally neutral law in order to protest some related evil.[4] The indirect civil disobedient may be protesting the *absence* of a law where a need for one is felt. The targets of indirect civil disobedience are in fact unlimited; the means are potentially as many as there are laws to break.

An indirect civil disobedient may, like the direct civil disobedient, seek his political goal for reasons of morality, but the disobedient form of his protest is usually a matter of political calculation, and he must look for his vindication to the political consequences of his conduct as well as to his conscience.

His political purposes may be to gain publicity for his

views, or to provoke a confrontation through the inconvenience and embarrassment his law breaking causes others. The draft-board raids of the Catholic Left were not carried out to question the morality of laws against breaking and entering, trespass, or destruction of government property: they were attempts to communicate a political protest indirectly but in as dramatic a way as possible.

Blacks who have unsuccessfully petitioned their city hall for installation of traffic lights at a dangerous intersection in the ghetto have sharpened bureaucratic awareness of their demand by organizing groups to block the intersection with their bodies. Here too the political pressure is clear and limited; it can be weighed against the consequences, good and bad, by protester and critic alike. But traffic law violations have been chosen as the vehicle for much more ambitious protests. In the Mayday demonstrations which disrupted Washington in the spring of 1971, protesters who believed that no political business was more urgent than bringing an immediate end to the war immobilized traffic to protest government "business as usual." Here the purpose of the conduct was less clear, the message was harder to hear through the disorder, and the consequences, good and bad, harder to weigh.

At the furthest edge, indirect civil disobedience merges into revolution. The Whisky Rebels had a powerful argument that the Federalist liquor excise tax was unjust, but in their protest they interfered with the federal mail, fired on troops, tarred and feathered excise collectors, and set fire to the home of the man charged with executing the obnoxious law. Today, antiwar elements have been frustrated by the continuing carnage in Indochina, but in their search for peace some have moved from dissent through protest and civil disobedience to indiscriminate criminality. Indiscriminate lawbreaking may be political in motivation, but by denying completely the authority of civil government, it is not civil disobedience whatever its results.

Thoreau believed that the rule, "Let your life be a counter friction to stop the machine," applied only when the law *directly* "requires you to be the agent of injustice to another." Mario Savio was speaking for a more militant view when he attempted to update Thoreau for the 1960s:

> There's a time when the operation of the machine becomes so odious, makes you so sick at heart, that you can't take part. And you've got to put your bodies upon the gears and upon the wheels, upon the levers, upon all the apparatus, and you've got to make it stop.

By the end of the sixties, civil disobedience was frequently so indirect that it seemed to aim, not at the reform of some mechanism of government, but at incapacitating and discrediting the power of the people behind it. "Shut it down!" tended to replace "Freedom Now!" as the rallying cry of the civil disobedients.

Because indirect civil disobedience is a thoroughly political art, negative reactions in the body politic serve as a kind of corrective to irrational excesses. In the last two years we have seen, I think, a return to more discriminating and politically sensitive uses of the tactic. The crewmen who jumped into the Pacific from the carrier *Constellation* as it sailed for Vietnam in October 1971, and the veterans who seized one of the nation's dearest symbols—the Statue of Liberty—in New York's harbor in December of that year were indirect civil disobedients who understood the political limits and potentials of the device.[5]

How can we know when civil disobedience is politically creative and when it is merely disruptive? In a way, if a man breaks the law for a cause vindicated years later, he may be said to have been justified. But the problem is infinitely more complex. A saint may go to jail for a lost cause. An individual with a fanatical commitment to some genuinely good end might employ extreme and reprehensible means. Does the historical judgment that slavery is immoral vindicate both the underground railroaders *and* John Brown?

Our insensitivity to these problems is getting us into trouble. The war in Vietnam evoked such resentment, disgust, and political frustration that civil disobedience became almost the norm. Yet we have no way to distinguish between the personal affirmations of conscience by draft resisters, the symbolic disobedience of the Catonsville Nine, the limited trespass of a sit-in at the Capitol, the mayhem of the Mayday Tribe, and dangerous disruption such as the burning of ROTC buildings and the bombing of the Capitol. In our system, they are all simply criminal.

As a result, some of the best men of our time, men of conscience and intelligence committed to serving right and opposing evil, are imprisoned as common criminals. Muggers, rapists, and murderers, jailed for unprincipled lawlessness committed in the course of some heinous pursuit, inevitably claim equal moral status as political prisoners. By his deliberate blindness to the difference, Vice-President Agnew demonstrated a lack of intelligent discrimination dangerous in a leader of public opinion when he castigated "the whole damn zoo" of "deserters, malcontents, radicals, incendiaries, the civil and uncivil disobedients." This is no more proper or helpful than the rhetoric of the far left that views every trial as a political contest and every law as an instrument of repression. By ignoring the obvious distinctions between a Berrigan and a bomber, between a Martin Luther King and a mugger, political leaders encourage a kind of romanticism about unprincipled lawbreaking which has already infected our youth and the editorial columns of some of our leading newspapers.

Ordinary crime may be politically motivated in a sort of psycho-sociological sense; like the ghetto riots of the 1960s, it may be the unthinking reflex of individuals frustrated beyond endurance by the failure of the political system to deliver on the American dream. Such lawbreaking is likely to have political consequences, but it is obviously different, both morally and politically, from self-sacrificing disobedience compelled by conscience or chosen carefully for a limited political purpose.

One reason for these confusions is that while disobedients may attempt to offer a justifying rationale, only some justifications are actually respectful and preserving of the rule of law. Perhaps we can find, in the debates over justification which have flared up around each civil disobedience protest movement, some rules to guide us.

19

In Search of Justification

> No rules can tell us how this disobedience may be done and by whom, when and where, nor can they tell us which laws foster untruth. It is only experience that can guide us.
> —Mohandas Gandhi

By far the most common feature of civil disobedience is that the protester claims his conduct is *justified*, that under the circumstances his lawbreaking serves some value more important to society than the value protected by the law he breaks. These justifications challenge our system in the performance of its most important political function: recognizing and regulating the interplay of conscience and law. A government "by the people and for the people" must rely on the individual citizen's conscience, his faculty for making moral judgments, both to secure his obedience to its laws and to keep law and policy congruent with its civilizing ethical values.

From time immemorial, civil disobedients have been advancing theories of justification and their critics have been knocking them down. Neither side has come off very well.

Instead of developing a technique for showing that their protest can be worth the cost it exacts, civil disobedients have relied on what they say are self-evident moral principles. But the principles are *not* self-evident to their critics who view all civil disobedience as antidemocratic and anarchistic. With the emergence of civil disobedience as an apparently permanent feature of our system of government, our conventional understandings can no longer bear the strain of the debate.

The architects of the American system of government were not absolutists about obedience to law. Men like Thomas Jefferson and James Madison spoke both of a right and of a duty to disobey. The American experiment in government was, after all, made possible by an escalating campaign of civil disobedience which culminated in a revolution. "Should we have ever gained our Revolution," Jefferson asked, "if we had bound our hands by the manacles of the law not only in the beginning but in any part of the revolutionary conflict?"[1]

Political thinkers at the time needed a theory that would entitle new institutions of self-government to obedience while justifying revolution against the previously established authority of the British Crown. They perceived their American Revolution as proceeding from the then novel notions that government derives its just powers from the consent of the governed and that the ends of government are to secure to the governed their natural rights to life, liberty, and the pursuit of happiness. Jefferson, in the Declaration of Independence, set forth what he believed were the fundamental conditions for obedience and disobedience, for the giving or withdrawal of that consent:

> [W]henever any Form of Government becomes destructive of these ends, it is the Right of the People to alter or to abolish it, and to institute new Government . . . Govern-

ments long established should not be changed for light and transient causes . . . But when a long train of abuses and usurpations, pursuing invariably the same Object evinces a design to reduce them under absolute Despotism, it is their right, it is their duty to throw off such Government.

At first glance, the Declaration of Independence seems an ideal touchstone for a theory explaining when citizens are justified in disobeying civil authority. The Constitution, after all, embodies principles according to which we control a majority's efforts to influence the political process through *enforcement* of the criminal law. There would be a pleasing symmetry to the documents of American history if the Declaration of Independence could stand as a source of principles by which to judge and guide the discretion of citizens attempting to influence the political process through *disobedience* of the criminal law.

Jefferson's stirring words, however, contributed to the confusion of our thinking on civil disobedience. The central notion of the Declaration of Independence—that men are obliged to obey laws because they have given their consent—is merely metaphorical and circular. And when a civil disobedient describes himself as one who has withdrawn his consent to the entire system, he casts his protest as an act of revolution.

The American Revolution was atypical in its causes, its conduct, and its consequences. In the years since Jefferson lived and died we have learned that revolution seems fated to undermine the purposes of even the purest revolutionaries, leaving country after country bloodied and ready for dictatorship rather than liberty. So long as our own system of government does not become completely moribund, so long as it continues to permit changes going to the roots of political, cultural, and economic arrangements, revolution will be impossible to justify.

More important, civil disobedience is not revolution; it is a form of protest. The Boston Tea Party was an attack upon the status quo in an intellectually organized way; the Revolution was an all-out attempt by force of arms to destroy, or at least to capture control of, the very framework of government. Despite the rhetoric labeling the civil rights movement a "nonviolent revolution," the changes sought in that struggle were won in the courts, in Congress, and in the court of public opinion. The civil disobedients forced the nation to toe moral, legal, and Constitutional lines—and to draw some new ones. They did not overthrow the Constitution.

The Declaration of Independence restated the argument of John Locke's *The Second Treatise of Civil Government,* perhaps the most influential work ever written on the subject of natural law.[2] John Locke's reason had informed him that men were created naturally equal and free; that an individual's freedom could not be taken from him without violation of the law of nature; and that a government could command a citizen's obedience only if he had consented to its dominion over him.

In order to reconcile man's duty as a citizen to obey the laws of legitimate authority with his "natural right" to rebel, Locke likened government to a contract drawn up and agreed to by the governed. The contract theory of government, embodied in the Declaration of Independence, was not devised with civil disobedience in mind. A citizen either accepted the covenant of his society, abided by the agreed procedures for formulating laws, and obeyed the resulting rules, or he rebelled.

But one of the lessons of our history is that there *is* a whole spectrum of citizen action lying between unqualified consent and actual rebellion. When Jefferson wrote in the Declaration of Independence of a "right" to overthrow despotic government, he was not suggesting that our government is obliged to push the collapse button whenever it is confronted by a body of aggrieved citizens. The "natural right" to revolution is very limited: citizens can overturn governments which no longer command their respect only when they are, in fact, sufficiently powerful to overwhelm antirevolutionary forces; and as a "right" to tear up the social contract, but not to change it, it is valueless to citizens who remain an ignored minority, or who desire to correct some particular wrongful exercise of authority by an otherwise acceptable government.

It should be no surprise that the Declaration of Independence overlooks the possibilities of civil disobedience as a limited withdrawal of consent. Our ideological forebears hoped they had constructed a system so carefully checked and balanced that majorities would not be able to impose policies or laws which were fundamentally unacceptable to minorities. Almost immediately, however, Americans began to argue about what conditions would justify the disobedience of those who felt government had to *earn* their consent.

Thomas Jefferson was in an awkward position when he condoned violation of the Sedition Act of 1798 by anti-Federalist editors and pamphleteers. As vice-president, he could hardly justify resistance on the ground of impending despotism! But he stuck to the "contract theory." He argued in the Kentucky Resolutions that the states, as the parties to the constitutional contract, had by the First Amendment forbidden the federal government from exercising *any* power over speech and press freedoms. The Sedition Act, he concluded, "is not law, but is altogether void and of no effect." The Resolutions were greeted in Federalist strongholds with dire predictions that "civil discord" must inevitably follow if any lesser authority than the Supreme Court attempted to rule on the contractual validity of federal laws.[3]

The Sedition Act of 1798 was never declared unconstitutional, in part because the federal judiciary at the time was pretty thoroughly in the Federalist camp. But in 1964, the Supreme Court wrote that "the attack upon its validity has carried the day in the court of history."[4] If the Jeffersonians' disobedience was vindicated, how well did the theory by which they attempted to justify it fare?

It was adopted in the 1830s by southerners who opposed federal tariff laws which they believed discriminated unfairly in favor of northern manufacturing interests. South Carolina passed a law which purported to nullify the federal law and threatened to withdraw its consent, to secede from the union, should the federal government attempt to enforce it.

As a theory for justifying disobedience, nullification proved anarchical and constitutionally absurd; but it was not really buried until the Civil War resolved the dispute —the government's laws are backed up by more than contractual authority. Meanwhile, the Abolitionists had advanced an entirely different natural law theory of justification. The constitutional contract was clear, stating that escaping slaves "shall be delivered up on the claim of the Party to whom [their] Service or Labor may be due." When the Abolitionists appealed to a "higher law," they were castigated by administration officials as "anarchists" and "traitors."

The arguments of the nineteenth century were still unresolved when Martin Luther King wrote "Letter from Birmingham City Jail," perhaps the most widely read and debated justification of civil disobedience in our history. He began with the natural law distinction borrowed from Thoreau and the Abolitionists: "There are *just* and there are *unjust* laws . . . Any law that uplifts human personality is just. Any law that degrades human personality is unjust." But while the Abolitionists disobeyed directly, to vindicate their individual consciences and to frustrate enforcement of unjust laws, King's "direct action" disobedience was an indirect political tactic designed to bring an injustice to an end. In fashioning his justification, he relied on the principles of Mohandas Gandhi's nonviolent revolution in India. For the minority in a political battle, according to Gandhi, "Suffering is infinitely more powerful than the law of the jungle for converting the opponent and opening his ears, which are otherwise shut, to the voice of reason."[5] To justify this tactic, according to King, the "one who breaks an unjust law must do it *openly, lovingly* . . . and with a willingness to accept the penalty."

Dr. King's justification was greeted with the familiar criticism: who was to decide what was good for the human personality? If his conviction that segregation laws degraded human personality justified Dr. King's lawbreaking, were not Governors Wallace and Barnett justified in violating the law in Tuscaloosa and Oxford by standing in schoolhouse doors to prevent the court-ordered entry of black pupils? They believed, with a passion equal to King's, that integration was degrading. And although Dr. King's emphasis on the need for nonviolence and for acceptance of the legal penalty was more limiting than prior justifications, these requirements, too, met with criticism. Louis Waldman, a member of the New York Bar, published an influential article in which he wrote:

> Apparently Dr. King thinks that in violating laws "openly," he and his following are more virtuous than those who violate laws secretly. As a matter of fact, the reverse is true. The open violation of law is an open invitation to others to join in such violation. Disobedience to law is bad enough when done secretly, but it is far worse when done openly, especially when accompanied by clothing such acts in the mantle of virtue and organizing well-advertised and financed plans to carry out such violations.[6]

The truth is that for most lawyers violation of law can never be justified; their whole lives are devoted to the principle that obedience to law is of the highest value.

By the mid-sixties, however, it was apparent to some lawyers that at least some civil disobedience must be justifiable, because the moral sensitivity of the nation's political and legal institutions seemed to depend on it. Three New York lawyers, Harrison Tweed, Bernard G. Segal, and Herbert Packer, wrote an article focusing on the difference between King's direct action against segregation laws and the Southern Governors' defiance of court orders:

> It is no answer to say [as King had] that in one case the objective is "bad" and in the other it is "good." Orderly social living would be impossible if people only obeyed laws they happened to like. . . .
>
> The crucial difference lies in the fact that the Negro demonstrators were not violating any court order, but rather laws which had not been tested, which the Negro demonstrators *in good faith believed were invalid*, and which they were determined to challenge *through the process of law*. . . . A free society would be doomed unless it provided the citizen with a means for asserting the invalidity of laws and other official acts as measured against the fundamental law of the Constitution. . . .
>
> We may assume that both [Governor Wallace and Governor Barnett] believed that the Federal Court decrees were unconstitutional, [but they] did everything they could to delay and defeat the execution of the court orders without involving themselves in a legal contest; and they acted after the validity of the desegregation orders had been fully and unsuccessfully challenged in the courts.[7]

This attempt at justification worked very well in the context, for the segregation ordinances were held unconstitutional, and the trespass, breach of the peace, and disorderly conduct ordinances under which many "direct action" participants had been arrested were held unconstitutional as applied. But these liberal lawyers failed to remember the Abolitionists and the Jeffersonians when they wrote: "Continued resistance to a law that has been fully and fairly settled . . . is no part of the American tradition and is in the deepest sense subversive of the legal process." Under the Tweed–Segal–Packer theory, Dr. King's disobedience was justified, but not the disobedience of slaves and Abolitionists who had refused to settle for the *Dred Scott* decision.

The lawyers' constitutional theory of justification also ruled out indirect civil disobedience completely. Supreme Court Justice Abe Fortas put the ultimate liberal imprimatur on this view when he wrote in *Concerning Dissent and Civil Disobedience:* "In my judgment civil disobedience —the deliberate violation of law—is never justified in our nation, where the law being violated is not itself the focus or target of the protest."[8]

Thoreau might have been speaking for our time as much as for his own when he wrote of lawyers: "They may be [men] of a certain experience and discrimination, and have no doubt invented ingenious and even useful systems, for which we sincerely thank them; but all their wit and usefulness lie within certain not very wide limits." By limiting justifiable civil disobedience to good faith attempts to test the constitutionality of the law being broken, the liberal lawyers led themselves into a trap. The war in Vietnam, which they came to despise, was not a "law" which could be broken to be tested; in any event, the Supreme Court has refused to pass on its constitutionality. That, in the court's parlance, is a "political question."

The Supreme Court did strike the segregation ordinances from the statute books; but not every evil is similarly subject to a test by direct civil disobedience. There is no law obliging racial minorities to participate in the more subtle forms of discrimination against them, there is no law obliging poor people to remain poor, and there is no law compelling citizens over draft age to participate in an unjust war. By ruling out indirect civil disobedience even where direct civil disobedience is logically impossible and where free speech and petitions have proved ineffective, the liberal lawyers rule out the only form of protest likely to reach the most terrible evils of our time—racism, poverty, and purposeless war.

King's declared purpose had not been to change the law, or even to win constitutional points in the Supreme Court; it was, by a confrontation of conscience, to win a larger political reform. This unabashedly political element, woven into Dr. King's justification of civil disobedience, should really have changed the ground of the debate. In their rush to help Dr. King justify his disobedience, the liberals missed this opportunity entirely, and were woefully unprepared for Philip Berrigan's "Letter from a Baltimore Jail."[9]

Father Berrigan was not of draft age. His direct opportunities to protest the war were limited to speaking and writing. When he poured his blood over some draft-board records and napalm over others, it was not so much because he wanted the draft laws changed as because he felt there was no other way his voice could be brought to bear on the American consciousness. His disobedience was indirect, and when he modeled his statement of justification on King's "Letter," he was pointing to the actual similarity of their political purposes and means:

> We have seen legitimate dissent first ridiculed, then resisted, then absorbed. To become, in effect, an exercise in naivete.
>
> With ineffectual grievance machinery, there is little hope of redress . . . [W]e have experienced intimately the useless-

ness of legitimate dissent. The war grows in savagery, more American coffins come home, Vietnamese suffering would seem to have passed the limits of human endurance.

In face of these facts, for some Americans to ask others to restrict their dissent to legal channels is asking them to joust with a windmill.

Berrigan's symbolic disobedience was intended, as was Dr. King's "creative tension," not to raise legal issues but to raise the consciousness of wrong in the American conscience, to sharpen the urgency of public debate, and to force us to deal with our obligations to truth, to law, and to the humanity of our fellow men. We will not be able to see the action of a King or a Berrigan for what it is until we have a means to distinguish it from the unjustified lawbreaking which we justifiably fear. Our confusion obscures their message and subverts the important role civil disobedience can play in our political life.

20

Democracy and Anarchy

> We dare not pin our faith solely on civil disobedience. It is
> like the use of a knife, to be used most sparingly if at all. A
> man who cuts away without ceasing cuts at the very root,
> and finds himself without the substance he was trying to
> reach by cutting off the superficial hard crust.
> —Mohandas Gandhi

How can civil disobedience ever play a positive role in
American political life when breaking the law, refusing to
abide by the decisions of a majority, seems to violate the
fundamental rule of the game? In its crudest form, this
objection to civil disobedience holds that each citizen who
enjoys the benefits of living in this society must bear the
obligations imposed by it: that you have to pay for your
rights. There are, however, two edges to this.

When individuals feel that their due as citizens is being
denied them, why shouldn't they demand their rights as a
first condition of giving their obedience? Equality, justice,
and the "unalienable Rights" of "Life, Liberty and the
pursuit of Happiness" are a few of the promised benefits of
our political system. So long as they cannot be delivered to

all, there is a certain hypocrisy to insisting that those who are denied them have obligations based on having received them!

In a slightly different form, one might say that because everyone has the right to vote, the right to be part of the majority, no one can be justified in frustrating the majority's will: today's minority may win tomorrow's election. But this leaves civil disobedience as the only recourse of the disenfranchised—the suffragettes, the blacks in the South, the draft-age objectors who were not old enough to vote.

It seems to me that the point civil disobedients have to answer is that our political process is designed to preserve a kind of balance between conflicting interests in society, and that civil disobedience is unacceptable because it works as a threat, a kind of political blackmail, which makes voluntary bargaining and compromise impossible. Indeed, if the political effect of civil disobedience were to compel the acquiescence of others, its use in a system where the authority of government is grounded in consent would deprive the laws of their legitimacy. In fact, civil disobedience does not work that way. Successful civil disobedience persuades decision-making authorities in the courts, Congress, or the whole people that the established compromises of the political order fail to accommodate an important and rightful interest. Civil disobedients force a majority to change policy by forcing it first to be conscious of injustices hidden by neglect or apathy, and then, if necessary, by forcing the majority to change its mind.

The president has exclusive control over the conduct of most foreign and military policies. These policies are, and should be, major concerns of ordinary citizens. Democracy was not very much in evidence when two successive "peace" candidates for the presidency pursued military victory on the battlefields of Vietnam once they were installed in the White House. President Nixon simply shut off the noise of democracy by tuning in the Purdue–Ohio State football game when more than three hundred thousand citizens came to his house to petition for a redress of grievances. Yet the antiwar movement was not a strong-arm tactic; it was educational. It raised the political consciousness of the nation until antiwar sentiment penetrated to decision-making levels. Civil disobedient protest worked as a kind of people's veto over the discretionary power of the Executive Branch of government to wage war. Like Dr. King's "direct action" campaigns it restored to us some rough approximation of democracy.

Successful civil disobedience does not compel the majority to knuckle under, but compels it to recognize the depth of conviction with which the minority presses its claims. When antiwar demonstrators blocked the streets in front of induction centers, they forced their views on a reluctant political process, but they did not disrupt the process by which laws are made or wars are waged. When Jessica Mitford asked General Hershey what effect the Stop the Draft Week in Oakland had had on induction, Hershey replied: "[W]e ended up with everyone inducted—there was not a person who promised to come to Oakland for induction who failed to show up . . . They stopped them for some few *minutes* . . . that was all."[1] The educative force of civil disobedience in a democracy is perhaps best summed up by these words of Abraham Lincoln:

> Public sentiment is everything. With public sentiment, nothing can fail; without it nothing can succeed. Consequently he who moulds public sentiment goes deeper than he who enacts statutes or pronounces decision. He makes statutes and decision possible or impossible to be executed.[2]

Critics who argue that civil disobedience is incompatible with democracy's majority rule not only misstate how civil disobedience works, they misstate the "fundamental rule" of democracy. Any society requires obedience and must adopt some means of obtaining it. But our laws have commanded respect by generally reflecting popular notions of justice. The purpose of our political process is to make this possible, and majority rule is no more than the best device we know of to approximate an identity of law and justice. Democracies rest on the psychological assumption that an individual will develop a habit of obedience if he is given a fair measure of control over collective decision making: he cannot, theoretically, complain of injustice in a law he helps to make.

If our political process were a perfect democracy, if power were evenly distributed, if there were no permanent minorities, if each citizen could feel he had an equal hand in making laws and settling on policies, then civil disobedience would have no place in America. But our democracy is necessarily flawed. Our institutions are not always responsive to minority voices. Majorities seek to use their control of the administration of government to perpetuate majority support. There is no effective mechanism for popular participation in foreign policy decision making. Access to the critical decision-making bureaucracies in general is both too diffuse and too complicated.

Our democracy, flawed though it is, avoids fatally alienating minority groups by giving them not only the right to speak freely, but the power to be heard and the hope of prevailing in the end. It is here that civil disobedience has become one of the key checks and balances in the system. It helps identify grievances and areas of moral stress which have been unfairly rejected or ignored by aggressive or passive majorities and their representatives at the helm of government. Effective civil disobedience gives them a powerful motive to search for ways to accommodate the goals of dissenters, and to ask whether the law or policy under attack is as important to them as it is offensive to the minority. Civil disobedience is not only compatible with our democracy, it is essential.

We must remember that our Constitution does not commit our democracy to unconditional majority rule. We have a Bill of Rights precisely because, when the Constitution was being ratified, debate uncovered a widespread fear that natural checks and balances would not be enough to forestall a tyranny by the majority. The Bill of Rights sets forth fundamental rules of the game. There are limits on what is fair for majorities to do with their power, just as there must be limits on what minorities can do in pressing for change.

Law, particularly the fundamental law of the political process, is not really a set of precise and easily ascertained rules. The Fourth Amendment guarantees that "The right of the people to be secure . . . against unreasonable searches and seizures . . . shall not be violated." We have seen how difficult it continues to be to determine just what sort of government activity violates such rules. It is only the evolution of an agreeable tradition and the development of common-sense rules that give it meaning. *None* of the rules of the game can be stated as absolutes.

If the founding fathers had had the benefit of our history, if they had foreseen fully the possibility that minorities as well as majorities might use and abuse the criminal law in political conflicts, they might have provided that "The right of the majority to be secure against unreasonable political law-violation by the minority shall not be violated." This would have accurately stated the rule of the game as we actually play it; and it would have left for judicial interpretation the problem of when civil disobedience is reasonable. Had the dangers of unjustified civil disobedience been handled in the same way as the dangers of repressive law enforcement, the variety of justifications put forward for civil disobedience might have been carefully evaluated and distinguished by the courts. In that event, we could have developed agreeable rules of the game by which to guide citizen discretion. For instance, just as rules of reasonableness have evolved to govern the trespass of officials upon a man's home in search of evidence, rules might have evolved to determine the reasonableness of a citizen's trespass on government property to protest.

At least one rule should be clear. Civil disobedience cannot be compatible with our democracy if its effect is to curtail freedom of expression by preventing another from speaking. When the disruption of political debate goes so far beyond heckling that it shuts the debate down, it subverts the process.

Another rule might be that in a democracy, civil disobedience must not be the first resort. A civil disobedient ought to be able to make a good case for his claim that the normal procedures of free speech, press, and ballot have already failed or are inadequate. Furthermore, a romantic attachment to the sacrifices of civil disobedience would eventually sap the vitality of other elements of the system and actually bring about a real breakdown of political institutions. Each of us tends to favor the methods we know best and the tactics that have proved successful for us in the past. We have learned the hard way that military leaders favor military solutions, which do not always produce happy results for humanity. There may be trouble ahead for democracy if the political leaders coming out of these times of civil disobedience do not broaden their skills.

If reform becomes synonymous with civil disobedience, then civil disobedience will be ripped from its firm place in the American political tradition, where it has been justified as the last, not the first, resort of aggrieved minorities.

This danger becomes more acute as our society crowds in on itself and the changes in it come faster all the time. We are finding that there are innumerable conflicting visions of truth and justice. If civil disobedients batter at public sentiment with more causes, more claims, and more reforms than the legal and political processes can handle, the system will indeed break down.

It is equally dangerous, however, to argue, as many critics do, that civil disobedience must lead inevitably to anarchy because it fosters a general disrespect for all laws, the good as well as the bad.

The fury in the body politic which civil disobedience invariably provokes is not caused by the individual protester's violation of law; we are too well-accustomed in the mid-twentieth century to widespread crime of a much more serious nature. Disobedient protest does not often cause us more than minor inconvenience. Nor do the aims of the protesters explain the reaction, as their goals are often quite generally and genuinely shared by even their severest critics. Nor is it their character, for they are usually decent and courageous, even if occasionally morally arrogant or offensive.

Civil disobedients touch on a deep-seated fear of anarchy; and it is upon this fear that their critics seize. The civil disobedient claims "It is *right* to break this law, at this time, for this reason." "What would happen," asks the critic, "if everyone did that?" I do not know why Americans are so fond of the domino theory. It has seldom been shown to be valid except with dominos, yet it has long been the chosen metaphor of those advocating rigid foreign and domestic policies.

So long as we remain a free society, it will be the justice of our laws—not the firepower of our police forces—that will command the obedience of the ordinary law-abiding citizens. A civil disobedience movement will not grow unless the law and the law's enforcers are in fact caught between the ideals undergirding our civilization and an exercise of governmental power that mocks them.

As a result, protests invoking widespread civil disobedience have not in fact led to anarchy. Their political effect has been to strengthen the rule of law by restoring to the authority of government a legitimacy it had lost. Shifting majorities do sometimes make bad laws or pursue unworthy policies. When civil disobedience penetrates to the guiding mechanisms of the political system and causes a shift in the direction of greater justice, the laws receive *wider* acceptance. This is clear in the historical evidence. The anti-Federalists violated the Sedition Act, but there was no increase in homicide. The Abolitionists violated the Fugitive Slave Law, but did not set off an epidemic of petty theft. They were vindicated in the court of history as will be the freedom riders and draft resisters.

These groups, morally opposed to some particular act of government, did not encourage generalized lawbreaking. The fairness and the moral quality of most laws commanded their respect. An abolitionist preacher gave this as his answer to the charge of anarchy:

> The men that refuse obedience to such laws are the sure, the only defenders of the law. If they will shed their own blood rather than sin by keeping a wicked law, they will by the same principle shed their blood rather than break a law which is righteous. In short, such men are the only true law-abiding men.[3]

It is true, of course, that the last fifteen years have been marked by an increase in civil disorder as well as by an increase in civil disobedience. Many would condemn civil disobedience because they fear civil disorder. The criminal violence of ghetto riots was rooted in the same social sickness that fired Dr. King's justification of civil disobedience, but there is no foundation in fact for laying the disorders at Dr. King's door. Both were responses to the ossification of our political process, but they were distinctly different responses.

The National Advisory Commission on Civil Disorders, appointed by President Johnson to study the ghetto riots of 1967, concluded that the causes were imbedded in a complex aggregation of social, economic, political, and psychological deprivations—the heritage of centuries of white control and black powerlessness.[4] Dr. King was probably right when he wrote, in "Letter from Birmingham City Jail," "If [blacks'] repressed emotions do not come out in these nonviolent ways, they will come out in ominous expressions of violence." I think many people thought at the time that his portrayal of civil disobedience as an *alternative* to anarchy was really a threat. But social science research is gradually proving him right.

Boston University's Howard Zinn turned up the fact that the general crime rate actually dropped in Albany, Georgia, during the massive civil disobedience campaigns there in 1961 and 1962,[5] despite the frustrations of a sustained civil disobedience campaign that was lost. Scholars at the University of Michigan concluded from several studies that the number of violent crimes *declined* in black communities when direct action protest campaigns were underway.[6] It seems quite clear that in most communities where we experienced real breakdowns of law and order, the rioting was *not* preceded by civil disobedient protests on civil rights issues; and most communities which were subjected to the inconveniences of civil disobedience did not fall prey to civil disorder.

The record of the last fifteen years seems to me to show something quite different. Conscientious civil disobedience has, indeed, led to other violations of law but the violations have been by the government. Martin Luther King's direct action campaigns started a process which produced the unconstitutional Federal Anti-Riot Act, for which I cast the worst vote of my congressional career. Because civil disobedience is so often the political tactic of dissent, the FBI and Nixon's Justice Department felt justified in treating some ethnic and political minorities as threats to national security, on a par with agents of an enemy nation. That, in turn, led federal and local authorities to embark on a comprehensive program to suppress and to punish as "conspirators" those who encouraged, and some who merely talked about, civil disobedience. To do so, they violated the right to privacy, the right to freedom of speech, the right to equal protection of the laws, the right to assembly and association, the right to reasonable bail, and the right to fair trial. This governmental lawlessness has, in a sense, been caused by civil disobedience, and if anything is likely to provoke disrespect for law in general and lead to anarchy, it is not draft-card burning or sit-ins, but the violation of fundamental laws of the land by the highest elected officials sworn to uphold them.

Yet the cries of "anarchy" have hardly abated. Unthinking application of the domino theory to law-enforcement reached a new height of absurdity during the *Spock* trial. When the Boston Five were indicted for conspiracy, their conscientious commitment to lend financial, verbal, and moral support to the Resistance did indeed move thousands to sign statements of "complicity." Hundreds "aided" and "abetted" draft resisters by handing them money or accepting their draft cards at public ceremonies that were sometimes televised. But there was no crime wave; the disobedience remained limited and conscientious. As the trial was getting underway, the Solicitor General of the United States and the president of the American Bar Association suggested that ghetto rioting and looting was connected to the "indiscriminate" civil disobedience of men like Dr. Spock. Editorial writers agreed.[7] At sentencing, Judge Ford labelled their protest a "rebellion against the law . . . in the nature of treason."[8]

Those who argue that civil disobedients provoke anarchy, by encouraging others to decide for themselves which laws to obey, should consider the consequences of the blind obedience they seem to prefer. Civil disobedience, and the potential of injustice to provoke it, has been an important check on the tendency of the politically empowered to resist that necessary process of change and reform (whether from the right or the left) that makes our system worthy of respect and obedience. Dr. King accused the liberal ministers of Birmingham of preferring "a negative peace which is the absence of tension to a positive peace which is the presence of justice."

Unquestioning obedience is the habit of slaves, not of citizens; and slaves, as we have seen, do a lot more damage than demonstrators when they are finally moved to rebel.

Those who accuse all civil disobedients of moral arrogance and political irresponsibility should ask themselves: does their own silent acquiescence help bring justice and peace, or does it encourage the arrogance of the politically empowered who enforce racist laws and wage unjust wars with impunity? Is their political passivity motivated by an undue fondness for comfort and convenience, by a willingness to tolerate evil so long as it falls on someone else's shoulders, or is it really a genuine concern for "law and order"?

I cannot escape the conclusion that the reason that most middle-class, middle-aged community leaders resist the idea that civil disobedience can be justified is because they fear involvement, not because they fear anarchy. Too many of us want tranquillity and peace too much to want moral and political dilemmas raised in so dramatic a manner as by civil disobedience.

Like Thoreau, I do not believe that our nation, any nation, can rely for very much on the obedience of men who "serve the state . . . not as men mainly, but as machines." Thoreau shall have the last word:

A common and natural result of an undue respect for law is, that you may see a file of soldiers, colonel, captain, corporal, privates, powder-monkeys, and all, marching in admirable order over hill and dale to the wars, against their wills, ay, against their common sense and consciences, which makes it very steep marching indeed, and produces a palpitation of the heart.

21

Finding a Forum

Should the constituted authorities of the State unite in
usurping oppressive powers; should the constituent body
fail to arrest the progress of evil 'thro the elective process
according to the forms of the Constitution; and should the
authority which is above that of the Constitution, the
majority of the people, inflexibly support the oppression
inflicted on the minority, nothing would remain for the
minority but to rally to its reserved rights . . . and to decide
between acquiescence and resistance, according to [a] calculation . . . in which the degree of oppression, the means of
resistance, and the consequences of its success must be the
elements.

—James Madison

The two hundred years of debate about the function and
propriety of civil disobedience leaves us with a major legal
and political problem: how to bring within the rule of law
one of the most important components of our political
process, one that is, by definition, illegal. Disobedience is
always unjustified until the disobedient persuades us otherwise. But how is he to do so? James Madison suggested, in
his essay quoted above, a method which has been strangely
neglected.

If law is disobeyed in an attempt to remedy a trivial oppression or an imagined evil, we will not look with favor on the disobedient, no matter how sincere he may be. No matter how severe the motivating oppression, we will view as unjustified such extreme lawbreaking as homicide, arson, or rape. Recognizing that all disobedience destabilizes social order to some degree, we will tolerate a greater degree of destabilization when disobedient protest succeeds than when it fails to remedy the evil that provokes it. By and large, James Madison's essay correctly identifies the elements of our calculation: we balance the harmful consequences against the beneficial; we demand a modicum of congruence between ends and means; and we are not tolerant of poor judgment.

But whose calculation is to govern? Certainly not the protesters. Thoreau put the Abolitionists' position nicely when he wrote that there are "times in which the rule of expediency does not apply, in which a people, as well as an individual, must do justice, cost what it may;" but the Abolitionists, and Thoreau among them, found it possible to move from unqualified defiance of the Fugitive Slave Law to unqualified delight in John Brown's unsuccessful and bloody raid on Harper's Ferry.[1]

Similarly, the balance cannot be satisfactorily struck by the lawmakers and policy makers themselves, or the institutions under their control. It is their use of governmental power which provokes the question; their own interests, authority, and political fate are inextricably bound up in the answer.

Many states already make provision in their statutes for the justification of illegal acts under special circumstances. Typical is Section 3505 of New York's Penal Law which provides that a violation of law is justified—is not a crime at all—when it is "necessary as an emergency measure to avoid an imminent public or private injury . . . of such gravity that, according to ordinary standards of intelligence and morality, the desirability and urgency of avoiding such injury clearly outweigh" inaction.

Some fascinating cases have cropped up around this "choice of evils" doctrine. May shipwrecked sailors kill and eat a companion to avoid starving? A nineteenth-century case said no, because the sailors could not have known whether or not they would be rescued before they starved. The doctrine does justify breaking and entering a burning home to save a sleeping family. It justifies assault on a person with a dangerous disease in order to prevent him from wandering around and starting an epidemic. It justifies taking the life of an assailant who cannot otherwise be prevented from killing another innocent person—"justifiable homicide."

A terribly high degree of urgency and imminent danger is necessary to justify homicide, but why cannot antiwar protesters who block the sailing of a munitions ship or the processing of draftees use the same principle to justify their limited disobedience? Napalm falling on innocent Indochinese certainly causes them grave injury. If all ordinary political measures have failed to bring a stop to a senseless war, why shouldn't Section 3505 apply?

In the first place, civil disobedience works too indirectly on the conscience and self-interest of others. If the bombing were to stop after such a protest, who could say it would not have stopped anyway? Who could say that some milder form of protest would not have had the same result? Who could say that the particular tactics were "necessary as an emergency measure"? And no court in this country, so long as we are actually at war, is likely to rule that under "ordinary standards of intelligence and morality" it is "clearly" necessary to halt the war effort.

On October 15, 1965, antiwar demonstrators conducted a nonviolent protest at the offices of the Ann Arbor, Michigan draft board. They marched around the building, displayed signs bearing antiwar and antidraft slogans, and they exercised their right to picket on an important issue. At the end of the day, however, thirty-nine refused to leave the draft board waiting room. They were arrested and convicted of violating Michigan's trespass statute. At their trial and through several appeals, the courts rebuffed their argument that the trespass was "symbolic speech," protected by the First Amendment.[2] The argument has been advanced by other civil disobedients in many different contexts.

Does the First Amendment establish a "right" to civil disobedience? Mere words do seem to have lost much of their impact in today's world; symbolic action sometimes serves the same purpose as oratory. When civil disobedience is intended to communicate an important message, why refuse to protect it as a form of "symbolic speech"?

Saluting the American flag, or not saluting it, is not exactly talking, but the Supreme Court has labeled such conduct a "form of utterance" which is entitled to protection under the First Amendment.[3] Man communicates all sorts of ideas and opinions by gestures, symbols, and other nonverbal behavior, including trespass and other civil-disobedient conduct.

But how far can we afford to go with this? Certainly, some "conduct" is so removed from any interference with the rights of others and so clearly a substitute for conventional communication that it should be protected as verbal conduct is. Waving Viet Cong flags, devising disrespectful displays of the American flag, and burning draft cards are good examples of the "uninhibited . . . vehement, caustic, and sometimes unpleasantly sharp attacks on government" on which our system of freedom of expression thrives.[4] And I believe that the laws Congress has passed against desecrating the flag and burning draft cards violate the First Amendment.

But most civil disobedience is not of this kind. If we were to permit an individual to win First Amendment protection simply by portraying his violation of any law as an effort to "say" something, or even if we force the courts to hold hearings on such claims, the lines of permissible conduct would become even more difficult to draw and the criminal process would be further debased by the effort. Eldridge Cleaver argued that his compulsive desire to rape white women was actually an expression of his anger at a political system which oppresses blacks. The argument belongs where it is—in his provocative book, *Soul on Ice*—and not in a court of law.

I think that any serious attempt to guide political action must cope with the relationship of ends and means. The justifiable means for protesting the imminent death of thousands of people differ from the justifiable means for protesting bureaucratic irregularities in some unresponsive agency. The balance sheet for any particular protest will be complex, for justification is ultimately an ethical and political problem, not a legal question. The concept of a "legal illegality" is not likely to win much favor in any rational system, and evaluating justifications by code or appellate court rulings should be counted out. We should not use the lawyer's methods at all. Thoreau was right that "A lawyer's truth is not Truth, but consistency or a consistent expediency."

Yet the legal system's function is to serve the ethical and political needs of our society, and it is unwise to provide *no* place within it for evaluating a citizen's claim that a particular violation of law serves those needs better than obedience. If only to prevent the practice of civil disobedience from overflowing its historical and functional role, we need some pragmatic standards, or at least a method to find them and to perform the rough calculation in particular cases.

It seems to me, as an attorney and former legislator, that an American jury is about the best place to go for testing the justifiability of civil disobedience. It is as close as we come, in the criminal process, to a cross section of the concerns and values of the community in general. Civil disobedience is designed to provoke people, to persuade people, to attract and repel them, but it is ultimately an appeal to the peoples' conscience, an attempt to activate the moral sense of the community. Protestors insist that they *are* in tune with the most broadly based values, and they urge the rest of us to acknowledge that we share those values.

If we were to open the jury's ears to these attempts at justification, if we were to give a civil disobedient the opportunity to try in the focused forum of a courtroom to persuade a cross section of the body politic that he was right, we would add to the pre-protest calculations of civil disobedients an important element of reality. In anticipating a jury's likely response, their discretion would be guided by considerations serving our common interests.

Unhappily, the rules now governing criminal trials deny civil disobedients the opportunity to do this. Questions of motivation and purpose are ruled irrelevant, and political matters are invariably said to be "not on trial," even when the political purpose of the offense and the political consequences of the trial are obvious to us all. As we shall see, there are sound legal and historical arguments for remedying this, placing the questions in the jury's hands, and opening political trials up to rich possibilities.

A civil disobedient cannot *prove* that his breaking the rules was justified, that his judgment was right; but he can put forward, as the government does when it wants to curtail a constitutional right, the grounds for his exercise of discretion. With that information, a jury can do the job. Fully informed of the actual purpose of the protest, the political and factual circumstances, and the consequences, it could decide whether his violation of law was reasonable or not.

There are six considerations of "civility" which often frame (and frustrate) attempts at defining civil disobedience itself which a jury should consider:
(1) Was the disobedience conscientious?
(2) Was disobedience necessary?
(3) Was the protest well-designed to appeal to conscience?
(4) Did it succeed?
(5) Was it nonviolent?
(6) Does the disobedient eagerly accept the legal penalty?

These points are sterile when handled definitionally, as rigid general rules; but they could be flexible and dynamic in the hands of a jury. Let us explore them in more detail.

(1) Was the disobedience conscientious? The question whether a witness is credible is always left to the jury to decide. The jury could also be called upon to decide whether a deliberate violation of law stems from a defendant's genuine belief about right and wrong. We, of course, will not grant immunity from the law on the ground of sincerity alone; conscience is entitled to society's vindication only when it is consistent with our common ethical values. If a direct civil disobedient can convince a random dozen of his fellow citizens, a jury, that by breaking the law he was only doing what a conscientious citizen *ought* to do, then there is reason to believe we need a change in the law. It would be the equivalent of a finding that the essential conditions of social cooperation are not being met, the strongest sort of message to lawmakers to try again.

There will always be some, in a society as vast and heterogeneous as ours, who will be unwilling for genuine reasons of conscience to abide by some particular law which the vast majority of us believes is essential to protect an overriding interest. Even in a political system working

to perfection, where conscience is given the maximum lee-
way compatible with order, there will be structural political prisoners. We cannot for example, really accommodate
the values of a group that believes human sacrifice is right
or traffic lights are wrong. But our traditional respect for
the dignity of each individual demands that we give questions of conscience as much breathing space as possible. It
is not our custom to prohibit a genuine act of conscience
unless there is an overriding need to do so.

(2) Was disobedience necessary? The civil disobedient must
persuade the jurors in the first place that the issue of his
protest is one of fundamental importance, involving some
serious and immediate injustice. He must also convince
them that civil disobedience was the only means, or at least
the only effective means, to challenge the law or redirect
the political process. A civil disobedient ought to have the
chance to justify his methods even when other means are
technically open to him, if they really are mere technicalities which doom him to the powerlessness of a permanent
and oppressed minority.

(3) Was the protest well-designed to appeal to conscience? A civil
disobedient must justify his tactical choices. If he chooses,
from among all the alternatives, to disobey a law that cannot be connected in the public mind with the evil he aims
to protest, he will have a tough time persuading a jury that
he was justified in inconveniencing and destabilizing society. Or if he chooses a law, or a time, or a place that makes
his protest so controversial that the public doesn't see the
underlying issue, he is not likely to succeed in justifying his
conduct any more than in furthering his cause. As civil
disobedience can only be justified if it is calculated to advance some worthy end, it certainly cannot be justified if
it actually undermines it.

It is only fair to require that a civil disobedient make his
protest as clear as possible, for he can succeed only if his

conduct raises the issue in the conscience of the political community. For a direct civil disobedient this is no problem because his conduct is almost self-explanatory. But an indirect civil disobedient faces much more difficult problems and we should be careful not to demand an unrealistic degree of clarity. Sometimes it may take rather a long campaign before the larger society can be made to see the reach and force of an unjust law or an immoral policy. Sometimes innocent members of the public must endure a significant inconvenience before they make the connection between their nonpolitical daily existence and their responsibility as citizens and voters for the evil provoking the protest. An apparent political backlash may be quite misleading. If the lawbreaking is two or three times removed from the evil being protested, however, the obscurity of its message is multiplied beyond possibility of justification. Incorrigibly arbitrary disruption raises no issue in the political process or in the courtroom but how to put a stop to it.

A jury will inevitably give consideration to the status, character, and demeanor of a civil disobedient trying to justify himself on conscientious grounds. This is as it should be. The tactical effectiveness of political disobedience depends, in part, on the protester emerging in the public view as more attractive than the social value presumably embodied in the law he violates or the policy he protests. Civil disobedience will be wasteful and perhaps counterproductive if it does not, ultimately, discredit the alternative. When protest is within the scope of the First Amendment, it is constitutionally justified however unruly and offensive it is. But although we must protect expression even when it is unpersuasive, we are under no obligation to justify illegal conduct that is too unattractively packaged to succeed.

These facts of life can guide the discretion of civil disobedients only to the extent that their decisions are tactical. When I have spoken at campuses around the country about the Ellsberg case or about the Berrigans, I had all too easy an answer for the young men and women who asked questions such as "Why shouldn't I burn draft-board records?" I would respond that a student is not very likely to be effective with such a protest; instead of making others think, he would be condemned for breaking the law, partly because youth makes the action seem self-indulgent and partly because of existing prejudices against student activists. After all, the Berrigans were priests who had committed their lives to mankind. The answer was made even easier by my reluctance to counsel anyone to violate the law, just as my own values keep me pressing for change within the law.

But the student might be just as ready to sacrifice, might have weighed just as carefully the pros and cons and the potential consequences on society and on himself, as a Berrigan or an Ellsberg or a Martin Luther King. If so, I suspect my words seemed irrelevant, whatever their realism. Many civil disobedients are concerned primarily with the net impact of the action on their own lives, not on the political process. Even when they are not really obliged by their consciences to do so, they may take a stand involving noncollaboration with the war-making government, or active resistance to it in order to define and give substance to their lives. They do it because they have to live with themselves, not because they have to live with the society.

(4) Did it succeed? Obviously, a civil disobedient whose cause is almost immediately successful is going to have an easier time persuading a jury that the protest was justified. But civil disobedience functions primarily as a consciousness-raising device, and it would be unreasonable to demand immediate justifying changes in law or policy. Not only may change be delayed, but civil disobedience is often aimed at some mid-term purpose within a longer-term po-

litical campaign which involves both conventional and disobedient methods. Considered alone, Dr. King's "direct action" campaign in Albany, Georgia, was a failure. Yet the failure of Albany and the political lessons learned there made the success of Birmingham possible. Perhaps it is enough to say that civil disobedience may be justified on this count if it serves to focus public concern on an important issue in a productive way.

Sometimes civil disobedience is designed, not so much to mobilize support or to unmask oppression but to provoke repression, to bring about a repressive collapse of our political or legal institutions. The 1968 Chicago Convention Riots, Bobby Seale's verbal excess in Judge Hoffman's court, and the 1971 Mayday demonstration in Washington may have been protests of this kind. Success in such a purpose is a different matter altogether. Americans generally do not like to see their institutions abused by those without power even though they seem inured to seeing them abused by those wielding power. If protesters could be led to consider the likely response of a jury to their tactical choices, they would be encouraged to choose the demonstrative rather than the destructive method.

(5) Was it nonviolent? No criterion of "civility" is more often insisted upon than nonviolence. Indeed, the conventional wisdom for several decades has been that protest is not civil disobedience unless it is absolutely nonviolent. Americans are vastly confused about violence. A 1969 public opinion survey, conducted by the University of Michigan's Institute for Social Research, revealed that 35 percent of the males between sixteen and fifty-four thought it was "violent" for a policeman to shoot a looter, *but 57 percent did not!* Fifty-six percent thought it "violent" when policemen beat students, but 30 percent did not. A full 22 percent, on the other hand, considered sit-ins acts of violence and 58 percent considered draft-card burning violent.[5] When

more American men consider draft-card burning violent than consider beating students violent, we seem to be cut off from our anchor in the ordinary meaning of words. Just as a majority seems to view civil disobedience as a kind of violence and condemns it out of hand, a minority views violence as civil disobedience and attempts to justify it on that ground.

The problem is confusing enough even when we nail down the meaning of violence. The patriots destroyed thousands of dollars worth of property in the Boston Tea Party; the Abolitionists attacked jails and committed at least technical assaults on federal marshals in their efforts to free fugitive slaves; the Berrigans destroyed government property. Is it really true that these protests cannot be justified if they were violent?

Our thinking about the necessity of nonviolence has been unduly influenced by the philosophy of Mohandas Gandhi. By voluntarily undergoing suffering, he thought, one could force opponents to see the truth for which one suffers. To resort to violence, to inflict suffering on the persons one is trying to persuade, would tend only to confirm them in their error and to close their consciences to the justice of your cause.

I do not doubt that adherence to absolute nonviolence lends to protest a moral force it might otherwise lack; but there is a danger of being too romantic about how nonviolence functions and too rigid about its necessity. Despite the rhetoric of nonviolence, both Gandhi and Dr. King understood that civil disobedience involves force of a kind. Both men combined the "moral jujitsu" of patient suffering with more obviously compulsive, even if nonviolent, devices such as boycotts and strikes. The success of the Birmingham campaign depended on economic pressure as much as it did on moral righteousness.

Even the most scrupulously nonviolent civil disobedient

does not always rely exclusively on the passivity of his protest to win concessions. In a power-centered society nonviolence alone may simply be ignored. What often makes the public take proper notice is the potential for violence, the threat, implicit in most civil-disobedient protests, that the lid cannot be kept on forever. Sometimes civil disobedience aims less at unmasking the brutality of the status quo than at raising the price by inconveniencing or worrying everyone. Whatever his preference for melting hearts, a politically astute civil disobedient will know that, as Dr. King put it, "History is the long and tragic story of the fact that privileged groups seldom give up their privileges voluntarily."

With the variety of purposes of civil disobedience in mind, it is unconvincing to say, as so many liberals do, that violence cannot be justified because it does not work. Violence sometimes does work, and the ghetto riots of 1967 were a good example. There is no doubt that they were fueled by political frustration. There were many who argued that they were justified because violence was the only language understood in the American political system. Indeed, to have continued to ignore the grievances of inner-city blacks after that summer would have cost the system more than anyone was willing to pay. The riots were followed, in April of 1968, by the passage of a federal open-housing statute which had been kicking around Congress since 1966.

Ramsey Clark was undoubtedly right when he said that "shocked and frightened and even outraged as white America thought it was about the 1967 riots, it found a new awareness of the problems that underlay those disturbances."[6] But several years have passed, and it seems clear that the riots did not lead to improvement of the ghetto conditions, whatever they did for raising the consciousness of white America. The scars are more prominent in the cities than the remedies. We have the Anti-Riot Act and a much expanded political surveillance program as a result, but the concrete advances predicted by apologists for the riots have not yet appeared.

The real question is not whether violent protest can pry results from the political process, but whether and to what extent protest must be nonviolent to be *justified*. The importance of nonviolence in this regard is that, as a form of political coercion, only nonviolence is truly compatible with the ends which a justifiable protest aims to advance. Any protest that is in touch with the fundamental moral precepts of our society must be as nonviolent as possible. Even if violence is successful in compelling reform in the short term, its spirit will infect the result. A civil disobedient, one whose sense of obligation to society is at the heart of his lawbreaking, must be concerned about the kind of society he is building with the "creative tension" of his protest.

One protesting society's brutality cannot seize as his tactic the application of a countervailing brutality; such disobedience is simply not conscientious. But when a civil disobedient brings his means into line with socially responsible ends, he demonstrates to us all what our ideals really are when they are put into practice. His conduct stands not only as an accusation, but as an example.

Nonviolence is not merely a tactical necessity, nor is it a moral absolute. To insist on absolute nonviolence may be to surrender an opportunity to purge some gross injustice from the system. To seek justice at any cost might plunge society into a bloodbath, or at least tighten the circles of violence. The means are the end in the making, and violence—even symbolic violence such as the Berrigans'—must be kept to a minimum. Nonviolence is a balancing problem within the discretion of a civil disobedient. There must be, as always, a reasonable relationship between the degree of disorder and the significance of the issue at stake. The distinction between injury to people and injury to property should be a paramount consideration. And the force must be clearly focused on the object of the protest.

(6) *Does the civil disobedient eagerly accept the legal penalty?* Gandhi said a civil disobedient must "cheerfully suffer imprisonment," and Dr. King said that "One who breaks an unjust law must do it *openly, lovingly* . . . and with a willingness to accept the penalty . . . to arouse the conscience of the community." For Gandhi, and for Dr. King, it was essential to undergo imprisonment to demonstrate the seriousness of their purpose and to unmask the hypocrisy and error of their foes. But not all civil disobedience aims to open hearts through the protesters' suffering. Sometimes laws are broken in order to get before the public information which it needs to know. Sometimes the purpose is to obstruct the enforcement of an unjust law or raise the price of an unjust policy. Sometimes it is an organizational device. Would a slave who made his escape in the 1850s be unjustified in breaking the law unless he gave himself up and paid the price of re-enslavement? Would it have been more moral for an Abolitionist working on the underground railway, aiding tens of slaves each week, to go to prison and leave the railroad unattended?

For Gandhi and King, paying the price helped win widespread and conscientious consideration of their cause, but it had another value. It was a way of emphasizing the "civility" of the protest. A respectful acceptance of the punishment provided by law was a way of broadcasting their deep respect for the rule of law, even while they violated a particular ordinance. It was proof of their sincerity and conscientious purpose, and an attempt to ward off accusations of anarchy.

"Paying the price" is, at least to some extent, a matter of

fitting tactics to the purpose of the protest. Certainly a lawbreaker is not justified simply *because* he is willing to accept prison. The criminal law is not a price system designed to help shop for our favorite crime and pay the going price.

The problem was posed most spectacularly by the Berrigans. When the Supreme Court rejected the appeal of the Catonsville Nine, Daniel, Philip, and two others refused to turn themselves in and to begin serving prison sentences. Philip was captured after two weeks, but Daniel eluded capture for four months and during that time had been sheltered by three dozen families in a dozen cities. He appeared at meetings, interviews, taped and filmed discussions and, after speaking at a rally at Cornell University, added symbolic insult to symbolic disobedience by eluding the FBI while costumed as one of the twelve apostles.

Daniel Berrigan's period underground is a reminder that it is not just by accepting the punishment that a civil disobedient justifies and emphasizes the "civility" of his conduct. It is also by the public, demonstrative nature of the act and the public explanation and defense of it in terms of widely shared ethical beliefs. Father Berrigan believed that a three-year sentence was unjust, he wanted to demythify the power of the government and the omnipotence of the FBI when they are resisted by a determined gadfly. Most of all he wanted to extend his opportunity to speak of the propriety of civil disobedience in the political circumstances and to continue the consciousness-raising activity that he knew the prison walls would cut off. His going underground was a further violation of law, requiring further justification. It was, in my estimation, consistent and effective civil disobedience.

Most of us know about the price exacted by the criminal process only from paying parking tickets. Very few of those who write glowingly of the necessity of "paying the price" have themselves been subjected to major penalties. Thoreau, for instance, spent but *one night* in the Concord jail, an experience he found "novel and interesting." His jailer was "a first-rate fellow and a clever man," and his cell "the whitest, most simply furnished, and probably the neatest apartment in town." This gives a special meaning to Thoreau's oft-quoted remark, "Under a government which imprisons unjustly, the true place for a just man is also in prison."

It was only after several talks with the Berrigan brothers, while they were serving their sentences together at the federal prison in Danbury, that I found a partial answer for those young men and women who express a desire to go to prison to give life substance and meaning in a time when the state imprisons men unjustly. Unless prison reform is your bag, or unless you can make an effective and justifiable protest through some minor infraction that carries a minor sentence, your obligation to yourself, your generation, and your society is to stay clear of prison and its grinding dehumanization, and to work for a better society where your work can be effective.

Going to jail may be valuable—even indispensable—to an effective protest. There will be situations in which an unwillingness to go to jail will render an act of civil disobedience unjustifiable. This is no reason to insist on a rule that civil disobedients *must* go to jail, or that they must do so willingly or even cheerfully.[7] Such a rule runs counter to the very idea that the question of justification should be put before a jury and that a jury should be entitled to release civil disobedients from punishment when the protest is reasonable, in their view.

It seems to me that a more fitting generalization than "a civil disobedient must eagerly accept the penalty" would be "a civil disobedient must be willing to submit his exercise of discretion to an authority higher than himself." The real mark of "civility" is that the protester does not insist on being the ultimate judge of the social reasonableness of his lawbreaking, or of the question of his legal and moral obligation in a civil society.

22

Political Trials

JUDGE HOFFMAN: This is not a political case as far as I am
concerned.
KUNSTLER: Well, Your Honor, as far as some of the rest of us
are concerned, it is quite a political case.
JUDGE HOFFMAN: It is a criminal case. There is an indictment
here. I have the indictment right up here. I can't go into
politics here in this court.
KUNSTLER: Your Honor, Jesus was accused criminally, too,
and we understand really that was not truly a criminal
case in the sense that it is just an ordinary . . .
JUDGE HOFFMAN: I didn't live at that time. I don't know
. . . Some people think I go back that far, but I really
didn't.
KUNSTLER: Well, I was assuming Your Honor had read of the
incident.

—from the Chicago
Conspiracy Trial

A political trial need not be handled with the blind stub-
bornness Judge Hoffman displayed throughout the
Chicago Conspiracy Trial by insisting that it was a routine
criminal case. Hoffman's conduct made the federal judici-

ary look ridiculous and brought the system of justice into far greater disrepute than the defendants could have hoped for from their antics alone. When a trial mixes legal and factual questions with political and moral issues which divide the society, it is dangerous as well as perverse to ignore it.

In the Chicago case and at some of the Black Panther trials, pandemonium in the courtroom and tumult in the streets were fueled by the frustration of the defendants' supporters. When attempts to mask the political nature of these legal proceedings failed, they took on an apocalyptic air—sometimes of carnival and sometimes of war. The integrity of the criminal process would be much better served if judges would face the realities unique to political trials.

Judge Damon Keith, the black judge assigned to the 1970 federal conspiracy trial of John Sinclair and several members of his White Panther Party in Michigan, tried to do just that. When Sinclair asked permission to make a pretrial statement to the White Panthers gathered in the spectators' gallery, the judge said "Go ahead." A bit surprised, perhaps, to be given the courtroom forum for a political harangue, Sinclair turned and said to his edgy supporters, "I come into this trial with a presumption of innocence. You owe the court a presumption of innocence too—don't disrupt the proceedings."[1]

I am not suggesting that to recognize the existence of political trials is enough to conform our criminal and political processes to the constitutional ideal, but Judge Keith's realism points in a hopeful direction. Political trials will never just go away, for there is no combination of remedies which would actually control the protean urge to repress dissent, and there is no simple way to cure, once and for all, the imperfections in our political system which have made civil disobedience an integral part of our process of government.

There is, however, a step we can take which would greatly reduce the discomfort of the recurrent intercourse between our criminal and political systems. At the heart of the criminal justice system is a properly political institution, the American jury. If we restore to the jury its historic right to decide criminal cases according to conscience, the underlying issues in political trials can be faced directly and resolved.

Whenever authorities or dissenters enter the criminal process seeking political gains beyond the halls of justice, the real issue is not one of fact but one of motive: the motive of the defendant, the prosecutor, or the legislature. A jury, functioning as a distillation of society's moral sense, is ideally suited to weigh those motives. When it finds that the law or the particular prosecution is repressive, or when it finds that an act of civil disobedience is justified, I believe a jury should vote to acquit a defendant. Juries, however, are not permitted to exercise such power.

Any one of hundreds of trials from the past decade would serve to illustrate the unreality which now pervades political trials and the procedural difficulties which arise when politics and morals are at the heart of a conflict between a criminally accused citizen and his accusing government. Rick Boardman's trial in 1969 is one of the less well known. He gave up the security of his conscientious objector's draft exemption by returning his draft card and refusing to cooperate further with the Selective Service System. We saw earlier, from the letter he wrote to his draft board, that he was capable of advancing an eloquent moral and political defense for his action.

At his trial, however, the only issue to be resolved was whether he had violated the draft laws knowingly and willfully, whether he did it with the required "criminal intent." Judge Ford, the judge who also presided over the *Spock* trial, drew the conventional legalistic distinction between "intent" and "motive" and refused to let witnesses testify about Boardman's reasons for resistance. In the end, Boardman's own brief testimony on this score led to the following exchange with the prosecutor:

> Q: Do you say you may decide for yourself whether a law is good or bad, and that you are free to disobey it?
> A: I do not say that.
> Q: What is it that you do say?
> A: I say, sir, that there are higher laws . . . to be obeyed at all times, [and] my intent is to follow those higher laws, whenever and in whatever way I can.
> Q: Yes, sir, but wasn't your intent also to disobey the Military Selective Service Act when you sent in the classification and the registration card?
> A: My intent isn't to disobey, it is to obey. It is to obey the laws of life, the laws of love, as I understand them, the laws of brotherhood.

After all the testimony, Boardman's lawyer asked Judge Ford to tell the jury that it should not convict him unless he had the "bad purpose" which would make his conduct criminal. Not only did the judge reject this request, but he also forbade the lawyer to suggest it to the jury: "You will not argue," the judge told him, "that the jury can decide this case in accordance with their consciences." To the jury, the judge delivered the usual instructions:

> We serve here in two domains. You decide the facts, and I lay down the law . . . you must take the law laid down by the Court, and none other.
> The only question for you to decide here is whether or not . . . Boardman knowingly and willfully violated the Military Selective Service Act of 1967.
> Motive, no matter how laudable or praiseworthy that motive may be . . . [is] never a defense where the act committed was an intentional violation of law—a crime.

Now some jurors may believe that the Vietnam war is immoral or unconstitutional or illegal. . . . If you allow your personal beliefs as to the legality or immorality of the war in Vietnam or any political opinions with respect to the Vietnam war to affect your judgment in this case, you will be violating your oath as a juror.

By excluding from evidence the reasons for Boardman's action, by ordering the jurors to consider his motive irrelevant, and by ordering them not to consider the political views which were at the heart of the case from start to finish, Judge Ford left them with nothing to do but decide what Boardman had already admitted—that he violated the draft laws and knew what he was doing. He was convicted and given a three-year sentence. The proceedings were typical of political trials today.

Originally, the American jury was conceived of as an essential feature of our popular democracy. It was thought that no other institution could so effectively temper the rigor of unjust laws, check the limitless power of politically motivated prosecutors, and support those who resisted government oppression. The power of an independent jury to acquit, where the letter of the law demanded conviction but justice demanded acquittal, was prized as a way to confront government with the people's judgment that certain laws or policies were out of line with the underlying principles of the Republic.

In 1735, the trial of John Peter Zenger for seditious libel established the American jury as the judge of the merits of laws and of the motives of prosecutors, as well as the finder of the facts. Zenger was technically guilty, but his jury dealt Governor Cosby a political blow, effectively nullified the repressive law, and acquitted Zenger. Throughout the colonial period, politically aware juries shielded Americans from enforcement of British mercantile laws which they felt were oppressive. It was for this important political role that Alexander Hamilton termed the jury "the very palladium of free government."

The founding fathers wanted to build that kind of jury power into the American system of justice. John Adams wrote of the juror that it is "not only his right, but his duty," in cases where enforcement of a law conflicts with other important values, "to find the verdict according to his own best understanding, judgment, and conscience, though in direct opposition to the direction of the court."

In 1788, Theophilus Parsons told the Massachusetts Constitutional Convention that "any man may be justified in his resistance" to an act of government which usurps the rights of the people.

> Let him be considered as a criminal by the general government, yet only his fellow citizens can convict him; they are his jury; and if they pronounce him innocent, not all the powers of Congress can hurt him; and innocent they will pronounce him, if the supposed law he resisted was an act of usurpation.

Theophilus Parsons later became Chief Justice of Massachusetts, but today a lawyer would be cited for contempt should he use the same words in trying to inform a jury of its political role.

The jury's role changed during the nineteenth century as judges cut way back on its power. A rigid rule was evolved: questions of fact are for the jury to resolve and questions of law are for the judge alone. Gradually, jurors were reduced to diggers after facts in the testimonial bog; the right of a political defendant to submit the question of his guilt or innocence to a jury was trivialized; and the jury was stripped of its historic power to ignore the judge's instructions in particular cases. The capstone came in 1895 when the Supreme Court concluded that because jurors cannot be allowed to create laws on their own, they cannot be allowed to nullify them.[2]

Indeed, we do not want juries to be able to make up new crimes on the spot, but we have come to treat them as incapable of exercising *any* discretion responsibly. We entrust to policemen, prosecutors, judges, and parole officers an unchecked discretion over the lives of others. Justice demands, as I have suggested in earlier chapters, that we cut back the sweep of the discretionary power now lodged with such officials; but I believe that a jury of citizens is the institution best suited to temper law with justice, to exercise a discretion informed by the larger society's deepest moral and political values.

We empanel more than a million jurors in America every year for some eighty thousand criminal trials. This is an extraordinarily expensive and cumbersome mechanism for finding facts—a task most nations leave to their judges. Although juries have been told since 1895 that they are duty-bound to follow the judge's instructions mechanically, the rhetoric of even recent Supreme Court opinions resonates with reminders of the larger role that independent jurors used to play. "The right to jury trial is granted," wrote the Court in 1968, "in order to prevent oppression by the Government. [It is] an inestimable safeguard against the corrupt or overzealous prosecutor and against the compliant, biased, or eccentric judge."[3] A few weeks later, in another opinion, the Court wrote that "one of the most important [functions a] jury can perform . . . is to maintain a link between contemporary community values and the penal system."[4] We thus have today the anomalous situation of courts extolling the inherent power of the jury to do justice, while refusing to tell the jury it has that power.

It seems obvious that we should now move to restore this

jury power. Some people object that a return to the original design of our jury system would lead to *injustice* in cases where the prosecution stands on the side of the oppressed and where popular passions are misdirected. Juries have, in the recent past, routinely acquitted white defendants who proudly admitted committing violent crimes against blacks. But even if judges were to tell racist juries of their power to nullify the law, would it increase abuses which are already a sad tradition? The truth is that biased and irresponsible jurors do not need to be told that they have the power to ignore a judge's instructions. They reach these verdicts, not because of anything that transpires in open court, but on the basis of the baggage of prejudices they carry with them into the jury box. The proper remedy is to make juries truly representative of society. Even to-day, as all-white juries are disappearing throughout the country, crimes against blacks go unpunished less often.

Another objection to enlarged jury power is that a jury of laymen lacks the specialized training necessary to interpret the meaning of laws. The objection misses the real point: defendants in today's political trials are not asking for juries to be told that they can interpret laws or overrule court decisions. They simply say that, accepting the judge's instructions on what a law means, the jury should refuse to enforce that law when, in the particular case, there is no other way to reconcile their verdict with the demands of conscience and justice.

The fear that juries will run away with their power if they are formally told they have it should be laid to rest by the experience of the State of Maryland. The State's Constitution provides that, in criminal trials, "the Jury shall be the Judges of Law, as well as of fact." Even today, judges in that state tell jurors that the legal instructions are "not binding upon you . . . and you may accept the law as you apprehend it to be in the case."[5] This license to judge the

merits of the law as well as to find the facts has not led
Maryland juries to create "peoples' crimes" out of the blue
or to engage in wholesale acquittals of the guilty.

I cannot believe any social value is really well-served by
continuing to keep juries in the dark about their power to
look to conscience as well as to fact in deciding whether or
not to acquit. After the conviction of Dr. Spock, one juror
in the case told a reporter, "The paradox was that I agree
wholeheartedly with these defendants but . . . I felt that
technically they did break the law."[6] The convictions were
reversed on appeal because the judge's instructions led the
jurors step by step to an inevitable guilty verdict. In reversing Spock's conviction the First Circuit Court of Appeals
emphasized that "the jury, as the conscience of the community, must be permitted to look at more than logic."[7] But
the *Spock* court stopped short of permitting the jury to be
told of the existence of its power or its sweep; and attempts
to expand the ruling and to remove from our courtrooms
the remaining barriers between conscience and logic have
failed. Judges continue to prevent defendants from elabo-
rating the moral and political grounds for acquittal and
their lawyers still face contempt if they urge jurors to ignore the judge's instructions.

When a defendant requests him to do so, I believe that
no judge should refuse to include in his charge to the jury
a caveat along these lines:

> It is your duty to accept my instructions as a correct state-
> ment of the legal principles which generally apply to a case
> of this type.
> But these principles are intended only to help you reach
> a fair result. You are entitled to act upon your own con-
> science, knowing that general rules do not always apply to
> what happens in a specific case. I tell you what the law
> means. You must accept that. But you have heard all the

evidence and you know that what the law seeks is justice—
what is right and fair and consistent with the values we
accept. If the law as I define it to you technically requires
you to convict this defendant, but you believe that under the
circumstances of this case justice requires that you let him
off, then you must vote for acquittal.

The defendant may be technically guilty as the law is
ordinarily applied, but justice may in your opinion require
that you find him not guilty. That is your power as a jury,
as representatives of society as a whole, in seeing to it that
our values are upheld and justice is done in this case.

It is obviously not enough to tack such an instruction on
at the end of a trial conducted along conventional lines. If
jurors are to go beyond the letter of the law and conform
their verdicts in particular cases to the principles upon
which our nation was founded, a defendant must be permitted to give them evidence of his worthy political motives or of the prosecution's unworthy ones.

Lawyers draw a distinction, however, between motive
and intent. A man's intent, his state of mind when he acts,
is relevant at a trial because "unlawful intent" is an element of almost every criminal charge. On the other hand,
the merits of a man's motives, the ultimate purposes
prompting him to act, are technically irrelevant.

When the Catonsville Nine were tried, the factual issues
were settled: they admitted performing the acts on which
the charges against them were based. The legal issue was
whether they "intended" to destroy federal property and
to interfere with the draft, and the Nine tried to expand the
limiting notion of "intent" to encompass the whole range
of motivating moral and political concerns. A bit of this
testimony, drawn from the court record by Daniel Berrigan for his play, *The Trial of the Catonsville Nine*, captures
the frustration of trying to do so:

PROSECUTION:
  I think the question could be answered yes or no, could it
  not? Yes or no, were you aware that it was against the law
  to take records from the Selective Service, and burn them?

  *   *   *   *   *

DANIEL BERRIGAN:
  My intention on that day
  was
  to save the innocent
  from death by fire
  I was trying to save the poor
  who are mainly charged with
  dying in this war
  I poured napalm
  on behalf of the prosecutor's
  and the jury's children
  It seems to me quite logical
  If my way of putting the facts
  is inadmissible
  then so be it
  But I was trying to be concrete
  about death because death
  is a concrete fact.[8]

Daniel Berrigan and his co-defendants at that trial were
self-possessed and articulate enough to take questions about
"intent" unusually far afield. The judge was also exceptional: he ordered them not to do it, he interrupted them
when they did, and he instructed the jury to ignore the
testimony, but because he was a decent man, who conceded
that "as a person" he agreed with them, he gave them
considerable latitude when they were on the stand.

Even this limited success of the Catonsville Nine is
unusual. Other political defendants, faced by aggressively
hostile judges, have had their motive defense shut off completely within the artificial confines of the rules of evidence.[9]

The word games must end. A defendant's motives do not come through clearly when they are forced into the awkward mold of "intent," and the contrivance is of no use to a defendant wanting to introduce the jury to the motives of the men who pass repressive laws or the motive of a prosecutor who brings a political case to trial.

I believe that an accused should always have the right to introduce motive evidence if he chooses to do so. That right will not, as some say, hand defense attorneys a device to impose additional burdens on courts by pressing frivolous claims of good motive or by impugning the motives of a prosecutor who is acting in obvious good faith. Direct evidence of a prosecutor's motives is hard to come by, and would certainly not consume much trial time in any event. In my experience as a defense attorney, it is not normally in a defendant's interest to raise the issue of his own motive at all, except perhaps to deny that he had one. It is the prosecutor who usually raises that issue in order to bind together circumstantial evidence that would otherwise leave a jury unpersuaded that it is the defendant who did the deed. If a defendant takes the stand, he can expect to be cross-examined intensively about any facts which suggest he has a motive for the crime. A prosecutor always tries to answer the jury's question: "*Why* would the defendant have done that?"

Yet, if the defendant does not deny violating the law, the prosecutor can be expected to object strenuously to any evidence of the defendant's good motive and the objections will be sustained. Why should a prosecutor have it both ways? Why shouldn't the accused have a right to give the jury his reasons for doing what he did? A defendant who tied up his trial by abusing this right would risk antagonizing the jury, and no court is really at his mercy because the ordinary rules excluding redundant and cumulative evidence give a judge ample power to keep a trial on the track.

Admittedly there will be some embittered defendants so bent on irritating the system that, casting caution to the wind, they will press absurd claims against their obvious interest. A defendant might insist on presenting evidence of some social injustice completely unrelated to a crime on which the prosecutor has him dead to rights. When this happens, it *will* waste some trial time, but it will be an occasional excess which a judge has the power to contain within tolerable limits.

On the other hand, once it becomes possible to bring a prosecutor's motives to a jury's attention, a prosecutor would be foolhardy not to select the laws he will enforce and the violators he will prosecute according to the community's legitimate law-enforcement needs. Once it becomes possible to introduce evidence of patterns of police harassment, as a defense against the panoply of harassment charges now thrown at dissenters, police departments might move to control individual officers who abuse their discretionary arrest power. Viewed in this light, a greater latitude in admitting motive evidence will lead to fewer political trials and, to that degree, to a saving of the court's time and its integrity as well.

If juries today were informed of their historic power to nullify laws, those in power would less often try to force a resolution of political conflict in the courts. The courtroom would become the forum we need to help set guidelines for determining when civil disobedience is justified, and we would bring the courts and the law into contact with the reality they should reflect and shape. The process by which government responds to popular will, and by which popular opinion matures and manifests itself, encompasses more political institutions than the television screen and the voting booth at election time. The political trial is one.

The jury is a political institution, one of the checks and

balances in our scheme of government. Its use could be of critical importance when our government becomes so wedded to an unacceptable policy that no other public institution is as uncompromised, as immediately available, or as appropriately constituted for putting alternatives before the people, as twelve random citizens. At such times, civil disobedients *should* be acquitted if the disobedience is justified in the view of a jury; there *should* be acquittals for dissenters who are victimized by repressive manipulation of the laws and by discriminatory prosecution. Defendants should be permitted to encourage jurors to perform this political function and judges should inform them that it is their right to do so.

Injustice is constantly with us and, to a degree, it is inevitable in any political system. Freedom of speech, press, and assembly, as well as other fundamental individual rights of citizens, tend to make the injustices visible and to move those in power to correct them. Segments of our people regularly find, however, that even when they utilize their conventional freedoms fully, the injustices they suffer remain invisible to society as a whole. If they succeed in making the injustices visible, those in power may still be unmoved. The congenital unresponsiveness of our system is compounded when the intense pressure of unacknowledged changes in values and shifts of power balances make society even more rigid in its reaction. Under such circumstances, the incidence of civil disobedience is bound to rise. Civil disobedience upsets social stability, providing a convenient justification for repression. Thus, the system directs its energies against symptoms rather than causes, and a calculated campaign against symptoms fuels itself with a visceral, unthinking popular support in the short run. This process, reenacted many times in our history, is further complicated today by the more sophisticated and less visible techniques for repressing the exercise of conventional forms of protest against injustice.

Our task is, as it always is, to preserve the unique flexibility of our system of government without abandoning its integrity. In periods of great political stress, when the overlap of the criminal and political systems is visible and provokes widespread concern, both public officials and dissenters strive, for different reasons, to politicize the criminal process even further. It is unrealistic to expect that we will come across some self-implementing device which can systematically contain these recurrent pressures and maintain a well-defined separation of criminal and political systems.

I put forward earlier a number of suggestions which would substantially reduce the vulnerability of the criminal system to the urge to repress dissent. I have also offered one man's view of a conceptual framework which both recognizes and regularizes the necessary play of civil disobedience within our political process. But much more is needed. We need to put officials in control of our institutions of government who are committed to the principle that it is improper and dangerous to exact criminal sanctions from citizens for lawfully pursuing political change or agitating for the acceptance of a novel view of the world. We need institutional methods to delimit the decision-making of citizens when the failure of conventional political recourse moves them to use the drama of disobedient protest. These are long-range and only imperfectly attainable goals. What we must do immediately is to add a touch of reality to the process, and I think the American jury can help us to do that.

Victims of repression, civil disobedients, political trials, and political prisoners—the fallout from the imperfections of our system—are important indicators of how it actually works, but not of how we want it to work. We want to preserve popular government and a high degree of stability. On the one hand, whatever form repression takes, whether sedition or conspiracy laws, frame-up or surveillance, a systematic attempt to treat dissent as criminal activity is an attempt to build a temporary tranquillity on the ruins of popular government. On the other hand, however rich the tradition of civil disobedience and however ameliorative its impact can be, it threatens severe social destabilization should it begin to replace rather than supplement our conventional political remedies.

I think of the "political prisoner" issue as a kind of Geiger counter; as the noise increases, it suggests that a critical mass, an explosive situation, lies ahead. Because there always seems to be more than enough life in the body politic to change course before the final explosion, we cannot really know how dangerous any particular conflict is or how much stress our system can take before finally losing its resiliency.

It is important to remember, however, that we rely on our criminal system to deter conduct that threatens our fundamental moral and social values. Its capacity to do that rests on the moral authority of the laws and on the integrity of the criminal process. To the extent that the criminal process is perceived as an instrument of political repression, and to the extent that the rigidity of political institutions diverts political energies into disobedient protest, the law loses its moral authority and the stigma of a criminal conviction is dissipated. When disobedience becomes a widely respected mode and arrest becomes an honor, the danger of social instability becomes acute.

I reject the apocalyptic prophecies issued by those who would welcome a repressive collapse of our system as its proper comeuppance. America is not ready for the Last Judgment. Hiroshima, polluted rivers on fire, and a thousand other images of apocalyptic possibilities have suffused the American consciousness with horrific visions of the End. Apathy has always been endemic in America, but I believe the aggravated apathy evident almost everywhere today is, in part, a defense against the pressure of these cataclysmic anxieties. I also believe, however, that the potential for creativity in citizenship, art in government, and flexibility in our system makes it likely that we have at hand the raw material of renewal, not the signs of an imminent collapse.

In spite of my optimistic bias, I cannot add my voice to the complacent chorus, often joined by liberals, which exults at how well our system works, how repression fails except when the target is trivial, and how justifiable civil disobedience is always vindicated by some future turn of the wheel. Their outlook is too simple, too satisfied, and historically inaccurate.

In truth, the agony of today flows less from a breakdown of formerly stable and perfected institutions of government than from our growing awareness of failings and imperfections which have been with us from the beginning. In its actual operations, our system of government does not track the constitutional model as closely as legislators, prosecutors, judges, and other actors in the process maintain. Nonetheless, the ideals of that model are of enduring importance to a liberty-loving people, and they endure in the American mind. They need defense at each turn of the wheel.

Notes

PART I

1. POLITICAL PRISONERS AT THE BEGINNING

The epigraph is from Thomas Jefferson's letter to Dr. Benjamin Rush, September 23, 1800, in *The Life and Selected Writings of Thomas Jefferson*, Modern Library ed. (New York: Random House, 1944) p. 558.

1. Leonard W. Levy, *Jefferson & Civil Liberties: The Darker Side* (Cambridge: Belknap Press, 1963) pp. 25–31.

2. Peter Brock, *Pacifism in the United States from the Colonial Era to the First World War* (Princeton: Princeton University Press, 1968) pp. 238–242, 250–253.

3. This account draws on the pamphlet written by one of Zenger's lawyers, James Alexander, *A Brief Narrative of the Case and Trial of John Peter Zenger: Printer of the New York Weekly Journal*, Stanley N. Katz, ed. (Cambridge: Belknap Press, 1963).

4. Harold L. Nelson, "Seditious Libel in Colonial America," *American Journal of Legal History* (1959): pp. 160, 164, 170.

5. This account of the Boston Tea Party is drawn from Donald B. Chidsey, *The Great Separation* (New York: Crown, 1965).

2. OPENING MOVES

1. This account of the Whisky Rebellion and the First Smear Campaign draws on Leon Friedman, *The Wise Minority* (New York: Dial, 1971).

2. This section draws on James M. Smith, *Freedom's Fetters* (Ithaca: Cornell University Press, 1956).

3. Thomas I. Emerson, *The System of Freedom of Expression* (New York: Random House, 1971) p. 100. (See ch. 11, n. 4.)

4. Friedman, p. 24.

5. Leonard W. Levy, *Jefferson & Civil Liberties: The Darker Side* (Cambridge: Belknap Press, 1963) Other material in the preceding paragraphs is found in Levy, pp. 56–58, 167.

6. Alexander Hamilton's argument for freedom to publish the truth was adopted by the appellate court which reversed Croswell's conviction.

3. OBEYING THE "HIGHER LAW"

1. John Hope Franklin, *From Slavery to Freedom: A History of Negro Americans* 3rd ed. (New York: Vintage, 1969) pp. 187–88.

2. This account draws on Russell B. Nye, *Fettered Freedom: Civil Liberties and the Slavery Question 1830–1860* (Lansing: Michigan State University Press, 1963), Leon Friedman, *The Wise Minority* (New York: Dial, 1971), and Richard D. Younger, *The People's Panel* (Providence: Brown University Press, 1963).

3. Younger, pp. 90–92.

4. Younger, pp. 99–100; see also *United States* v. *Reed,* 17 Fed. Cas. 727 (1852).

5. Friedman, p. 38; Younger, pp. 98–99. See, *United States* v. *Scott,* 26 Fed. Cas. 990 (1851) and *Charge of Judge Sprague to the Grand Jury,* 30 Fed. Cas. 1015 (1851).

6. Younger, pp. 103–105; see *United States* v. *Stowell,* 27 Fed. Cas. 1350 (1854).

7. *Ex parte Milligan,* 71 U.S. 2 (1866). Lamdin Milligan was arrested in October, 1864, on charges of conspiracy against the government, inciting insurrection, and giving aid and comfort to the rebels. Specifically, he had become a member of the Order of American Knights. He was found guilty and was sentenced to be hanged, although a civilian grand jury, convened during his imprisonment, had not indicted him. Milligan petitioned the Supreme Court for a writ of *habeas corpus.* The Court, ordering him freed, said that denying Milligan a trial by jury was "a gross usurpation of power. Martial rule can never exist when the courts are open and in the proper and unobstructed exercise of their jurisdiction; [the power to suspend the writ of *habeas corpus*] is also confined to the locality of actual war."

8. *Minor* v. *Happersett,* 88 U.S. 162 (1894).

9. This account and the quotation are from Friedman, pp. 91–93.

4. POLITICAL PRISONERS AND THE "WAR TO END ALL WARS"

Except where I have indicated in the notes, I have drawn this account from Zechariah Chafee, Jr., *Free Speech in the United States* (Cambridge: Harvard University Press, 1941), and Emerson, Haber and Dorsen, *Political and Civil Rights in the United States* (Boston: Little, Brown & Co., 1970) 3rd ed., vol. 1, pp. 55–66. The epigraph is taken from the transcript of the testimony of the Hon. Jacob Panken, Justice of the Municipal Court of New York City, before a Senate subcommittee conducting hearings in December 1920, on a proposed joint resolution recommending a grant of amnesty and pardon to persons convicted under the Espionage and Selective Service Acts during World War I; *Amnesty and Pardon for Political Prisoners: Hearings before a Subcommittee of the Committee on the Judiciary, United States Senate* (Washington, D.C.: Government Printing Office, 1927) p. 64.

1. Peterson & Fite, *Opponents of the War, 1917–1918* (Madison: University of Wisconsin Press, 1957) p. 5.
2. Quoted in Peterson & Fite, pp. 8–9.
3. He was later released on a writ of *habeas corpus*. Peterson & Fite, p. 31.
4. *Amnesty Hearings*, p. 54, testimony of Mr. Algernon Lee, testifying for the national executive committee of the Socialist Party.
5. *State v. Freerks*, 140 Minn. 349 (1918).
6. *Ex Parte Starr*, 263 F. 145 (D. Mont. 1920).
7. *Report of the Attorney General*, 1918, p. 48.
8. *Debs v. United States*, 249 U.S. 211 (1919); the Holmes letters are quoted in Leon Friedman, *The Wise Minority* (New York: Dial, 1971) p. 113–114, n. 19.
9. *Abrams v. United States*, 250 U.S. 616 (1919).
10. *United States v. Steene*, 263 F. 130 (N.D.N.Y. 1920).

5. REPRESSION OF THE INTERNATIONAL WORKERS OF THE WORLD

This account is drawn from Zechariah Chafee, Jr., *Free Speech in the United States* (Cambridge: Harvard University Press, 1941); William Preston, *Aliens and Dissenters: Federal Supression of Radicals, 1903–1933* (Cambridge: Harvard University Press, 1963); Leon Whipple, *The Story of Civil Liberty in the United States* (Westport, Conn.: Greenwood Press, 1970). The epigraph from the IWW constitution is quoted in Chafee, p. 225.

1. *Ex Parte Jackson*, 263 F. 110 (1920) in Chafee, p. 227.
2. Preston, pp. 122, 311 n. 9.
3. Jason Epstein, *The Great Conspiracy Trial* (New York: Random House, 1970) p. 100.
4. *Fiske v. Kansas*, 274 U.S. 380 (1927). For proceedings below, see 117 Kan. 69 (1924).

6. THE RED SCARE AND THE PALMER RAIDS

Except where indicated in these notes, I have relied for this account of postwar repression on William Preston, *Aliens and Dissenters: Federal Suppression of Radicals, 1903–1933* (Cambridge: Harvard University Press, 1963).

1. This account of the events of 1919 is drawn from Vern Countryman, "History of the F.B.I.," (a paper delivered on October 30, 1971, at the FBI Conference held in Princeton, N.J. under the auspices of the Committee for Public Justice) pp. 11–14. It is soon to be published in book form along with the other important papers delivered at the conference.

2. *Colyer* v. *Skeffington*, 265 Fed. 17, 50 (D. Mass., 1920).

3. *Fong Yue Ting* v. *United States*, 149 U.S. 698, 709, (1893).

4. Zechariah Chafee, Jr., *Free Speech in the United States* (Cambridge: Harvard University Press, 1941), p. 222, where Chafee points out that "Francis Place, the tailor, overturned the government of England in 1832 and precipitated a revolution which the voters had failed to accomplish simply by posting placards urging the people to start a run on the banks. There is a middle method of political change between the ballot and the bomb, namely economic pressure, and that, however unwise or injurious in nature, may very well be the method of the Communist Party. It advocates the overthrow of our government, but not by force and violence."

5. See the opinion in *Bosny* v. *Williams*, 185 Fed. 598 (S.D.N.Y. 1911) for a description of the procedures developed by the inspectors of the Immigration Bureau.

6. Mitchell Palmer's instructions are reprinted in Chafee, pp. 209–11.

7. *Colyer*, 265 Fed. at 43.

8. Chafee, p. 593.

9. Emerson, Haber & Dorsen, *Political and Civil Rights in the United States* (Boston: Little Brown & Co., 1967) 3rd. ed., vol. 1, p. 62.

7. COMMUNISTS AS POLITICAL PRISONERS

1. *Taylor* v. *Mississippi*, 319 U.S. 583 (1943).

2. Jack Levine, "Hoover and the Red Scare," 195 *The Nation* (1962): pp. 232, 233.

3. Zechariah Chafee, Jr., *Free Speech in the United States* (Cambridge: Harvard University Press, 1941), p. 446.

4. The following review of the Communist Party's strength in the United States is drawn from Irving Howe and Lewis Coser, *The American Communist Party, A Critical History (1917–1957)* (Boston: Beacon, 1957).

5. See *United States* v. *Dennis*, 183 F. 2d at 201, 206 (2 Cir. 1949).

6. *Dennis* v. *United States*, 341 U.S. 494, at 500 (1951).

7. Robert Mollan, "Smith Act Prosecutions: The Effect of the *Dennis* and *Yates* Decisions," 26 *University of Pittsburgh Law Review* 705 (1965): pp. 709–10.

8. *Yates* v. *United States*, 354 U.S. 298 (1957).
9. *United States* v. *Silverman*, 248 F. 2d 671, 686 (2 Cir. 1957).

8. MODERN POLITICAL PRISONERS: RACE

In sketching the early period of the civil rights struggle, I have drawn on John Hope Franklin, *From Slavery to Freedom: A History of Negro Americans*, 3rd ed. (New York: Vintage, 1969); William Kunstler, *Deep in My Heart* (New York: William Morrow & Co., 1971); Howard Zinn, *SNCC: The New Abolitionists* (Boston: Beacon, 1965); and, particularly, the fine biography of Dr. Martin Luther King, Jr., David L. Lewis, *King: A Critical Biography* (New York: Praeger, 1970). Particularly helpful in sorting out the Black Panther story are Paul Chevigny, *Cops and Rebels: A Study of Provocation* (New York: Pantheon, 1972); Philip S. Foner, ed., *The Black Panthers Speak* (Philadelphia: J.B. Lippincott Co., 1970); and Gilbert Moore, *A Special Rage* (New York: Harper & Row, 1971). The epigraph is from *The Autobiography of Malcolm X* (1965), excerpted in Leon Friedman, ed., *The Civil Rights Reader* (New York: Walker & Co., 1968) p. 115.

1. Zinn, p. 45.
2. Kunstler, p. 63.
3. Lewis, p. 169.
4. I have used the text of "Letter from Birmingham City Jail," reprinted from *Liberation* (June, 1963) pp. 10–16, in Hugo Adam Bedau, ed., *Civil Disobedience: Theory and Practice* (New York: Pegasus, 1970) pp. 72–89, at pp. 76–77.
5. Martin Duberman, "Black Power and the American Radical Tradition," in Duberman, *The Uncompleted Past* (New York: Random House, 1969) pp. 234–253, at p. 237.
6. Moore, p. 52.
7. Moore, p. 53.
8. Moore, p. 55.
9. Huey P. Newton, "Functional Definition of Politics," *The Black Panther*, January 17, 1969, reprinted in Foner, pp. 45–47, at p. 46.
10. In a report for the National Commission on the Causes and Prevention of Violence, Jerome H. Skolnick acknowledges that the Panthers had to be "given credit for keeping Oakland cool after the assassination of Martin Luther King ... [not] from any desire on their part to suppress black protest in the community [but] from a sense that the police are waiting for a chance to shoot down blacks in the streets." Foner, xxiv.
11. Judge Sherman's opinion in the Cleaver case is quoted in Moore, pp. 78–79.
12. The exchanges between Seale and Hoffman are set out in very readable form by Jason Epstein, "The Trial of Bobby Seale," in *Trials of the Resistance* (New York: New York Review/ Vintage, 1970) pp. 189–246, at p. 227.

13. "The Black Panthers in Court: The Lonnie McLucas Trial," 1 *Yale Review of Law and Social Action* 4, 46 (Winter, 1970).

14. *The New York Times*, May 25, 1971.

15. *The New York Times*, May 26, 1971.

16. See, House Committee on Internal Security, *Gun Barrel Politics: The Black Panther Party, 1966–67*, House Report No. 92–470, 92nd Congress, 2nd Session (Washington: Government Printing Office, 1971) Minority Opinion, p. 147, for the view that the Panthers' political rhetoric and social service programs were a facade for crimes of violence, crimes against property, and extortion; and see the testimony of Jean Powell and Larry Clayton Powell, in *Riots, Civil and Criminal Disorders: Hearings Before the Permanent Subcommittee on Investigations of the Committee on Government Operations, United States Senate*, Part 19, 91st Congress, 1st Session (Washington: Government Printing Office, 1969) pp. 3783–3826, for the view that David Hilliard's stewardship of the Black Panther Party led to a perversion of Huey Newton's ideas and ideals.

17. *The Wall Street Journal*, January 13, 1970.

18. Bond's remarks were made in reply to a question from Edward Morgan of ABC-TV; Bond relates the interview in his Preface to Foner, p. ix.

19. Quoted in Moore, p. 57–58.

20. Roy Wilkins, "The New Panthers," *New York Post*, September 30, 1972.

9. MODERN POLITICAL PRISONERS: WAR

For this account of the anti-war and anti-draft movement I have found particularly useful: Michael Ferber and Staughton Lynd, *The Resistance* (Boston: Beacon, 1971); Leon Friedman, *The Wise Minority* (New York: Dial, 1971); Jessica Mitford, *The Trial of Dr. Spock* (New York: Vintage, 1970); and *Trials of the Resistance* (New York: New York Review/ Vintage, 1970).

1. Ferber and Lynd, p. 4.

2. Ferber and Lynd, p. 22.

3. 110 *Congressional Record* 18132 (August 5, 1964).

4. Friedman, p. 122. General Hershey's view of his responsibilities was eventually to win many supporters for the Resistance. In 1965, the Selective Service System circulated to local draft boards a confidential memorandum which spoke of the threat of induction as a "club" with which to control the lives of young American men:

The psychology of granting wide choice under pressure to take action is the American or indirect way of achieving what is done by direction in foreign countries where choice is not permitted. Here, choice is limited but not denied, and it is fundamental that an individual generally applies himself better to do something he has decided to do rather than something he has been told to do.

The draft, according to this memo, employs a system of deferments for "channelling manpower" so that each student deferred is "impelled to pursue his skill . . . in the national interest" by the "pressurized guidance" of the threat of induction. The cynical memorandum found its way into the hands of student organizers at the beginning of 1967, when the anti-war movement was on the verge of launching massive disobedience of the draft laws. The suggestion that even the deferred were being manipulated and silenced by the threat of induction raised the level of hostility on the nation's campuses and helped focus anti-war protest on the war machine's one vulnerable spot—the draft.

5. Ferber and Lynd, p. 23.

6. *United States* v. *O'Brien,* 391 U.S. 367 (1968). Chief Justice Warren, writing for the Court, summarized the reasons why the Justices would not invalidate a law on account of the repressive motivation of the legislators responsible for passing it:

Inquiries into congressional motives or purposes are a hazardous matter. When the issue is simply the interpretation of legislation, the Court will look to statements by legislators for guidance as to the purpose of the legislature, because the benefit to sound decision-making in this circumstance is thought sufficient to risk the possibility of misreading Congress' purpose. It is entirely a different matter when we are asked to void a statute that is, under well-settled criteria, constitutional on its face, on the basis of what fewer than a handful of Congressmen said about it. What motivates one legislator to make a speech about a statute is not necessarily what motivates scores of others to enact it, and the stakes are sufficiently high for us to eschew guesswork. 391 U.S., at 383–84.

7. Richard M. Baordman, "Letter to Local Board No. 114," reprinted in Hugo Adam Bedau, ed., *Civil Disobedience: Theory and Practice* (New York: Pegasus, 1970) pp. 178–186, at p. 180–182.

8. This account of "Stop the Draft Week" and of the trial of the Oakland Seven draws on Emma Rothschild, "Notes from a Political Trial," in *Trials of the Resistance,* pp. 106–124.

9. Ferber and Lynd, p. 146.

10. *Gutnecht* v. *United States,* 396 U.S. 295, 306–307 (1970); see also, *Oestereich* v. *Selective Service Board,* 393 U.S. 233 (1969).

11. See, Willard Gaylin, M.D., *In the Service of Their Country: War Resisters in Prison* (New York: Viking, 1970).

12. *Rights in Conflict* (Bantam ed., 1968).

13. According to J. Anthony Lukas, in *The Barnyard Epithet and other Obscenities* (New York: Harper & Row, 1970) Perennial Library edition, p. 32, Foran told the Loyola Academy Boosters Club, after the trial, that all of the defendants except Bobby Seale were "fags," and that "We've lost our kids to the freaking fag revolution."

14. The apt phrase seems to have originated with Francine Du Plessix Gray, "The Ultra-Resistance," in *Trials of the Resistance,* pp. 125–161.

PART II

II. THE URGE TO REPRESS DISSENT

1. I have drawn this account of Socrates' trial from Gerald Dickler, *Man on Trial* (Garden City, N.Y.: Doubleday, 1962) pp. 15–32.
2. *West Virginia State Board of Education* v. *Barnette*, 319 U.S. 624, 641–42 (1943).
3. *Whitney* v. *California*, 274 U.S. 357, 376 (1927) (concurring opinion).
4. Thomas I. Emerson, *The System of Freedom of Expression* (New York: Random House, 1971) pp. 6–8, 12. Except for the opinions of the Supreme Court (and as a lucid exposition and evaluation of those opinions) I have found no work on the subject of repression and the First Amendment superior to this comprehensive book.
5. *The New York Times*, June 24, 1970.
6. *Abrams* v. *United States*, 250 U.S. 616, 630 (1919).

12. FIDDLING WITH THE FIRST AMENDMENT

The epigraph comes from Cromwell's reply to a beseiged Roman Catholic town in Ireland when it offered to surrender on the condition that he grant the inhabitants freedom of conscience. Cromwell is quoted in Zechariah Chafee, Jr., *Free Speech in the United States* (Cambridge: Harvard University Press, 1941) p. 529.

1. *New York Times Co.* v. *Sullivan*, 376 U.S. 254, 270 (1964).
2. *Schenck* v. *United States*, 249 U.S. 47, 52 (1919) (emphasis added).
3. *Debs* v. *United States*, 249 U.S. 211, 215 (1919) (emphasis added).
4. *Whitney* v. *California*, 274 U.S. 357, 371 (1927).
5. 274 U.S. at 375–377 (concerning in the court's decision to affirm only on the ground that Miss Whitney had not properly raised the First Amendment issue in the proceedings below).
6. *Stromberg* v. *California*, 283 U.S. 359 (1931) (holding California's "red flag" law unconstitutional); *Herndon* v. *Lowry*, 301 U.S. 242 (1937) (reversing the conviction of a member of the Communist Party under a state insurrection law).
7. *DeJonge* v. *Oregon*, 299 U.S. 353 (1937) (reversing the conviction, under state criminal syndicalism law, of a Communist Party member whose offense had been to serve as chairman of a peaceful meeting called by the Communist Party to protest police brutality in a longshoreman's strike).
8. *Dennis* v. *United States*, 341 U.S. 494, 510 (1951).
9. *Brandenberg* v. *Ohio*, 395 U.S. 444, 454 (1969) (concurring opinion).
10. 341 U.S. at 549.
11. 341 U.S. at 588–89.
12. *Yates* v. *United States*, 354, U.S. 298, 324–27 (1957).

13. *United States* v. *Spock*, 416 F. 2d 165, 172 (1 Cir. 1969).
14. *Brandenberg* v. *Ohio*, 395 U.S. 444, 447 (1969) (*per curiam* opinion) (emphasis added).

13. ABUSE OF DISCRETION

Useful sources for this chapter were Kenneth Culp Davis, *Discretionary Justice: A Preliminary Inquiry* (Baton Rouge: Louisiana State University Press, 1969): Paul Chevigny, *Police Power* (New York: Vintage, 1969); and Abe Goldstein, "Police Discretion Not to Invoke the Criminal Process: Low Visibility Decisions in the Administration of Justice," 69 *Yale Law Review* 543 (1960). The title of this chapter was suggested by Alan Dershowitz's article, " 'Stretch Points' of Liberty," *The Nation*, March 15, 1971, pp. 329–34.

1. The quote appeared in Dershowitz's article. Six weeks later the Mayday Tribe launched its quixotic attempt to shut down the government by tying up rush hour traffic in Washington D.C. The anti-war protest, irritating and illegal though it was, was not a national emergency; but on the morning of May 3rd, when the protest began, the Washington police department's standard operating procedures for making arrests during civil disorders were suspended. The use of "field arrest forms" and polaroid photographs, a procedure designed to satisfy the minimum constitutional requirements in a mass arrest situation, was scrapped. From May 3rd to May 5th, over 13,000 people were swept up off the streets of the capital. Virtually all of the arrests were illegal, and participants, passersby, tourists, spectators, and newsmen were herded together in overcrowded cells and make-shift detention centers. Not only were the innocent caught up in the net, but because the field arrest forms had been abandoned, those who had been arrested violating the laws could not be prosecuted. Virtually all the cases were thrown out of court. On May 5, Assistant Attorney General William Rehnquist, now Supreme Court Justice Rehnquist, defended the suspension of constitutional procedures by invoking a doctrine of "qualified martial law." There is, of course, no such doctrine. Deputy Attorney General Kleindienst, Attorney General Mitchell, and President Nixon himself praised the methods used and held them up as a "model" to be followed in the future. The conclusion is inescapable that the operation was devised and authorized at the highest levels of the administration. See, American Civil Liberties Union of the National Capital Area, *Mayday 1971: Order Without Law* (July, 1972).

2. See, ch. 3, n. 7.

3. The UFO story is drawn from *The New York Times*, August 12, 1968, and August 28, 1968; *The Washington Post*, April 18, 1970, April 24, 1970, April 28, 1970, and April 29, 1970; Brief of Appellants in *The State of South Carolina* v. *The UFO, Inc.*, et al; and a telephone conversation with Reber

Bolt, who prepared this brief for the appeal to the Supreme Court of South Carolina.

4. Miss Davis was released on $102,500 bail shortly before her trial began. A California law denies bail to defendants charged with "capital crimes" where "the proof is evident or the presumption great." It was the judge's view of the evidence that kept her behind bars for sixteen months. When, in February 1972, the United States Supreme Court ruled the death penalty unconstitutional, California's "capital crimes" provision was nullified, in the judge's view, and he set the bail.

5. Robert Jackson, "The Federal Prosecutor," *24 Journal of the American Judiciary Society* 18, 19 (1940).

6. *Yick Wo* v. *Hopkins*, 118 U.S. 356, 373 (1896).

14. WHAT'S WRONG WITH CONSPIRACY?

I have found the following materials helpful in developing an understanding of conspiracy law: Thomas I. Emerson, *The System of Freedom of Expression* (New York: Vintage, 1971) pp. 401–412; Jessica Mitford, *The Trial of Dr. Spock* (New York: Vintage, 1970) pp. 61–72; Nathaniel L. Nathanson, "Freedom of Association and the Quest for Internal Security: Conspiracy from Dennis to Dr. Spock," 65 *Northwestern University Law Review* 153 (1970); Herbert L. Packer, "The Conspiracy Weapon," in *Trial of the Resistance* (New York: New York Review Book/Vintage, 1970) pp. 170–188; Francis B. Sayre, "Criminal Conspiracy," 35 *Harvard Law Review* 393 (1922); "Conspiracy and the First Amendment," 79 *Yale Law Journal* 872 (1970); and "Developments in the Law: Criminal Conspiracy," 72 *Harvard Law Review* 920 (1959). I am also indebted to my co-counsel in the Ellsberg case, Leonard Boudin, and to Arthur Kinoy and Chuck Jones of the Rutgers Law School faculty for their insights. The epigraph is quoted from Mitford, p. 161.

1. *Krulewitch* v. *United States*, 336 U.S. 440, 446, 447 (1949) (concurring opinion).

2. *Harrison* v. *United States*, 7 F. 2d 259, 263 (2 Cir. 1925).

3. *Poulterers Case,* 77 Eng Rep. 813 (Star Chamber, 1611).

4. *Philadelphia Cordwainers' Case* (1806). A report of the case, printed as a pamphlet in 1806 was reprinted in Commons and Gilmore, 3 *Documentary History of American Industrial Society*, pp. 59–248. See, Sayre, p. 413.

5. *Commonwealth* v. *Carlisle*, Brightly's N.P. Rep. (Pa.) 36, 42 (1821). See, Sayre, p. 414–15.

6. See, Paul Chevigny, *Cops and Rebels: A Study of Provocation* (New York: Pantheon, 1972), an excellent book written around the case of Alfred Cain, Jr., Ricardo De Leon, and Jerome West, Black Panthers charged, twice tried, and finally acquitted of conspiracy to rob the New Dunston Hotel in Harlem. Although they were acquitted of the conspiracy charges, all three were convicted of "possession" of a loaded

sawed-off shotgun. The arresting officers testified that they found the gun in a gunny sack on the floor of the back seat of the undercover agent's car when they picked up the defendants. There was no evidence proving that any one of them—or that all three—owned the gun or even knew it was there, but under New York law everyone riding in an automobile is *presumed* to possess any illegal weapon in the car, no matter who placed it there. On the strength of this presumption, De Leon was sentenced to seven years in prison—the maximum. Jerome West got an indefinite term up to three years, and Alfred Cain got off with five years probation. But even Cain had endured two major trials and had already spent over a year in jail in the process.

7. *Krulewitch*, 336 U.S. 440, 453.

8. *United States* v. *Bufalino*, 285 F. 2d 408, 420 (2 Cir. 1960).

9. See, Trial Transcript of the Record in *The People of the State of New York* v. *Lumumba Abdul Shakur, et al.* (Sup. Ct., NY.Y Co. No. 1848–69) pp. 15452–15472.

10. *The New York Post*, May 14, 1971.

11. *The New York Times*, May 15, 1971.

12. *Bond* v. *Floyd*, 385 U.S. 116, 133 (1966). The Court went on to say: "Bond's statements were at worst unclear on the means to be adopted to avoid the draft. While the SNCC statement said 'We are in sympathy with, and support, the men in this country who are unwilling to respond to a military draft,' this statement alone cannot be interpreted as a call to unlawful refusal to be drafted. Moreover, Bond's supplementary statements tend to resolve the opaqueness in favor of legal alternatives to the draft."

13. Mitford, p. 56.

14. Quoted in Emerson, p. 407.

15. Mitford, p. 201.

16. Michael Ferber and Staughton Lynd, *The Resistance* (Boston: Beacon, 1971) p. 146.

17. Mitford, pp. 160–61.

18. Mitford, pp. 225, 231.

19. *United States* v. *Spock*, 416 F. 2d 165 (1 Cir. 1969).

20. 416 F. 2d 165, 184, 186, 188.

21. See, *N.A.A.C.P.* v. *Alabama ex rel Patterson*, 375 U.S. 449, 460–461, 463 (1958); *Bates* v. *City of Little Rock*, 361 U.S. 516, 523–24 (1960); *Shelton* v. *Tucker*, 364 U.S. 479, 485, 490 (1960); *N.A.A.C.P.* v. *Button*, 371 U.S. 415, 429–30 (1963); *N.A.A.C.P.* v. *Alabama ex rel Flowers*, 377 U.S. 288, 309 (1964).

22. 416 F. 2d 172–74.

15. WHERE DID THE GRAND JURY GO?

An invaluable source on the history of the grand jury is Richard D. Younger, *The People's Panel* (Providence: Brown University Press, 1963).

The McCarthy period is covered in Leonard Boudin, "The Federal Grand Jury," an unpublished paper, delivered at Georgetown Law Center, September 17, 1971. The Nixon Administration's innovations are well-documented in Frank J. Donner and Eugene Cerruti, "The Grand Jury Network," *The Nation*, January 3, 1972, pp. 5–20. The legal aspects of recent developments are covered nicely in "Federal Grand Jury Investigation of Political Dissidents," 7 *Harvard Civil Rights Civil Liberties Law Review* 432 (1972). Also helpful were two papers presented at a conference sponsored by the Committee for Public Justice in New York City on April 30, 1972: Sanford Jay Rosen, "Grand Juries: A Contemporary Perspective" and Leon Friedman, "The Grand Jury: Shield or Sword." I also received some timely assistance from Jim Rief of the Center for Constitutional Rights in gathering and analyzing this information. The epigraph is quoted from Donner and Cerruti, p. 6.

1. Younger, p. 50.
2. *Newsweek*, December 20, 1971.
3. Donner and Cerruti, p. 6.
4. *Bacon* v. *United States*, 449 F. 2d 993 (9 Cir. 1971).
5. *In re Grand Jury Proceedings, Harrisburg, Pa.*, 450 F. 2d 199 (3 Cir. 1971).
6. *The New York Times*, October 10, 1971, and February 27, 1972.
7. *United States* v. *Caldwell*, 92 Sup. Ct. 2686 (1972).
8. See, *Bursey* v. *United States*, 466 F. 2d 1059 (9 Cir. 1972); *Gibson* v. *Legislative Investigating Committee*, 372 U.S. 539 (1963); *Sweezy* v. *New Hampshire*, 354 U.S. 234 (1957); and *Watkins* v. *United States*, 345 U.S. 178 (1947); · but see, *United States* v. *Weinberg*, 439 F. 2d 734 (9 Cir. 1971).
9. *United States* v. *Costello*, 350 U.S. 359 (1956).

16. THE DARK AT THE END OF THE TUNNEL

By far the most useful material to date on the FBI is contained in the various papers presented to the Committee for Public Justice at its Conference on the FBI at Princeton, New Jersey, on October 30, 1971. The papers are to be published soon in book form. I found the following particularly useful: Vern Countryman, "History of the FBI"; Frank J. Donner, "The FBI Informer, His Role in the American Political Intelligence System;" John T. Elliff, "The Scope and Basis of FBI Domestic Intelligence Data Collection"; Thomas I. Emerson, "The Federal Bureau of Investigation and the Bill of Rights"; and William W. Turner, "An Insider's View of the FBI."

1. See the "Advisory Statement" on the subject prepared in 1970 by the Executive Board of the American Library Association, and Reese Cleghorn, "A Federal Intrusion: When Readers Become Suspects," *South Today*, July 9, 1970.
2. Lee Lockwood, "How the 'Kidnap Conspiracy' Was Hatched," *Life*, May 21, 1971.

3. See, Paul Chevigny, *Cops and Rebels: A Study of Provocation* (New York: Pantheon, 1972), particularly in Chapter 10, "State and Revolution: Political Provocation in Europe and the United States," pp. 223–76; Frank Donner, "The Theory and Practice of American Political Intelligence," *New York Review of Books* (April 22, 1971) pp. 27–38 (hereafter, "Donner-NYR").

4. Robert J. Lifton, who hosted the fund-raiser, reports the incidents in "To Frighten and Stifle," *The New York Times* (March 6, 1972).

5. *Richmond Times-Dispatch*, August 1, 1971.

6. The full text of the memorandum is reprinted in Donner-NYR, p. 31.

7. "Police states" are not the exclusive creations of extreme right-wing or left-wing dictatorships; a police state is the repressive system of government adopted by a whole range of authoritarian governments seeking to eliminate real or imagined resistance. Joseph II of Austria was an enlightened eighteenth-century ruler, but he mistrusted both the men who worked for him and the masses. Operating under secret instructions from the emperor, and accountable only to him, Austria's ubiquitous, silent, and secret police penetrated and gathered intelligence data on all classes of citizens—including the government officials, the army, and the judiciary. The clergy were particularly watched to see that they did not disseminate views hostile to the emperor. He had the best of motives for creating his eighteenth-century *Polizeistadt:* he wanted to modernize his government, he wanted a dedicated and efficient bureaucracy, and, in order to make government responsive to his people's needs, he wanted to keep tabs on all aspects of public opinion.

As one student of the early *Polizeistadt* reminds us, Joseph II "did not wish to tyrannize his people; he wished to free them, by supervision, of the danger of falling prey to agitators, demagogues, and revolutionaries."

Political police were a major feature of nineteenth-century European governments. In post-Revolutionary France, Napoleon's minister of police, Joseph Fouché, elevated the political police into a position of unparalled primacy as the chief protector, censor, and moral guide of society. In 1805 he wrote that the political police was "the regulating power which is felt everywhere, without ever being seen, and which, at the center of the state, holds the place which the power which sustains the harmony of the celestial bodies holds in the universe, a power whose regularity strikes us although we are unable to devine the cause. . . . Every branch of the administration has a part which subordinates it to the police."

Fouché made it no secret that the job of his police included "uncovering and dissolving coalitions and *legal* opposition . . . as well as the murky plots of royalists and foreign agents." His technique was to use informers to ensure that there were no secrets, and *agents provocateurs* to expose, to discredit, or to set up for prosecution groups on the right and on the left.

A secret police thrives on plots, both to eliminate political enemies and to build popular support for the government. A problem for a successful police state is the dearth of conspiracies against it. According to his secretary, Bonaparte personally authorized the secret police to organize a conspiracy to assassinate him. In the resulting prosecution, mere political enemies were tried and were convicted together with the real conspirators (who had been provoked by the police). After the Restoration, provocation was made even easier by more repressive laws. In the reign of Louis XVIII, the mere artistic representation of Napoleon I became a crime. Some artisans were arrested after they executed busts of the late emperor; the order for the busts had been placed by police undercover agents.

The police state with which we are perhaps most familiar is Hitler's National Socialist Regime in Germany. The methods were cruder; the political police were not just ubiquitous and omnipotent, but sadistic as well, and murder and concentration camps were added to their enforcement arsenal. We must not forget, however, how Hitler established a rule by Gestapo without directly confronting the safeguards of the liberal Weimar Constitution. Like many constitutions, it provided the Executive with "reserve powers" in the event of extreme emergencies. On February 28, 1933, following the Reichstag fire, Hitler promulgated an "Ordinance for the Protection of the People and the State," declaring a permanent state of emergency. The Gestapo was built systematically until it had amassed the full power of a political police in parallel to or in place of the normal police authorities. [My source for this footnote is Brian Chapman, *Police State* (New York: Praeger, 1970).]

In recent years we have seen political incarceration in the Soviet Union guised as psychiatric observation. It may signal the coming thing in police state methods; but a midwestern friend tells me that this practice has been far from unknown in America. The records of Cleveland State Hospital, where he worked for seven years, show that in the mid-1800s the discovery of a mental disorder known as "Millerism" resulted in the incarceration there of anyone who was found to support a notorious socialist named Miller.

8. Robert Barkin, "War Toys for Adults," *The New Republic*, December 11, 1971.

9. Donner-NYR, p. 36.

10. Vin McLellan, "Surveilling Civilians: Old Dossiers Never Die," *The Village Voice*, November 11, 1971.

11. The Ervin-Rehnquist exchange is printed in *The Congressional Record*, June 20, 1971, pp. s10224–226.

12. *Tatum* v. *Laird*, 408 U.S. 1 (1972)

13. Emerson, p. 30.

14. William Preston, *Aliens and Dissenters: Federal Suppression of Radicals,* 1903–1933 (Cambridge: Harvard University Press, 1963) pp. 242–43.

15. The Hoover memorandum is quoted in Elliff, p. 39.

16. Turner, pp. 20–24.

17. These Media files are quoted in Elliff, p. 52–54.

18. Elliff, p. 35.

19. Wall testified at the Princton FBI Conference, and was interviewed in *The New York Times,* January 13, 1972.

20. A copy of this memorandum has surfaced and is in the possession of attorneys for the American Civil Liberties Union.

21. Arthur R. Miller, *The Assault on Privacy* (Ann Arbor: University of Michigan Press, 1971) p. 56.

17. FIGHTING BACK—FIVE DAYS IN THE LIFE

1. Quoted by Justice Douglas, dissenting in *Scales* v. *United States,* 367 U.S. 203, 271 (1971).

2. *Alderman* v. *United States,* 394 U.S. 165 (1969).

PART III

The writing on civil disobedience is voluminous, and I have not attempted to survey all of it. I have found the following particularly useful: Francis A. Allen, "Civil Disobedience and the Legal Order," 36 *University of Cincinnati Law Review* 1, 175 (1967); Hugo Adam Bedau, ed., *Civil Disobedience: Theory and Practice* (New York: Pegasus, 1970); Peter Brock, *Twentieth-Century Pacifism* (New York: Van Nostrand Reinhold, 1970); Carl Cohen, *Civil Disobedience: Conscience, Tactics, and the Law* (New York: Columbia University Press, 1971); Abe Fortas, *Concerning Dissent and Civil Disobedience* (New York: World, 1968); Harrop A. Freeman, "The Right of Protest and Civil Disobedience," 41 *Indiana Law Journal* 255 (1966); Robert H. Freilich, "The Emerging General Theory of Civil Disobedience Within the Legal Order," 45 *Journal of Urban Law* 563 (1968); Leon Friedman, *The Wise Minority* (New York: Dial, 1971); Wilson Carey McWilliams, "On Violence and Legitimacy," 79 *Yale Law Journal* 623 (1970); Reinhold Niebuhr, "The Preservation of Moral Values in Politics" reprinted from *Moral Man and Immoral Society* (Charles Scribner's Sons, 1960) in Staughton Lynd, ed., *Nonviolence in America: A Documentary History* (Indianapolis: Bobbs-Merrill, 1966) pp. 499–519; Paul E. Sigmund, *Natural Law in Political Thought* (Cambridge: Winthrop, 1971); Michael Walzer, *Obligations: Essays on Disobedience, War, and Citizenship* (Cambridge: Harvard University Press, 1970); and Howard Zinn, *Disobedience and Democracy: Nine Fallacies on Law and Order* (New York: Vintage, 1968).

In Part III, all quotations from Dr. Martin Luther King, Jr. are from his "Letter from Birmingham City Jail," reprinted in Bedau, pp. 72–89: all quotations from Henry David Thoreau are from his essay, "Civil Disobedience," reprinted in Bedau, pp. 27–48; and all quotations from Mohandas Gandhi are from his *Non-Violent Resistance* (Kumarappa ed. 1961).

18. CIVIL DISOBEDIENCE

1. Poplin was not court-martialed for refusing to obey the order to write the pamphlet. Instead, he was harassed with petty orders and charged with nit-picking infractions until he went AWOL for eleven days. The ordinary sentence for such an unauthorized absence is two weeks in the stockade, but Poplin's special court-martial punished him by restricting him to his unit and busting him to private. He requested the court, in vain, to order him imprisoned rather than returned to "PsyOps" duty, for he felt he could no longer conscientiously participate in the unit's psychological warfare operations. Once back in his unit, he refused to obey further orders, and he finally refused to don his uniform or salute his superior officers. A general court martial on fifteen charges for such offenses ended with a compromise sentence of nine months in the stockade. His appeals were exhausted in November 1972. The Poplin case received a great deal of attention in the Japanese press but, strangely, very little attention in the United States. Peter Weiss and Mark Amsterdam of the Center for Constitutional Rights, who handled his general court-martial and appeals, related the history of the case to me.
2. Leon Friedman, *The Wise Minority* (New York: Dial, 1971) p. 87.
3. *Griswold* v. *Connecticut*, 381 U.S. 479 (1965).
4. For the useful distinction between direct and indirect civil disobedience, and for much of the analytic basis of this part of the discussion, I am indebted to Carl Cohen, *Civil Disobedience: Conscience, Tactics and the Law* (New York: Columbia University Press, 1971) pp. 51–75.
5. See, Steven R. Weisman, "How Are We Doing On the Networks?" *The New York Times*, January 2, 1972; Vin McLellan, "The Statue of Liberty: Captive or Compatriot?" *The Village Voice*, January 6, 1972.

19. IN SEARCH OF JUSTIFICATION

1. Leon Friedman, *The Wise Minority* (New York: Dial, 1971) p. 28.
2. Natural law philosophy has been with us since ancient Greece, and most civil disobedients continue to draw on its rich traditions today. As the Second Continental Congress aligned us with that tradition by adopting the Declaration of Independence, it is not so farfetched to examine it for some common ground between the civil disobedients and the defenders of American law and order.

Originally, natural law had nothing to do with disobedience; philosophers were searching for an answer to the opposite puzzle—what is it about law that deserves obedience? Greeks and Romans found the answer in the concept that existing legal order reflected the principles inherent in human nature. It was simply against man's nature to disobey the law. Cicero summed it up: "There is a true law, right reason in accord with nature, it is of universal application, unchanging and everlasting . . . binding at all times upon all people." (*The Commonwealth*, 3.22) For men who believed that the universe is saturated with natural law, it was easy to believe that governments had, simply by human reason, distilled and codified its specific commands. The Christian tradition adapted this scheme to its own view of nature: God's creation was permeated with his reason, and the commands of his law could be known through conscience.

But the immutability of natural law was always resting on an unsteady foundation. When an individual exercises "right reason" or conscience to distinguish between what is good and what is evil for him and for his society, his perception of the natural order of things is a function of his time, his culture, and his status. It was an obviously close-cropped St. Paul who asked, "Doth not even nature itself teach you, that, if a man have long hair, it is a shame unto him?" (I Cor. 11:14). To men who held slaves, slavery seemed as natural as rain.

Natural law answered the need of legal conservatives of the ancient world, but once social and legal arrangements came to depend on some "higher law" for their legitimacy, it was open to radicals to use *their* view of what is natural to justify reform, disobedience, or even revolution. The seeds of conscientious disobedience were sown by St. Thomas Aquinas. He argued then there were two sources of moral obligation higher than the law of the state: divine law (God's revelation in scripture) and natural law (God's commands revealed in his creation). What if man's laws did *not* reflect God's laws? "Human law," wrote Aquinas, "does not bind a man in conscience and if it conflicts with the higher law human law should not be obeyed." (See, Paul E. Sigmund, *Natural Law In Political Thought* (Cambridge: Winthrop, 1971) from which this account is drawn.)

3. See, "The Legislature of Rhode Island on the Virginia Resolutions, February, 1799," in Richard Hofstadter, ed., *Great Issues in American History*, Vol. I (New York: Vintage, 1960) pp. 184–86.

4. *New York Times Company* v. *Sullivan*, 376 U.S. 254, 276 (1964).

5. Gandhi is quoted in Harris Wofford, Jr., "Non-Violence and the Law: The Law Needs Help," 15 *The Journal of Religious Thought* 25 (1957–58), reprinted in Hugo Adam Bedau, ed., *Civil Disobedience: Theory and Practice* (New York: Pegasus, 1970) pp. 59–71, at p. 67.

6. Louis Waldman, "Civil Rights—yes: Civil Disobedience—no," 37

New York State Bar Journal 331 (1963), reprinted in Bedau, pp. 106–12, at pp. 108–9.

7. Harrison Tweed, Bernard G. Segal, and Herbert L. Packer, "Civil Rights and Disobedience to Law," *Presbyterian Life* (February 1, 1964) pp. 6–9, reprinted in Bedau, pp. 90–7, at pp. 91–2.

8. Abe Fortas, *Concerning Dissent and Civil Disobedience* (New York: World, 1968) p. 108.

9. Philip Berrigan, "Letter from a Baltimore Jail," in *Prison Journals of a Priest Revolutionary* (New York: Ballantine, 1971) pp. 15–22.

20. DEMOCRACY AND ANARCHY

1. Jessica Mitford, *The Trial of Dr. Spock* (New York: Vintage, 1970) p. 67.

2. Lincoln is quoted in Harris Woffard, Jr., "Non-Violence and the Law: The Law Needs Help," 15 *The Journal of Religious Thought* 25 (1957–58), reprinted in Hugo Adam Bedau, ed., *Civil Disobedience: Theory and Practice* (New York: Pegasus, 1970) pp. 59–71, at p. 60.

3. Lyman Beecher, "The Duty of Disobedience to Wicked Laws." The influential Presbyterian minister's sermon is excerpted in Leon Friedman, *The Wise Minority* (New York: Dial, 1971) p. 35.

4. *Report of the National Advisory Commission on Civil Disorders* (Bantam ed. 1968) p. 35.

5. Howard Zinn, *Disobedience and Democracy: Nine Fallacies on Law and Order* (New York: Vintage, 1968) p. 13.

6. Solomon, Walker, O'Connor & Fishman, "Civil Rights Activity and Reduction in Crime Among Negroes," 12 *Archives General Psychiatry* 227 (1965), reported in Francis A. Allen, "Civil Disobedience and the Legal Order," 36 *University of Cincinnati Law Review* 1, 31–32 (1967).

7. Noam Chomsky, Paul Lauter and Florence Howe, "Reflections on a Political Trial," in *Trials of the Resistance* (New York: New York Review/ Vintage, 1970) pp. 74–105, at p. 93.

8. Mitford, p. 208.

21. FINDING A FORUM

The epigraph is from James Madison, "Against Nullification" (1835) which can be found in Adrienne Koch, ed., *The American Enlightenment* (New York, 1965) pp. 532–33. The passage is excerpted in Leon Friedman, *The Wise Minority* (New York: Dial, 1971) p. 26.

1. See, Francis A. Allen, "Civil Disobedience and the Legal Order," 36 *University of Cincinnati Law Review* 1, 175, at p. 180 (1967), citing Thoreau's essays: "Slavery in Massachusetts" and "The Last Days of John Brown" from Thoreau, *A Yankee in Canada, Anti-Slavery and Reform Papers* (1891).

2. The facts of the Ann Arbor case, and the legal arguments they

advanced are set forth in detail in Carl Cohen, "Law, Speech, and Disobedience," in Hugo Adam Bedau, ed., *Civil Disobedience: Theory and Practice* (New York: Pegasus, 1970) pp. 162–177.

3. *West Virginia State Board of Education* v. *Barnette*, 319 U.S. 624, 632 (1943) (requirement of flag salute, in connection with recitation of pledge of allegiance in school, struck down as compelling "a form of utterance"); see, *Stromberg* v. *California*, 283 U.S. 359 (1931) (displaying red flag is protected by the First Amendment); *Tinker* v. *Des Moines Independent Community School District*, 393 U.S. 503, 514 (1969) (armbands worn by students in school to "exhibit their disapproval of the Vietnam hostilities and their advocacy of a truce, to make their views known, and, by their example, to influence others to adopt them" are termed a "form of expression" protected by the First Amendment); but see, *United States* v. *O'Brien*, 391 U.S. 367 (1968) (draft-card burning, although it is assumed to be a form of "symbolic speech," can nevertheless be prohibited by a regulation directed at some other, legitimate purpose).

5. *The New York Times*, May 26, 1971.

6. Interview, *Center Magazine* (Vol. 3, 1970).

7. Howard Zinn writes: "If a specific act of civil disobedience is a morally justifiable act of protest, then the jailing of those engaged in that act is immoral and should be opposed, contested to the very end. The protester need be no more willing to accept the rule of punishment than to accept the rule he broke. There may be many times when protesters *choose* to go to jail, as a way of continuing their protest, as a way of reminding their country-men of injustice. But that is different than the notion that they *must* go to jail as part of a rule connected with civil disobedience. The key point is that the spirit of protest should be maintained all the way, whether it is done by remaining in jail, or by evading it. To accept jail penitentially as an accession to "the rules" is to switch suddenly to a spirit of subservience, to demean the seriousness of the protest." (*Disobedience and Democracy: Nine Fallacies on Law and Order* (New York: Vintage, 1968) pp. 120–21)

22. POLITICAL TRIALS

The increase in the number of political trials in recent years has generated some good literature on jury nullification. I have drawn on Joseph L. Sax, "Conscience and Anarchy: The Prosecution of War Resisters," 57 *Yale Review* 481 (June, 1968); J. M. Van Dyke, "The Jury as a Political Institution," 16 *Catholic Lawyer* 224 (Summer, 1970); "The Changing Role of the Jury in the Nineteenth Century," 74 *Yale Law Journal* 170 (1964); and Brief for Appellant, *United States* v. *Boardman* (1 Cir. 1969) No. 7355. Thomas Weiskel's article, "Notes on Living with End," *The New Journal* (May 9, 1971): pp. 3–5, nicely dissects America's current fascination with images of the Apocalypse. The epigraph is from the Trial Transcript of the Record in the Case of *United States* v. *David T. Dellinger et al.*, pp. 11359–60, quoted in Theodore L. Becker, ed., *Political Trials* (Indianapolis: Bobbs-Merrill, 1971) p. 167.

1. These proceedings were not transcribed and I have relied on the recollections of Sinclair's attorneys, Lennie Weinglass and Buck Davis. Judge Keith broke new ground in another element of that case as well: he ruled that the President and his Attorney General could not, as they had hoped, evade the requirements of the Fourth Amendment to gather intelligence on domestic dissidents through warrantless wiretaps. He ordered the Justice Department to disclose whatever conversations had been overheard. The Supreme Court upheld him unanimously in *United States* v. *United States District Court for the Eastern District of Michigan*, 92 S. Ct. 2125 (1972).

2. *Sparf* v. *United States*, 156 U.S. 51 (1895).

3. *Duncan* v. *Louisiana*, 391 U.S. 145, 155–56 (1968).

4. *Witherspoon* v. *Illinois*, 391 U.S. 510, 519, n. 19 (1968).

5. *Wiley* v. *Warden*, 372 F. 2d 742, 743, n. 1 (4th Cir. 1969): Indiana is the only other state retaining for its juries some measure of nullification power.

6. *The Boston Globe*, September 8, 1968.

7. *United States* v. *Spock*, 416 F. 2d 165, 182 (1 Cir. 1969). Judge Ford had required the jurors to answer a series of questions designed to explain their verdict. By requiring these answers (called "special verdicts") as well as a general verdict ("guilty" or "not guilty"), Judge Ford virtually ensured the convictions. The First Circuit Court of Appeals put it this way:

There is no easier way to reach, and perhaps force, a verdict of guilty than to approach it step by step. A juror, wishing to acquit, may be formally catechized. By a progression of questions each of which seems to require an answer unfavorable to the defendant, a reluctant juror may be led to vote for a conviction which, in the large, he would have resisted. The result may be accomplished by a majority of the jury, but the course has been initiated by the judge, and directed by him through the frame of the questions. . . .

Here, whereas, as we have pointed out, some defendants could be found to have exceeded the bounds of free speech, the issue was peculiarly one to which a community standard of conscience was, in the jury's discretion, to be applied. (Id, 182, 183.)

8. Daniel Berrigan, *The Trial of the Catonsville Nine* (Boston: Beacon Press, 1970) pp. 48, 82–3.

9. Thomas Bowen was convicted of willfully failing to report for induction. When Bowen took the stand at his trial, the judge permitted him to testify that he refused induction because he did not want to get into the army, but the judge refused to let him answer his attorney's next question: "Why?" The Fourth Circuit Court of Appeals reversed the conviction and sent the case back for another trial in which Bowen

would be able to explain his conduct as best he could. The appellate judges said "we think that he should not have been deprived of the opportunity to . . . offer any possible explanation for his conduct." (*United States* v. *Bowen*, 421 F. 2d 193, 197 (4th Cir. 1970).) It should be obvious, however, that the trial judge's ruling in this case was unusually strict: that even though Bowen will be allowed to answer, he will not be allowed to present the testimony of others to buttress his claim of good motive.

Index